MODEST HOPES

Don Loucks & Leslie Valpy

MODEST HOPES

Homes and Stories of Toronto's
Workers from the 1820s to the 1920s

DUNDURN
PRESS

Publisher: Scott Fraser | Acquiring editor: Kathryn Lane | Editor: Michael Carroll
Cover designer: Sophie Paas-Lang | Interior designer: Laura Boyle
Cover image: Don Loucks
All Toronto home illustrations © Don Loucks
Printer: Marquis

Library and Archives Canada Cataloguing in Publication

Title: Modest hopes : homes and stories of Toronto's workers from the 1820s to the 1920s / Don Loucks & Leslie Valpy.
Names: Loucks, Don, author. | Valpy, Leslie, author.
Description: Includes bibliographical references and index.
Identifiers: Canadiana (print) 20210194502 | Canadiana (ebook) 20210194979 | ISBN 9781459745544 (softcover) | ISBN 9781459745551 (PDF) | ISBN 9781459745568 (EPUB)
Subjects: LCSH: Working class—Dwellings—Ontario—Toronto—History. | LCSH: Row houses—Ontario—Toronto— History. | LCSH: Semi-detached houses—Ontario—Toronto—History. | LCSH: Historic buildings— Ontario—Toronto. | LCSH: Working class—Ontario—Toronto—History. | LCSH: Toronto (Ont.)— Buildings, structures, etc. | LCSH: Toronto (Ont.)—History.
Classification: LCC FC3097.7 L68 2021 | DDC 971.3/541—dc23

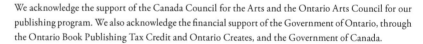

We acknowledge the support of the Canada Council for the Arts and the Ontario Arts Council for our publishing program. We also acknowledge the financial support of the Government of Ontario, through the Ontario Book Publishing Tax Credit and Ontario Creates, and the Government of Canada.

Dundurn Press
1382 Queen Street East
Toronto, Ontario, Canada M4L 1C9
dundurn.com, @dundurnpress ✆ f ◎

To Lynda, Naomi, Alanna, and Emma
— Don Loucks

To Aaron, Robbie, and Matthew
— Leslie Valpy

CONTENTS

AUTHORS' NOTE

The all-too-often voiceless and forgotten people who built Toronto are silent, their lives and achievements routinely ignored and erased. *Modest Hopes* was written with the idea that after introducing the cottages that were their homes, the importance of their lives and contributions to the city will be better understood.

These small, 400- to 900-square-foot, one- to three-bedroom houses were often built on the less desirable and inexpensive land close to the industries where the people who lived in them worked. For every Rosedale mansion, there were hundreds of these workers' cottages. Their small size, lowly status, and poor location, crowded onto streets downtown and in the west and east ends, have made these houses vulnerable to neglect and demolition, too often replaced by larger "modern" homes and commercial development. Their disappearance is like the erasing of our history, like the tearing out of pages from the Toronto storybook.

In the 19th century, Toronto was a young city that greeted many thousands of new arrivals, most with very few possessions. Their dreams of a new home must have been as powerful and all-consuming as were their hopes for a better future for themselves and their families. The cottages that still remain embody and remind us of these hopes and dreams — they are modest in size but grand in hope.

We hope that with the pen-and-ink drawings, photographs of the modest houses, and the telling of the stories of the successful trajectory of the lives of some of the immigrants and workers who flourished in them, the value of these homes will become evident. Their worth should be measured less by their size and architectural antecedents and more by how these "vessels" were able to shelter, support, and enable so many families to flourish.

Each of these cottages has a story.

After reading *Modest Hopes*, we hope readers will think differently about these workers' cottages. When walking or driving by one, a pair, or a long or short row of these little houses, the reader might wonder who lived in them, where did they come from, what did they accomplish, what part of our city did they build, and how did they contribute to the Toronto we know today? In *Modest Hopes*, these stories are told.

Fig. 1 Hamilton Street.

INTRODUCTION

Home Is Where the Heart Is

There is little thought for the past, especially the past of the working poor, those who lived in tiny homes and laboured in the traditional industries and trades. Memory or acknowledgement of those who truly built the country with their hands and their skill and fortitude is obliterated. We just romanticize them as an idea and pave over their existence.

— John Doyle, *Globe and Mail* [1]

The purpose of *Modest Hopes* is coincidentally summarized in the preface of George H. Rust-D'Eye's *Cabbagetown Remembered*, where he writes that his book "is intended to remedy, in some small way, the imbalance of attention to the lower social orders and their environment, caused by the perspective of the early writers on the history of this city." [2]

In the early 1800s, the Town of York was defined by John Graves Simcoe's 1793 "Plan of York Harbour," which consisted of a 10-square-block grid just west of the Don River. The geography of the lake, river, and rising ground to the north contained the small community of one- and two-storey log, frame, and later brick buildings. "Muddy York," named after the condition of its streets, had a population of 700 in 1812, made up mostly of English, Scottish, and Irish settlers; Loyalists who had fled the American Revolution; and a small number of escaped slaves from the U.S. South. By 1852, the Town of York had a new name, Toronto, had been designated a city, and had a population of 30,000.

Visitors to the city in the early part of the century often remarked on the clouds of wood and later coal smoke that obscured the community and its few church steeples. They were also assailed by the noise of industry and the yelling of carters and merchants in the streets, as well as the unavoidable smell of horse dung and backyard privies.

These were some of the conditions that greeted the thousands of newcomers who began to flood into Toronto at this time. As primitive and unsavoury as this environment was, it did not dim the hopes of those who arrived looking for a better life. With almost inconceivable sacrifice and commitment, tens of thousands of immigrants came to Toronto in search of a brighter future. Their sense of dislocation, their fear of the unknown, and the utter strangeness of this community in the wilderness must have been almost overwhelming. The fact that most of the newcomers spoke English, the language of their new home, would have helped them adjust to their new surroundings. Connections with family and friends already living in Toronto with whom they could live until they found their own homes would have made the transition from the old to the new easier. But for most of the newcomers, adjusting to life in their adoptive city must have been a struggle only comparable to the experience of immigrants today.

The enduring need for and dream of a "home" as a safe and nurturing place to live and raise families in the New World must have helped sustain them. So many of these new arrivals to Toronto had been in desperate conditions. Most had fled appalling poverty; many were driven out of their homes and off ancestral lands they and their families had lived in and worked on for countless generations. From the peasants' stone huts or hovels of rural Scotland and Ireland to the crowded tenements of cities such as Edinburgh, Dublin, and London, immigrants from Britain arrived hoping for better futures in Upper and Lower Canada and cities such as Toronto and Montreal.

The conditions they left behind, the experiences of their passage across the ocean or the trek from other parts of the continent, the expectations they had for Toronto, and the actual conditions they met upon arrival affected their progress and success in their new home.

A city can be seen as a collection of neighbourhood communities. Each one consists of physical and tangible contexts made up of streets, buildings, open spaces, and natural features. Each also has an intangible character that comprises the events, stories, and lives of the people who lived there. Many factors affected the quality of immigrants' daily lives both outside and inside homes — community environments such as places of employment, schools, religious institutions, and shopping. But equally important, the quality of their daily lives was shaped inside their homes, such as the requirements of washing and of bodily functions, sleeping, clothing storage, laundry, food storage and preparation, and family interactions met within these houses. These contexts and the individual elements within them are reflected in their stories.

The earliest workers' homes still seen in Toronto are the Scadding Cabin, built in 1794 and moved to its current location at the Canadian National Exhibition in 1879, and the Osterhout Log Cabin, built in 1795 and moved to Guildwood Park in 1934.[3]

Still scattered throughout the older parts of Toronto, however, are some of the city's first "workers' cottages." These modest houses are squeezed between their larger, newer neighbours, or exist in rows hidden behind decades of change and "modernization." The layers of porches and second-storey additions, clapboard fronts, angel stone, and vinyl siding disguise the original modest homes that sheltered and nurtured the families of immigrants and labourers who built Toronto.

Newcomers who arrived in Toronto and lived in crowded temporary conditions and then worked and saved enough money to move into, for example, a self-contained 12- to 16-foot-wide frame-and-brick rowhouse

Fig. ii *Osterhout Log Cabin, built circa 1795 and moved to Guildwood Park in 1934.*

was the result of unimaginably strong hopes, beliefs, and commitments to their futures. For workers and their families, these houses were far from modest; they improved quality of life, embodied social and economic advancement, and served as signs of ambition and values.

Historically, and continuing today, from the perspective of many Torontonians, these tiny, modest couplets and rowhouses are considered cramped, poorly constructed, unlivable, and unimportant "teardowns," as John Doyle in the *Globe and Mail* has commented.

Chapter One in *Modest Hopes* offers an overview of the traditional British structures that served as models for Toronto's workers' cottages.

The innovative, historic antecedents conceived in the 19th century to serve as plans for improving workers' housing are also presented. This context is intended to put into perspective the five house types that evolved from 1820 to 1920.

These house types, whether single, side-by-side duplex, or row, are identified and explored in Chapter Two. Building descriptions, photographs, illustrations, and elevations are included in that chapter to provide an understanding of the houses themselves, their layout, and the spaces inside.

Chapter Three introduces the range of immigrant groups that came to Toronto from the 1820s to the 1920s, describing who they were, where they came from, and the housing conditions they left behind. Understanding how these people lived before coming to Toronto helps readers to appreciate the enormity and scale of the achievements of many who were able to purchase or rent and live in a Modest Hope.

Chapter Four outlines the history of Toronto from 1820 to 1920. As well as examining the physical and economic growth of the city, the chapter also looks at the social conditions faced by the poor who arrived in Toronto searching for better lives. What was Toronto like when the thousands of immigrants who migrated to the city between 1820 and 1920 arrived? During this period, Toronto's great symbols of empire and power, such as St. James Cathedral, Osgoode Hall, and the University of Toronto, were built. At the same time, Toronto became a "city of cottages." The reactions of Toronto's citizenry and ruling elite to these waves of new arrivals are also discussed.

Chapter Five considers some of the neighbourhoods that contained — and some still contain — great numbers of workers' cottages, such as Lombard Street,[4] The Junction,[5] The Ward,[6] Cabbagetown,[7] Corktown,[8] Leslieville,[9] and Riverside.[10]

In Chapter Six, the stories of eight individuals and their families who lived and flourished in some of these workers' cottages are told. And finally, the Conclusion reviews the reasons why these vulnerable buildings are valuable, what they represent, and why they should be preserved.

Fig. 1.1 Sackville Street.

1

ORIGINS

The History and Antecedents of Workers' Housing Movements

[T]he labourer is one of the most valuable members
of society.... His situation then should be considered,
and made at least comfortable.

— Nathaniel Kent, *Hints to Gentlemen
of Landed Property*

T he designs of Modest Hope prototypes were influenced by social movements whose goals were to improve the living conditions of the "poor" in cities and the country or on large estates. In
particular, Nathaniel Kent, an English land valuer and agriculturist,
was instrumental in fostering such movements. Kent's groundbreak-
ing book *Hints to Gentlemen of Landed Property* (1775) had a fundamental impact on the conceptual design of workers' housing and
affected the popularity of workers' cottages. Some important excerpts
from Kent's work are:

We are all careful of our horses, nay of our dogs, which are less valuable animals; we bestow considerable attention upon our stables and kennels, but we are apt to look upon cottages as incumbrances, and clogs to our property; when, in fact, those who occupy them are the very nerves and sinews of agriculture … more real advantages flow from cottages, than from any other source; for besides their great utility to landed property, they are the greatest support to the state, as being the most prolific cradles of population. Cottagers are indisputably the most beneficial race of people we have.[1]

Estates [are] of no value without hands to cultivate them, the labourer is one of the most valuable members of society; without him the richest soil is not worth owning. His situation then should be considered, and made at least comfortable, if it were merely out of good policy. There is certainly no object so highly deserving the country gentleman's attention; his interest, and his duty equally prompt him, to do all he can to place him upon a better footing than he is at present. The first point to be taken under consideration is the state of the cottages, which these useful people inhabit.[2]

The shattered hovels which half the poor of this kingdom are obliged to put up with is truly affecting to a heart fraught with humanity Those who condescend to visit these miserable tenements can testify that neither health nor decency can be preserved in them.[3]

Great towns are destructive both to morals, and health, and the greatest drains we have; for where many of the lower sort of people crowd together, as in London, Norwich, Birmingham, and other manufacturing towns, they are obliged to put up with bad accommodation, and an unwholesome, confined air, which breeds contagious distempers, debilitates their bodies, and shortens their lives.[4]

Kent's work revolutionized the conditions of workers' cottages throughout Britain. His book featured detailed descriptions of improved yet cost-effective cottages. He had the foresight to see value in improving the conditions of these cottages, which in turn increased productivity, pride, and a sense of home and place for the working class.

A few years later, heavily influenced by Nathaniel Kent, British architect John Wood published *A Series of Plans for Cottages or Habitations of the Labourer, Either in Husbandry, or the Mechanic Arts, Adapted as Well to Towns as to the Country* (1806). It is considered one of the earliest British pattern books for workers' cottages.

John Claudius Loudon's *Encyclopedia of Cottage, Farm, and Villa Architecture and Furniture* (1836) is considered by many scholars to be one of the best-known architectural treatments of workers' housing to follow Kent and Wood. A decade later, English social activist Edwin Chadwick took reference from Loudon's patterns for workers' cottages in his work to reform the Poor Laws in England. Chadwick's *Sanitary Report* (1842) instituted major reforms in urban sanitation, public health, and the designs of workers' cottages.[5]

The theories and work of Kent, Wood, Loudon, and Chadwick, among others, had a resounding impact. Gradually, rural estate and factory owners, railway magistrates, and small developers throughout England, Scotland, and Ireland saw value in improving both the conditions and aesthetics of housing for their workers. Designs of cottages started to reference larger, more stately homes, incorporating mansard roofs,[6] bay windows, fretwork,[7] transom windows, and two-toned brick patterns over doors and windows.

In 1840s Britain, several housing reform societies were established in which Queen Victoria's husband, Prince Albert, had a personal interest.[8] To many of these housing societies, he offered his support and advice, including serving as president for the Society for Improving the Condition of the Labouring Classes (SICLC). Its objective was to commission designs for affordable yet sanitary buildings for the working classes in large urban environments.

Fig. 1.2 Front elevations and floor plans from John Wood's *A Series of Plans for Cottages or Habitations of the Labourer.*

The Prince Albert Model Cottage was introduced at the Great Exhibition's Crystal Palace in London's Hyde Park in 1851. Prince Albert was a lead organizer of the exhibition, which was a celebration of modern industrial technology and design that aimed to provide the world with the promise of a better future.[9] The Exhibition was also a vehicle for Britain to make "clear to the world its role as industrial leader"[10] and it became a symbol of the Victorian Age.[11]

At the exhibition, the Prince Albert Model Cottage received the Gold Medal Class VII, the highest honour awarded for housing science at the time.[12] The Model Cottage's architect was Henry Roberts, who had designed many buildings that represented innovations in workers' housing. The cottage was designed to house four families, with two flats on each level. Each flat had a living room, a heating cupboard, a kitchen, a coal bin, and three bedrooms for privacy, allowing one for the parents and separate ones for boy and girl siblings.[13] Plus, they were purported to be soundproof, resistant to dampness, sanitary, and cheap to make.

The Great Exhibition's Model Cottage tour ended with an exhibit room where information on the display home and other similar types was made available in pamphlets, books, and model drawings. Hundreds of thousands of people from around the world walked through the exhibit and returned home with the cottage in print form. More importantly, they took away the idea that a home shapes its inhabitants and reflects the nation.[14,15]

The Model Cottage and its philanthropic ideals gave further momentum to workers' housing designs in British pattern books and magazines,[16] which were soon disseminated overseas to become a major influence on 19th-century architecture in Canada,[17] evident in the number of pattern-book-inspired cottages in cities, towns, and villages across Southern Ontario.

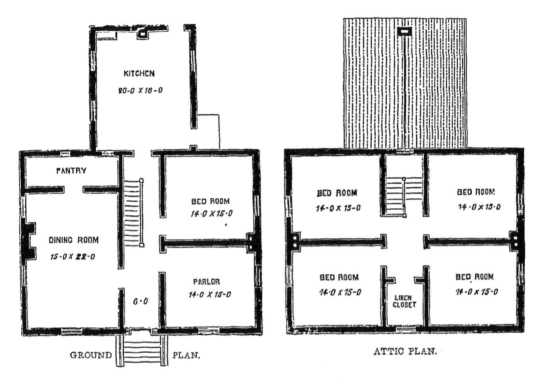

Fig. 1.3 Floor plan from the *Canada Farmer*, November 15, 1864, "A Cheap Farm House."

Fig. 1.4 An example of "A Cheap Farm House" style in Bognor, Ontario.

Fig. 1.5 "A Cheap Farm House" front elevation.

Model Workers' Cottages Canada-Style

In 1864, Canada's own series of house patterns was published for the first time in the "most successful home-grown print campaign [that] managed to infiltrate the vernacular"[18] in the "inconspicuous guise of a farming magazine."[19] That year, Toronto's *Globe* newspaper began publishing a biweekly journal called the *Canada Farmer*. It included a column entitled "Rural Architecture," written by the Scotland-born, Toronto-based architect James Avon Smith, who had designed a few churches, some houses, and several commercial buildings and warehouses.[20] Smith's *Canada Farmer* articles and patterns had a tremendous impact on Canadian designs. They were the only Canadian source for modern design ideas for Canadian architects and builders until the *Canadian Architect and Builder* appeared in 1888.[21]

Smith published two designs for rural homesteads in 1865 — "A Small Gothic Cottage" and "A Cheap Farm House" — that were easily adaptable to stylistic changes, tightly packed building sites, and city restrictions. With their simplicity and efficient layout, these plans effectively changed the architectural landscape of Ontario in the 1800s.[22] Their design is directly connected to many workers' cottages in Toronto.

Drawings and excerpts from late-19th-century advertisements reflect this movement to improve the living conditions of the "poor" in health and housing during that period. This idea that the improved home improved lives encompassed social values current at the time, and many of these values were attached to the idea of "home." The design of many of these small houses, especially those built in the latter half of the 1800s, often reflected these values and improvements. A good example of these ideas is found in the following excerpt from an advertisement representing a popular model for rural housing published in 1875:

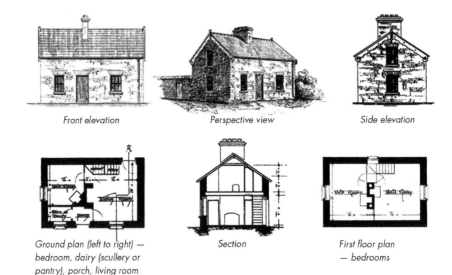

Front elevation   *Perspective view*   *Side elevation*

Ground plan (left to right) —
bedroom, dairy (scullery or
pantry), porch, living room   *Section*   *First floor plan*
— bedrooms

Fig. 1.6 Labourers'
dwellings, County
Mayo, Ireland,
1875, architect
E. Townsend.

We give with this number an illustration of a Labourer's Dwelling, designed by Mr. E. Townsend, C.E. A number of these cottages have recently been erected in the counties of Galway and Mayo, under the Board of Works. These cottages have the advantage of three bedrooms, which prevents the evil of the different sexes sleeping in one room, which only too often occurs in country places. To these cottages is attached a yard with ashpit, w.-c., and piggery at the further end, and other out-offices according to the means of the occupier. The walls are built of rubble masonry, and the floor of living room, porch, &c., is made of concrete in preference to tiles, it being often found difficult to repair the latter in remote country districts. The total cost of one of these cottages is £120.[23]

Although some of the more liberal-minded landowners at that time attempted to improve the living conditions of their tenants by providing "modern" houses, there continued to be a social stigma attached to these small homes that lasted well into the 20th century. The patronizing tone and sentiments expressed in the following sections from G.A. Dean's 1849 "Essay on Cottages for Labourers," when read today, help us to understand the basis of society's continual erasing of the history of these cottages and their social and cultural devaluation:

> The accommodation required is not such as would be looked for by persons moving in a higher sphere of life, and who are accustomed, comparatively, to luxuries; the labourer belongs to a totally distinct class of society, and what he most requires are warm, comfortable, and well-ventilated apartments. Let the dwellings of the poor be scientifically constructed, and much illness and misery will be prevented. In effecting this the whole community is interested, as parochial expenses are increased or diminished according to the healthy state of the labouring population.
>
> …
>
> Cottages should be warm, and substantial: judgment will also be displayed when the architectural character of the building is in harmony with its use.
>
> …
>
> The picturesque appearance of the cottage may be increased by entrance porches, overhanging roofs, and stacks of chimney shafts, having ornamental summits. The porch, independently of its architectural effect, affords both warmth and shelter, as does also the overhanging roof. The lofty chimney clustered shafts, besides assisting to prevent a smoky room, have a very pleasing appearance.
>
> …
>
> The taste for the beautiful, which formerly was confined exclusively to the upper and middle classes of society, is now partially extending to the labourer.

...

Facilitate the opportunity of the labourer for obtaining comforts, and the means of rational enjoyment, and you will create in him a relish for his frugal and homely fare and furnish him with the means of happiness in his home and family.

...

In surveying the state of the population of our agricultural districts, it will be generally observed, that the condition of the farm labourer is inferior to that of the mechanic, both as regards education and domestic comfort. This has already seriously engaged the attention of many benevolent landowners, who are strenuously endeavouring, not only to ameliorate that condition, but, by permanent improvement, to establish such a system of domestic economy, as will gradually and surely induce a feeling of morality, and which will always be accompanied with settled habits of industry.[24]

Fig. 1.7 Audley Avenue, the storey-and-a-half cottage pair.

The social organizations to improve living conditions for the less fortunate, and the examples of house designs that became popular in Britain and Ireland at this time and that resulted in healthier housing for workers, certainly impacted what was built in Toronto. Many, if not all, workers' cottages that can be seen in the older sections of the city today reflect in their designs aspects of this modern house movement.

Tens of thousands of displaced rural labourers and industrial workers from Britain, Ireland, Continental Europe, the U.S. South, the Caribbean, and China came to Toronto in the 19th and early 20th centuries to seek better lives. Whether they had lived in rural cottages or urban tenements, their expectations and frames of reference for housing were shaped by what they knew. The section that follows is intended to provide an idea of the living conditions Toronto's immigrants left behind and underscores the vast difference and improvement living in a Modest Hope meant.

Rural Workers' Housing

Living conditions and housing for rural workers in Britain, Ireland, and Continental Europe in the 17th, 18th, and early 19th centuries varied from region to region and country to country, but they generally shared a number of characteristics:

- They were built to protect the inhabitants and often their animals from weather, wild animals, and strangers.
- The small shelters were built to provide a home offering some family privacy, whether located on the landlord's property or on other land they worked.
- The cottages were generally constructed of building materials easily available nearby such as fieldstone, clay, turf, thatch, poles, and branches, easy to assemble into a functional shelter by people with few tools and domestic construction skills.

Fig. 1.8 A rural cottage in Donegal, Ireland, Victorian period.

These housing characteristics or requirements resulted in a range of huts and shelters that usually consisted of dry-laid (mortarless) stones piled on one another, with gaps allowing smoke from cooking fires inside to escape. More sophisticated cottages incorporated fieldstone as well as turf blocks stacked and then covered with mud or clay plaster to form the walls, while branches were used to frame a simple, sloping roof structure. Materials such as thatch, and later, flat stones and slate on more substantial roof framing systems, were also employed.

Figure 1.8 shows an archival photograph of a rural Irish cottage with white-painted stucco parging on the fieldstone walls and a thatch roof. It is difficult to determine the age of this particular cottage, but most likely it was built during the Victorian Era.

Exterior wall treatments such as wattle-and-daub, a construction technique involving branches woven together and filled with layers of wet clay applied to both sides of the vertical wattle structure and allowed to dry, were quite common. Stucco was also used on fieldstone walls to stabilize the dry-laid or mortarless walls and to water- and draft-proof them. These various building treatments evolved into the rural cottages seen in Figures 1.8 and 1.9. Such restored rural huts are still found throughout Britain and Ireland and were a precedent that helped form expectations for housing in the New World.

For many people, the living conditions in these small rectangular stone-and-stucco cottages consisted of a single dirt or flagstone ground floor that contained a communal fireplace for heating, cooking, eating, and living. There was often a curtained-off bed for adults on the ground floor and a loft or attic under the eaves for children to sleep. There was no running water, and the privy was outside. Usually, the family kept farm animals inside at night for the animals' protection and to provide warmth for the family.

Fig. 1.9 Cottage in Anstruther, Scotland.

Urban Workers' Housing and Urban Slums

Many of the immigrants to Toronto might have once lived in cities where housing conditions could be described as urban slums. The situation that existed in Dublin had parallels in cities throughout Britain, Ireland, and the rest of Europe. The exodus of the moneyed class might not have occurred elsewhere, but everywhere formerly fashionable areas became slums and new slums were created during the Industrial Revolution as workers flooded into the cities from the countryside and small towns.

Fig. 1.10 Dublin tenement housing of the early 20th century.

At the height of the 18th century, Dublin's inner city possessed an impressive variety of fine two-, three-, and four-storey Georgian townhouses and rowhouses built for wealthy merchants, lawyers, and members of high society. The Act of Union of 1801 shifted the Irish Parliament in Dublin to direct rule from London, which soon prompted many of Dublin's upper class to move to the outskirts of the city or to Britain's capital. Their large, abandoned inner-city homes were quickly turned into numerous small businesses, while landlords converted many into tenements and rooming houses, packing as many families as they could into the large homes and rooms.[25]

Ireland's Potato Famine from 1845 to 1852 brought many families into the city, seeking refuge from devastated rural areas. By the early 20th century, a third of Dublin's population lived in city centre tenement slums. By 1911, "Dublin had the worst housing conditions of any city in the United Kingdom."[26] According to statistics, "22,701 people lived in 'third-class' houses which were termed as unfit for human habitation."[27]

In the 19th-century Industrial Revolution in Britain and Ireland, working and living conditions of urban labourers changed dramatically and had a deep impact on home life. As workers migrated from the country to the city, their lives and the lives of their families were utterly and permanently transformed.[28]

During this period, the construction of terraced rows of small, inexpensive houses became a common means of providing shelter for factory workers. These were often built by employers who charged high rents

Fig. 1.11 Traditional cottage houses in North Strand, Dublin.

for poorly constructed cottages that too often became part of crowded, unhealthy, high-density slums. Most had privies in the rear yard, but in many parts of Ireland, rows were built as back-to-backs, resulting in the sharing of sanitary arrangements.[29] Too many of the poorest population lived in this overcrowded and inadequate housing, often even in cellars. It has been recorded that in one instance 17 people from different families resided in an area of 16 by 13 feet.

By the mid-1800s, these terraced houses had developed a negative reputation. Their lack of toilets and through-ventilation were feared as health hazards, so that they became "associated with high-density and extremely squalid living conditions in industrial towns and were strongly condemned by the more affluent members of the community."[30] By the 1930s, the Dublin tenements were considered "the worst slums in Europe."[31]

Dublin Tenement Life: An Oral History by Kevin C. Kearns provides a graphic picture of the creation and scale of the tenements that housed over one-third of Dublin's population — the urban poor at that time:

> The decline of Georgian Dublin from elegant abodes of the aristocracy to "human piggeries" is one of Dublin's saddest sagas. Myriad historical events contributed to the process of degeneration. A major force was the Act of Union in 1801 and the dissolution of the Irish Parliament that triggered a mass exodus of wealthy and prominent citizens. The departing gentry left their grand domiciles to be managed by agents as property values began a precipitous decline. Resplendent Georgian houses purchased for £8,000 in 1791 were sold for a paltry £500 in the 1840s. At mid-century when Ireland was in the cruel grip of the "Great Hunger" these spacious structures fell increasingly into the hands of the "profiteering landlords" who gradually came to rule the dark Dublin Slums. The downtrodden masses carried out what has been aptly termed the "colonization" of the brick Georgian terraces. Rack-renting landlords viewed their properties as little more than cattle-sheds to be packed with humanity. As the "respectable" classes fled to the suburbs in the second half of the 19th Century entire districts fell into tenement "slumdom." In 1900 there were over six thousand tenement houses in Dublin and one-third of the entire population lived in these "foul rookeries." By 1938 there were still 6,307 tenements in the capital occupied by 111,950 persons.[32]

Between 1800 and 1850, the population of England doubled as farm labour gave way to factory work, exacerbated by migration during the famine years. While urban centres swelled, a housing crisis ensued, and cities such as London struggled to house new residents. Massive overcrowding and filthy conditions prevailed throughout dense city districts and often down narrow alleys that were once passageways to give access to stables. Many could not afford even the worst housing and moved from place to place without a home.[33]

The *First Report of Her Majesty's Commissioners for Inquiring into the Housing of the Working Classes* was laid out before the British Houses of Commons and Lords in 1885. It stated that while conditions of working-class housing had improved over the past 30 or 40 years, many conditions remained dire and improvements were still necessary. An excerpt from the report reads as follows:

> In Clerkenwell, at 15, St. Helena Place, a house was described containing six rooms, which were occupied at that time by six families, and as many as eight persons inhabited one room. At 1, Wilmington Place, there were 11 families in 11 rooms, seven persons occupying one room. At 30, Noble Street, five families of 26 persons in all were found inhabiting six rooms. A small house in Allen Street was occupied by 38 persons, seven of whom lived in one room.

Fig. 1.12 Slum housing, Twine Court, Shadwell, London, circa 1899.

Fig. 1.13 East Terrace, South Queensferry, Edinburgh.

In Northampton Court there were 12 persons in a two-roomed house, eight of whom inhabited one room. In Northampton Street, there was a case of nine persons in one room. At 5, Bolton Court, a family of 10 persons occupied two small rooms. At 36, Bowling Green Lane, there were six persons in an underground kitchen. At 7, New Court, there were 22 persons in two rooms in which fowls also were kept. In Swan Alley, in an old, partly wooden and decayed house, there were 17 persons inhabiting three rooms.[34]

Similar to Dublin and London where middle- to upper-class terrace housing became lodging for the poor, the wealthy in Scottish cities also left the inner city and their former houses often became tenements.

Poorhouses

A great many working-class people had no real homes at all, just simple huts or miserable spaces in urban slums. In 1815, after the Napoleonic Wars, the problems of mass unemployment and homelessness required a solution. So the British government passed the Poor Law of 1834 to provide such an "answer." This law saw the creation of workhouses, or poorhouses, for the destitute. The institutions were designed to be "as like prisons as possible"[35] to discourage people from remaining on government relief. Families were separated upon entering the grounds and confined each night like inmates in a prison, working by day on tasks such as breaking stones or crushing bones to make fertilizer.

One assistant commissioner of the workhouses commented: "Our object … is to establish therein a discipline so severe and repulsive as to make them a terror to the poor and prevent them from entering."[36] These institutions "grew hand-in-glove with the Industrial Revolution as great swaths of people moved to urban areas to find work, but often fell victim to underemployment."[37] Despite these very harsh conditions, workhouse inmates increased from 78,536 in 1838 to 197,179 in 1843.[38] This rise reflected the degree of desperation among the poorest of the poor.[39]

Housing for Black Slaves in the U.S. South and Caribbean

In the Americas, a different kind of housing existed that was designed especially for the great many enslaved Black people forced to labour there. From the beginning of the 16th century to the middle of the 19th century, Africans seized by slave traders were taken to the western hemisphere. Housing for them varied widely depending on the context,

Fig. 1.14 A slave house in the U.S. South.

Fig. 1.15 Chattel plantation house in Barbados.

whether it was rural or urban. On farms and plantations, slaves working on the land usually lived in huts or barracks-style housing, while those tasked with jobs in homes, kitchens, laundries, or stables either in the country or cities simply resided where they worked.

Most slave cabins were constructed crudely of wood with no foundations and were typically a single storey with one or two rooms, depending on how many families lived in them.[40] Most of the housing was poorly built, since there was little expectation it would last for more than a few decades.[41] After slavery was officially abolished in the United States in 1865, many slaves became landless because most of the land was owned by the plantations. Some former slaves were subsequently allowed to build their humble homes on marginally productive plantation estates, paying very little rent; other former slaves left their "homes" and fled north, looking to build new and better lives elsewhere. Some of these came to Canada and settled in Toronto.

The chattel house, originating in Barbados, was a type of housing built for plantation slaves. It, too, had no foundation and was constructed of timber and supported by coral blocks, allowing it to be easily relocated and its inhabitants evicted on short notice.[42] Many immigrants to Toronto left behind such conditions and their memories of them. The eventual attainment of homes of their own in Canada, whether rented or owned, was an amazing achievement and transition as well as an undeniable improvement in their lives.

Fig. 2.1 Boulton Avenue.

2

THE ARCHITECTURE
Five Modest Hope House Types

For every Gooderham mansion, there were thousands of workers' cottages. In the grand scheme, not many of these remain in current day Toronto. But there are certainly enough to serve as a reminder of our forbearers and how they lived.
— Derek Flack, content strategist, editor, and instructor[1]

Architecturally, workers' cottages are vessels of history. Most were built in a style brought to Canada — to Toronto — by way of the many immigrants who moved there in the 19th and early 20th centuries. There are vestiges of much grander homes in their designs — the yellow brickwork around windows and doors, fretwork bordering windows and in the peaks of rooflines, the carefully laid-out slate roofs or simple bay windows — speak an architectural language of prosperity, pride, and modest hope.

Cultural and heritage values are embedded in these cottages and are reflected in their size and "look." Yet, "along with the architectural interest, there is a social element that one should note about this fading bit of Toronto's history. The people largely responsible for building this city lived in these humble properties that were not much larger than the apartments we so love to complain about today."[2] The foundation of Modest Hope homes is that the people who once lived in them made them important and gave them value. Furthermore, these small houses were a significant symbol of "home," a concept the urban middle classes of North America, from the 1820s, envisioned as "an embellished inner space cut off from the public world" and "an incubator of morals and family affections."[3]

Five Modest Hope house types can be identified, but first it is necessary to understand why they are important and to imagine what everyday life might have been like for the people who once lived in them. Essentially, their worth lies in their success containing and fostering so many accomplished lives. As Christopher Alexander comments in *The Timeless Way of Building*, "a person is so far formed by his surroundings that his state of harmony depends entirely on his harmony with his surroundings."[4]

These modest cottages were once homes that nurtured the lives of so many people who built Toronto. The actual physical space, the layout and size of each room, impacted the quality of their lives. The number of people who resided in each house, the interior temperature during different seasons, and access to natural light and views outside were also influential in the calibre of daily living for the occupants, as were the everyday requirements of washing and bodily functions, sleeping, clothing storage, laundry, food storage and preparation, and family interactions. Other factors included how the house was heated, what lighting was used at night, what cleaning was required, and what kind of furniture the people had.

Other aspects that affected their lives were more contextual and included where the house was located in the city, what the neighbourhood itself was like, how noisy it was, and who else lived on the street or next door. Social and cultural issues were also important: what people's country of origin was; where the employed members of the family, often fathers, sometimes young sons, daughters, and mothers, had to go to work; where children had to attend school and play; and how close everybody was to local markets, taverns, and churches.

Given the above considerations, the context of these houses and how they emotionally and physically touched all aspects of lives lived in them help us understand their value today. As the 19th century progressed, original one-storey, two-room cottages evolved into more substantial homes, some with brick veneer on the street-facing elevation replacing the earlier, less-expensive stucco or board. When demand for these houses grew, a half or full second storey was commonly added to the same narrow footprint, increasing the livable floor area from 800 to 1,000 square feet. As architectural styles and fashions changed in Britain and Ireland, classical and later Victorian and Second Empire styles and features were imported by the immigrant craftsmen who built what they knew. Bay windows, buff-coloured brick detailing, and carved bargeboards and brackets, as well as window, porch, and railing elements were built onto the basic and durable workers' house plans customary in Toronto for decades. Replication of these styles and details certainly reflected the builders' and owners' British heritage as well as their colonial loyalty to the mother country.

The design of most, if not all, these Modest Hopes was based on simple, shared characteristics. Each house was narrow and occupied very little land. The interior was used efficiently, while high ceilings added a sense of spaciousness. They were inexpensive and easy to construct, since the layout was based on familiar and often repeated designs that evolved throughout the late 18th and 19th centuries in England, Scotland, and Ireland.

Some factory owners in Toronto, such as the Gooderhams, built workers' cottages as a source of income. The Gooderhams built their cottages close to their distillery on the waterfront west of the Don River. Their workers represented a captive market for these cottages, since their proximity to the distillery reduced travel time to and from work. Some, like the 32 Garrison Common or Robinson Cottages in the city's west end, were built by the early real estate developer James Lukin Robinson in 1859 as a business investment. Workers' cottages were also provided for the Don Jail's staff, directly south of the institution below Gerrard Street on Munro and Hamilton Streets in the east end.

Workers sometimes built their own houses such as those on Erie Terrace (Craven Road) in the east end of Toronto. After saving as much as they could and purchasing the lot, they often erected temporary shelters or shacks at the rear of their properties to live in while they slowly constructed cottages after work and during layoffs. The new cottages were built from available materials and designed according to existing plans, or they were based on familiarity with similar houses they worked on as carpenters or masons or when helping neighbours or family members build homes.

When thousands of immigrants from Great Britain and Continental Europe arrived in Toronto in the late 1800s, there were limited housing options available. The more fortunate had relatives who had immigrated earlier and who had lodgings of some kind to share until the newcomers found their own homes. Single men often lived in one room with other males in a tenement, men's only lodgings, or flophouses. Some built shacks from scrounged wood and discarded crates along the Don River and on unclaimed land elsewhere, while others built backyard houses on the properties of family members or friends. For many families, housing of any kind was more problematic to find, a difficulty that increased as the number of family members expanded. If they could afford the expense, some immigrants rented or even purchased a house.

The cost of such cottages and the sacrifice required to rent or own one represented a commitment to the future that should be appreciated today. The following examples are based on average wages and commodity prices in the late 19th to early 20th centuries. The percentage of a single wage earner's income spent on housing can be compared to the recommended Canadian average today of 30 percent, and the cost of food is based on an average today of approximately 11 percent of the same annual income.

To rent a five- or six-room frame Modest Hope for two adults and four children, the father — a carpenter, mason, painter, or plasterer — faced certain difficult conditions. At 30 cents per hour for an eight-hour day, he earned $2.40 per day. For a six-day week, he earned $14.40, for a month $57.60, and for a year $691.20, given that he worked all year.

Since much of this type of work was seasonal and subject to market factors, let us assume an average annual wage of $450 for the worker. With rent likely between $8 to $12 per month or $100 to $150 per year, we can figure an average annual rent of $120. That meant such a family spent 27 percent of its gross annual income on housing, slightly lower than the recommended Canadian average today of 30 percent.

Using the same annual income, and based on today's average of 11 percent of a family of six's annual income spent on food, this meant that a family living in a Modest Hope likely had $50 per year or just 14 cents per day to feed the family. For the rest of the year, the family was left with 90 cents per day for all other living costs such as heat, furniture, tools, equipment, clothing, education, religion, socializing, recreation, and savings.

Fig. 2.2 Cottage advertisements in the *Toronto Evening Star,* January 12, 1894.

If the same worker bought the same five- or six-room frame cottage on a 30-by-100-foot lot, had the same annual income of $450, and the purchase price was $1,250, he would need to save a down payment of $100, say, over two years. That would mean he would have to save $50 a year before purchasing the house while probably renting or sharing another one. To buy a Modest Hope, he would pay annual interest of 6 percent or $6 per month plus a $12-per-month mortgage payment, the latter deducted from the purchase price until it was paid off. So, instead of paying rent of $10 per month, the house buyer paid $18 per month, representing 48 percent or almost half of his annual income. Using the same annual income, and based on today's average of a family spending 11 percent of that income on food, meant that the family living in a purchased Modest Hope also had $50 per year, or just 14 cents per day, to feed themselves. As such, this family was left with only 50 cents per day for all other living costs.

Although the above figures are merely estimated averages, what is clear is that in terms of the fundamental effort necessary to rent or own one of these small houses, the amount of work, the doing without, the making do, the sharing, and the faith in the future should be remembered when we see a Modest Hope today and contemplate what it represents.

1. THE ONE-STOREY COTTAGE

Fig. 2.3 Gerrard Street East, a one-storey cottage row.

The 400- to 500-square-foot, single-storey cottage was a very popular and affordable house in the early to mid-19th century in Toronto. Whether erected as a detached home, side-by-side duplex, or rowhouse, it generally had a wood frame construction often with brick veneer on the front elevation and clapboard, stucco, or later, asphalt brick shingles on the sides and back. Based on a side-hall plan, the front elevation of a pair of such houses was consistently symmetrical. Both entry doors were centred, and windows for the front room were located on each side. The interior was divided into four rooms: two bedrooms, a parlour, and the kitchen. Variations in this house type included a Gothic[5] centre gable, a front porch, rear kitchen additions, and a sleeping loft accessible by a ladder or steep stair (see Figs. 2.4 and 2.5).

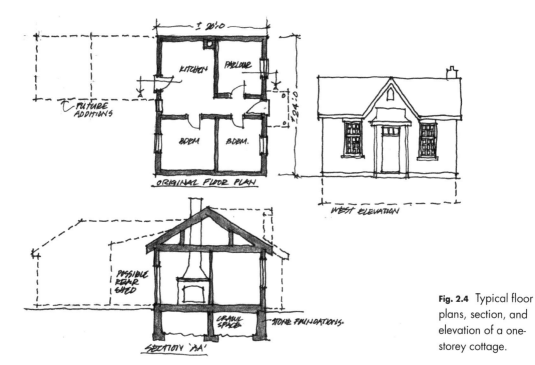

Fig. 2.4 Typical floor plans, section, and elevation of a one-storey cottage.

Fig. 2.5 Knox Street. Formerly called Lake Street, it became Knox in 1897. Originally, Lake Ontario was much closer to the house before the waterfront was infilled for industry. The street was once heavily occupied by bricklayers, labourers, and commercial fishermen, the last taking their families out in their schooners for cruises on the lake on Sunday afternoons.[6]

Fig. 2.6 Eastern Avenue.

Fig. 2.7 De Grassi Street.

Fig. 2.8 Lewis Street.

Fig. 2.9 Saulter Street.

Fig. 2.10 St. Paul Street.

Fig. 2.11 Audley Avenue.

Fig. 2.12 A side-by-side one-storey cottage pair.

Fig. 2.13

324 Ontario Street

Once the home of James and Susan Watt from Scotland, the Watts lived here with their seven children from 1878 to 1920. James worked as a travelling salesman with Samuel Trees & Company, an importer of saddlery and trunks and a manufacturer of collars and blankets. Upon James's death, Susan continued living here until 1920. "Strongman" Fred H. Beasley then lived at the address until 1922. Well known locally, he was frequently photographed demonstrating his impressive feats of strength. He also owned a local confectionary.

Fig. 2.14 Mitchell Avenue.

Fig. 2.15 Lewis Street.

Fig. 2.16 Dundas Street East.

Fig. 2.17 Lewis Street.

Fig. 2.18 This house at 38 St. Paul Street was once the home of Anne O'Rourke from Ireland. After moving to Canada with her husband and son in 1847, she had six more children in Toronto. Upon the early death of her husband, Anne was widowed with seven children. She found work at a nearby dairy (see pages 183–91).

2. THE STOREY-AND-A-HALF COTTAGE

Fig. 2.19 Coxwell Avenue.

The storey-and-a-half cottage evolved from earlier houses and was a variation of the single-storey cottage type. It relied on slightly higher ground or main floor walls to provide headroom in the attic storey. In the case of rowhouses, a window in the front centre gable provided light and some ventilation for the attic sleeping loft. For a detached house of this type, windows were also located in the upper gables of the sidewalls, allowing the upper half storey to be divided into two separate sleeping areas, each with its own window for light and ventilation. Access to the upper level was usually by steep narrow stairs located in the centre hall (see Fig. 2.20).

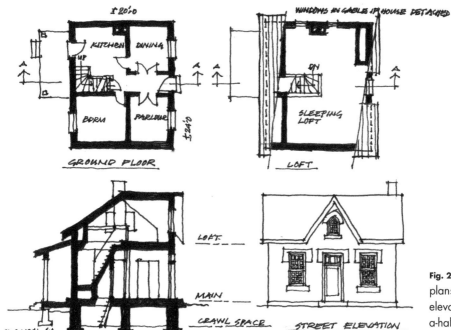

Fig. 2.20 Typical floor plans, section, and elevation of a storey-and-a-half cottage.

Fig. 2.21 Saulter Street.

Fig. 2.22 De Grassi Street.

Fig. 2.23 Hamilton Street.

Fig. 2.24 Morse Street.

Fig. 2.25 Ashdale Avenue.

Fig. 2.26 Silver Birch Avenue.

Fig. 2.27 Silver Birch Avenue.

3. THE TWO-STOREY MANSARD AND BAY-AND-GABLE ROWHOUSE

Fig. 2.28 Dundas Street East.

This house type was very popular from the middle to the late 19th century, and well-preserved examples are found throughout downtown Toronto today. They generally used a mansard-type roof profile or a roof shape that was straight, convex, bell-caste, or concave on the front elevation, with one or two projecting dormer windows. The ground floor was commonly a side-hall plan with a single window in the front parlour. Later models were constructed with a projecting three-sided bay with windows in the front and ground-floor room. This type, known as a bay-and-gable house, was usually constructed as detached, pairs, or rows. It was consistently wood frame construction with the use of a masonry veneer with contrasting detailing on the front wall. These decorative elements used soldier courses[7] on the first floor, blind arches[8] above the windows, and contrasting brick and/or limestone components, including keystones, stone sills, and decorative masonry features, all expressive of status and affluence referencing their British roots (see Figs. 2.28–2.30).

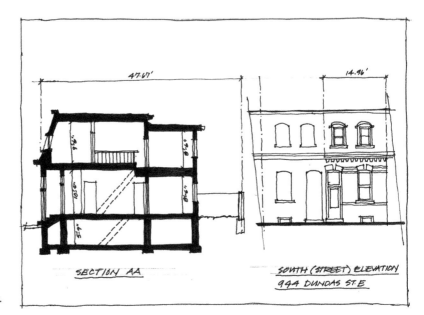

Fig. 2.29 Dundas Street East, typical section and elevation without main-floor bay window.

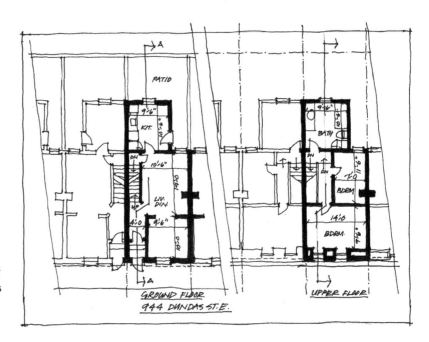

Fig. 2.30 Dundas Street East, section and plans without main-floor bay window.

Fig. 2.31 Saulter Street.

Fig. 2.32 St. Paul Street.

Fig. 2.33 Sackville Street.

Fig. 2.34 Eastern Avenue.

Fig. 2.35 Draper Street.

Fig. 2.36 21 Blackburn Street (right).

21 Blackburn Street

This was once the home of Henry Harwood-Jones and his wife, Jane (née Hourigan), who lived here with four of their eventual six children. They were a mixed English Protestant–Irish Catholic marriage, uncommon then, and their descendants believe that is partly why they came to Toronto in 1907 — to flee discrimination. Henry worked as a music teacher in their home and was also a popular organist at nearby Little Trinity Church. In 1916, he wrote the music for "My Soldier Dad" (words by Lewis Sinden). Henry later worked at Consumers' Gas as a meter reader but continued to play the organ at Little Trinity. Today, the descendants of Henry and Jane Harwood-Jones number upward of 225, and their very large family is spread across Canada, as well as in Australia and the United States, with careers that include police officers, hairdressers, assembly-line workers, clerks, military personnel, clerics, and music industry professionals.

Fig. 2.37 29 McGee Street (far right).

29 McGee Street

This was once the home of Hugh Kelly and Hugh Kelly Jr., father and son Irish Catholic butchers who had a stall in Toronto's St. Lawrence Market. Hugh Jr., along with Hugh Wise (a promising athlete who rowed with Ned Hanlan) and Charles Phillips, among others, were accused of beating to death a local resident, William Long, in his mother's back garden. Mysteriously, only Hugh Wise and Charles Phillips were charged, though William Long identified his attackers before dying of brain injuries days after the attack. The Kelly family continued to live on McGee Street at 29, 39, and 47.[9]

3 Ashby Place

This house was once the home of Jeremiah ("Jerry") Shea from 1906 to 1907, born in St. Catharines, Ontario, to Irish parents. Jerry dropped out of school to help his brother, Michael, develop a line of Shea theatres in Buffalo, realizing

the early potential of moving pictures. In 1899, Jerry left Buffalo and moved to Toronto where he soon opened the first Shea theatre, a small venue at Yonge and King Streets, which was an immediate success. In 1910, they opened a larger theatre called the Shea Victoria on Victoria Street at Richmond Street. In 1914, Jerry opened Shea's Hippodrome on Bay Street, north of Queen Street. In the early decades of the 20th century, the name "Shea" was synonymous with theatre excellence.

Fig. 2.38 3 Ashby Place (third house from the right)

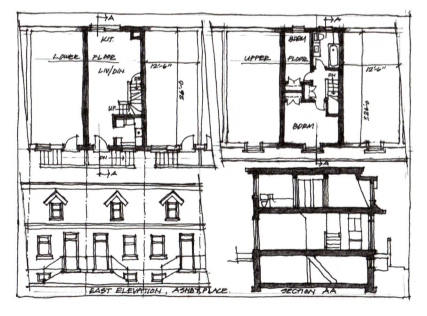

EAST ELEVATION, ASHBY PLACE.   SECTION AA

Fig. 2.39 Ashby Place floor plans, section, and front elevation.

4. THE TWO-STOREY TOWER-FORM OR GABLE-DORMER ROWHOUSE

Fig. 2.40 Mark Street.

These types of workers' cottages are more elaborate variations of the earlier bay-and-gable mansard two-storey houses. They were often 16 to 18 feet wide and 30 to 36 feet in depth, with a gross floor area of 1,200 to 1,300 square feet, though with a floor plan and size similar to the earlier types. These houses are characterized by tower-form dormers of different shapes, front porches, and a high level of decorative slate roofing, woodwork, and brick detailing. Again, they were generally built as detached, pairs or rows.

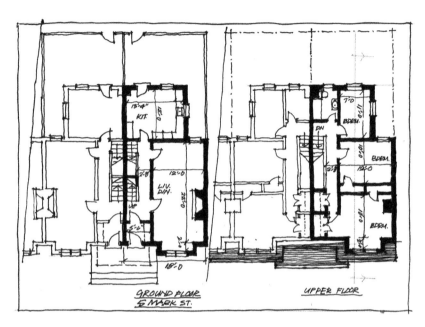

GROUND FLOOR
5 MARK ST.

UPPER FLOOR

Fig. 2.41 Mark Street, typical ground and upper floor plans.

SECTION AA

NORTH (STREET) ELEVATION
5 MARK ST.

Fig. 2.42 Mark Street, typical elevation and section.

Fig. 2.43 First Avenue.

Fig. 2.44 Pape Avenue.

Fig. 2.45 Tiverton Avenue.

Fig. 2.46 Geneva Avenue.

Fig. 2.47 Geneva Avenue.

5. THE TWO- AND THREE-STOREY TOWNHOUSE TERRACE

Fig. 2.48 Grant Street, a two-storey brick townhouse.

This compact terrace house had many precedents in Britain, Ireland, and Continental Europe and again evolved from the earlier, smaller house types. With either a simple low, sloped roof or a flat roof with a decorated parapet/cornice, these houses in many cases were also 16 to 18 feet wide and 30 feet in depth and provided a gross floor area of 1,200 to 1,300 square feet. A side-hall plan increased width and allowed for a larger front room or parlour and accommodated, on the second floor, either one or two bedrooms in the front or two bedrooms in the back. Some of these townhouses had a third floor under a mansard roof, adding an additional 400 to 600 square feet. This third floor typically had dormers, provided two to four extra bedrooms, and the stair was double-backed and extended. These rooms were often for servants who worked for affluent families with the means to live in these larger houses. Sometimes such houses were shared by several families or the rooms were rented.

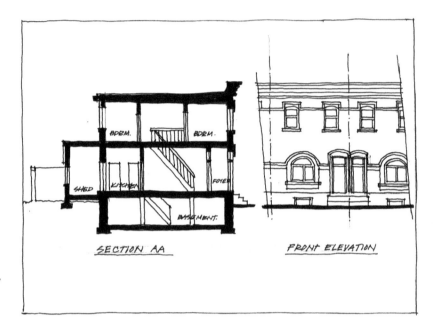

Fig. 2.49 Booth Avenue, typical section and elevation.

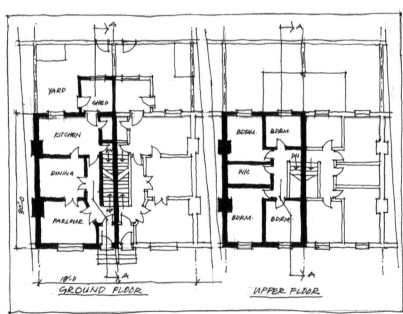

Fig. 2.50 Booth Avenue, typical ground and upper floor plans.

Fig. 2.51 Shuter Street.

Fig. 2.52 This house at 24 Allen Avenue (second house from right) was once the home of the Foden family, whose three sons fought in the First World War (see Fig. 2.58).

Fig. 2.53 Trinity Street.

Fig. 2.54 Booth Avenue.

Fig. 2.55 79 Allen Avenue (left).

79 Allen Avenue

A Victorian Gable version of the two-storey townhouse type. Robert Ferguson Jr. once lived here. He was originally from Scotland and worked at Elias Rogers & Company upon arriving in Toronto in 1892, ahead of his pregnant wife and their son. Maggie, Robert's wife, and Thomas, his son, joined him in Toronto from Northern Ireland when Thomas was only six months old. This was the first time Robert met his son. It was on Allen Avenue, years later, that Robert received notice that Thomas had been killed in the First World War. Robert outlived Maggie and two of his children (see pages 173–182).

Fig. 2.56 36 De Grassi Street (left).

36 De Grassi Street

This was the home of the Bewley family. Sons Stanley (born 1895) and Raymond Bewley (born 1897) attended Queen Alexandra Public School around the corner. Stanley worked at Woods Manufacturing Company at Logan Avenue and Dundas Street East as a cloth cutter. When the First World War began, both Raymond and Stanley enlisted. Raymond was injured but returned; Stanley died in the war in 1918. He was 23.

Fig. 2.57 73 Berkeley Street (left).

73 Berkeley Street

James E. Hynes once lived at 73 Berkeley Street in this workers' cottage housing block. Born in Kingston, Ontario, to Irish parents, the unmarried James resided at number 73 with his widowed mother, Mary. James's sister, Bridget, married Patrick Boyle, a printer. Hynes and Boyle shared an outrage over British colonialism in Ireland, prompting them to publish the *Irish Canadian* weekly newspaper, which forced Canadian political parties to recognize the emergence of a Catholic presence in English Canada. The 1868 Ottawa assassination of Thomas D'Arcy McGee, a Father of Confederation who opposed the Fenian presence in Canada, put Boyle and Hynes in jail for three months, suspending the publication of their newspaper. The partners' long-suspected Fenian sympathies had aroused suspicion of their guilt.[10] Hynes's home at 73 Berkeley was ransacked by police searching for evidence, but nothing was found, so he was released on bail and *The Irish Canadian* resumed publication. Patrick J. Whelan was eventually tried, convicted, and executed for McGee's murder.[11]

265 Booth Avenue

This address was once home to Herbert Ralph Foden, born in 1887, who attended Queen Alexandra Public School and worked at John Inglis and Company. He enlisted in the First World War with his two brothers, Sam and Jose, in the same battalion. In March 1917, Private Foden was reported missing and eventually presumed dead after all efforts to locate him failed. Only 29, he left behind his wife and two children.

Fig. 2.58 265 Booth Avenue (second house from left).

83 Boulton Avenue

The Holland family once lived in this house. They came to Toronto in 1834 before the Irish Potato Famine. Members of their extended family joined them when the famine ravaged Ireland. A family of butchers, there were five Terence Hollands, all of whom had that occupation.

Fig. 2.59 83 Boulton Avenue (centre).

Fig. 3.1 Kensington Market.

3

THE NEWCOMERS

Early Immigrants to Toronto Who Built and Lived in Modest Hopes

The most beautiful house in the world is the one that you build for yourself.
— Witold Rybczynski, The Most
Beautiful House in the World

A significant portion of the people who made Toronto their home in the 19th and early 20th centuries came to Canada as immigrants. The New World has always been a magnet for immigration as a chance to move beyond the traditional classes, economic constraints, and health crises of Britain, Ireland, Eastern Europe, and other homelands while enjoying seemingly unlimited space, new opportunities, and resources.

So many of these new arrivals to Toronto either left of their own accord or were driven out of their urban or village homes or off ancestral land their families had lived in and worked on for countless generations. Many had lived in peasants' un-mortared stone huts or wattle-and-daub thatched shelters in rural England, Scotland, and Ireland. Others resided in the crowded tenements of cities such as London, Birmingham, Edinburgh, and Dublin. Many new arrivals to Toronto had memories of wood-frame chattel houses in the Caribbean or slave cabins in the U.S. South. To come to Toronto, work, and save enough money to live in a 400- to 900-square-foot Modest Hope was an amazing achievement. For families to make a home with its own address and a front door, four walls, separate rooms, windows, and a roof was a breathtaking success and a vast improvement in the quality of their lives.

In *Immigrants: A Portrait of the Urban Experience, 1890–1930*, Robert Harney and Harold Troper provide an excellent summary of the forces that drove so many people to immigrate to Canada at that time. These reasons can be understood to also apply to some degree to those immigrants who came to Toronto in the early part of the 19th century and lived in some of Toronto's earliest Modest Hopes:

> Most Canadians, whether they approved of newcomers or not, saw the immigrant's desire to come here as the logical outcome of a simple set of push and pull factors. After all, they reasoned, in Europe there was oppression, economic misery and over-population, while in Canada there was freedom, employment opportunities and rich available land. Such a view of the arriving migrant assumed that all the newcomers wished to become permanent settlers — they were the peasants who dreamed of their own farms on the prairies or were the victims of political and religious persecution seeking the protection of the British crown. Before the 1900s the Canadian experience seemed to confirm this view of migration and the immigrant's motives.[1]

The importance, impact, and contributions these tens of thousands of men and women made to the communities they settled in to establish new homes for themselves and their families cannot be underestimated. The combination of their work and hope for the future helped foster the construction of the physical Toronto as well as the inclusive socio-cultural character of the city. These accomplishments are sometimes invisible and forgotten and often buried under centuries of growth, change, and edited narrative. The few remaining workers' cottages scattered throughout older Toronto neighbourhoods can and should be understood to represent, embody, and reflect, among their many attributes, their early owners' commitments to and success in achieving their own modest hopes for the future.

Focusing on workers' homes does not mean forgetting, of course, the original European settlers and their families who were the first to live and work in the Town of York. However, for the purpose of this book, the emphasis is on describing the large number of immigrants who came to Toronto between the 1820s and 1920s, many of whom were eventually able to call Modest Hopes their homes. Certainly, while Toronto has received many immigrant groups throughout its history, we concentrate here on some of the largest and most impactful ones who arrived in the aforementioned time period.

English Immigration to Canada

Writers Patrick A. Dunae and George Woodcock point out that "The English were among the first Europeans to reach Canadian shores."[2] A substantial wave of United Empire Loyalists during and after the American Revolutionary War (1775–83) boosted the population of the future Canada. This group was significant in the founding of Upper Canada (now Ontario) and profoundly shaped the politics and culture that later created Canada.

By the outbreak of the War of 1812, the roughly 110,000 inhabitants of Upper Canada were comprised of about 80,000 early and late Loyalists, while the remaining number largely consisted of immigrants or their descendants from the United Kingdom. After the end of the Napoleonic Wars in 1815, an even greater influx of English people

Fig. 3.2 British immigrants standing on the Bridge of Sighs to Simcoe Street from Union Station, Toronto, 1911.

immigrated to British North America to seek relief from job losses due to the introduction of new technologies, augmented by a series of bad harvests, high unemployment, and low wages. This situation soon highlighted an unstable system that did not support the poor in England. Immigration to the colonies became an attractive alternative to low pay, no pay, or starvation. Also, many English farm workers came to Ontario with the assistance of agricultural trade unions.

Among the upper and middle classes, "younger sons and discharged officers emigrated because they were unable to keep up appearances at home."[3] Many British immigrants travelled to Canada with "official encouragement" led by the English social hierarchy in Canada, who induced ex-officers and other members of the gentry to emigrate, offering generous grants of land and hoping to establish a kind of aristocracy in the British colony.

The Canada Company, a large British land development firm formed in 1826, played a significant role in bringing "suitable" British settlers to Canada through the enticement of free land. It provided schemes aimed at the working class, "the victims of crop failures and economic recession," who arrived in Canada "with no money and none of the skills they needed in a pioneer environment."[4]

While the English were the earliest and largest immigrant group from Britain to settle in Canada, they represented only 25 percent of the total from there to Canada before Confederation in 1867. However, between Confederation and 1915, they dominated the immigrant numbers from England, Scotland, and Ireland.

After Confederation, another significant wave of British immigration occurred. Between 1868 and the late 1930s, British Home Children, mostly English, were sent to Canada. More than 100,000 orphaned, abandoned, and pauper children were given free passage and homes in various communities in the country.

The opening of the Prairie provinces triggered another wave of English immigration to Canada between 1890 and 1914. This one over-lapped with a government-led campaign in the early 1900s launched by the Dominion of Canada to entice British immigrants with "British ideals" to go to short-handed farms experiencing rural depopulation as farm workers moved to Toronto to take advantage of its economic boom. The campaign reached out to people in areas such as the poor suburbs of East London, among other targeted areas, and claimed their money problems would disappear in Canada and that jobs, land, and housing were abundant.

The Canadian government's Immigration Branch commissioned organizations such as the Salvation Army and steamship lines to help promote and encourage immigration to Canada. The government paid a commission, the "British Bonus," to steamship booking agents for each "suitable immigrant" who purchased a ticket to sail to Canada. The campaign was a success, causing scores of English immigrants to come to Canada, but it was also flawed. Steamship agents were supposed to recruit farm labourers and rural-bound settlers, not urban factory work-ers, mechanics, and skilled tradesmen, since there was little demand for them.[5] A steady stream of English immigrants poured into Toronto and stayed there. Ten thousand arrived in Canada in 1901 alone, followed by 65,000 more in 1906, peaking at 113,000 in 1913.[6] Toronto's 1901 population was 208,040, of which 24,901 (or 12 percent) were from England. In 1911, Toronto's population was 376,538, of which 71,116 (or 18.9 percent) were from England.[7]

In the early 1900s, as Allan Levine writes in *Toronto: Biography of a City*, the city's "population remained more than 85 percent white

Fig. 3.3 British immigrants from Halstead, Kent, 1913.

Anglo-Saxon, either British or Canadian born, and overwhelmingly Protestant. The vast majority of the 100,000 or so British immigrants who settled in Toronto between 1900 and 1914 found a niche in their new Canadian homeland."[8] Some ended up in what disdainfully became known as "shacktowns," with eight being developed just outside Toronto's city limits to form a sort of "horseshoe of poverty" where city regulations did not reach. These areas provided cheap building lots during the housing shortage at that time and quickly became populated with new immigrants from Britain, some experiencing unexpected lives of poverty in their new country.

But these shacks were far from transient hovels; for many, they were their first homes in Canada. Alice Randle wrote in *Saturday Night* magazine in 1914 that "The small cabins … 'had curtained windows [that] showed a thrifty woman's care…. Each cottage seemed to have a personality all its own.'"[9] Whether living in shacktowns, or working-class, east-end neighbourhoods off Queen, King, or Parliament Streets, most British immigrants found jobs in factories, industries, and stores, imbuing "Toronto with both trade unionism and a deep affection for and pride in the mighty British empire."[10] The year 1922 saw another wave of English immigrants to Canada. Under the Empire Settlement Act, the British government helped a total of 165,000 British, mostly English, immigrants settle in Canada after the First World War.[11]

For those who were English-born or born of English-born parents living in Toronto, their expectations regarding housing in their new city were influenced by what they had known and left behind in the Old

World. The Toronto Modest Hopes many of them eventually lived in or aspired to live in reflected familiar English cottages whose architectural form and detailing referenced traditional British imperial styles. This familiarity gave these new arrivals a sense of comfort and reduced the strangeness of this "alien" new place.

Scottish Immigration to Canada

As J.M. Bumsted has noted in *The Scots in Canada*, initial Scottish emigrants "were not so much harried out of Scotland as attracted to other places. As with other immigrant groups to Canada, those Scots who arrived were on the whole the ambitious and energetic members of their home society, individuals who had made a conscious decision that the future was more promising elsewhere."[12]

Scots began arriving in Canada as early as the 17th century,[13] when a Scottish settlement, named New Scotland or Nova Scotia, was created by Sir William Alexander in 1622.[14] These early settlers were a collective of Roman Catholics seeking political and religious refuge, fur traders, merchants, and decommissioned soldiers.

Initially, the British government objected to emigration, fearing that the loss of agricultural and industrial workers would impact Scotland's economy. So obstacles were placed in the way of departure — the government even raised the price of overseas passage to make it beyond the means of most seeking to leave.[15] Those who could afford to go paid inflated ticket prices, while others left covertly on less-than-ideal ships that were overcrowded and under-provisioned. As a result, outbreaks of epidemics were common.

Between 1770 and 1815, Scottish Highlanders settled in considerable numbers in Prince Edward Island, Upper Canada, and Nova Scotia, creating distinct ethnic enclaves in their respective provinces. However, as the economy in the British Isles declined after 1815, combined with a rapid population growth in the early 19th century, emigration was viewed increasingly as a solution to the problems of job loss and homelessness.

The Scottish or Highland Clearances contributed to the next wave of immigration to Canada from Scotland. The Clearances ultimately destroyed traditional clan society and were the catalyst for rural depopulation of and emigration from Scotland on a grand scale, changing the character and culture of the Scottish Highlands forever.[16]

Thousands of rural labourers, whole families, and clans were forcibly removed and evicted from land they had worked and lived on for more than 500 years. For the landlord, this action made sense: the raising of sheep was far more profitable and less trouble than having serfs work the land. Varying accounts maintain that at the peak of the Clearances as many as 2,000 cottages were burned down every day. These stone and thatch-roofed houses were made uninhabitable so that their occupants could never return home once their fields were combined and enclosed and sheep were brought in to graze their ancestral lands.

Between 1811 and 1821, around 15,000 people were removed from land owned by the Duchess of Sutherland and her husband, the Marquis of Stafford, to make room for 200,000 sheep. Some of those turned out had nowhere else to go; many were old and infirm and starved or froze to death when left to the mercy of the elements. In 1814, two elderly people in Strathnaver who did not get out of their cottage in time were burned alive. The Isle of Rum in 1826 was cleared of its tenants, who were paid to immigrate to Canada, travelling on the ship *James*. Every one of the passengers contracted typhus by the time they arrived in Halifax. This "transportation" was not that uncommon, since it was often cheaper for landowners to pay the passage of immigrants to the New World than to try to find their tenants other land or save them from starvation. In 1851, 1,500 tenants in Barra were led to believe they were attending a meeting about land rents. Once there, they were overpowered, tied up, and forced onto ships to America.[17]

During the Clearances period, emigration from Scotland climbed steadily. With the further decline of the kelp industry, falling cattle prices, and by the mid-1840s, a potato famine in the Highlands, financial devastation of the subsistence economy hit the remaining crofters hard, quickly spreading starvation and disease. Mass migrations of Scots ensued from the Highlands, some to the Scottish Lowlands in search of factory work, and if possible, to Canada, the United States, or Australia.

Fig. 3.4 Immigrant family upon arrival from Scotland, 1911.

In desperation, many Highlanders left as indentured servants.[18] Some landowners paid the way for their evicted tenants, choosing the price of a passage over prolonged monetary support. "Many Scottish immigrants were brought to British North America through resettlement schemes sponsored by the government or by private charitable organizations" to help rid the Highlands of excess population. Some Scots left on their own accord, scrounging what little they had left while leaving nothing behind. They scraped just enough together to finance their own passage to British North America, their motives in line with the desires of most immigrants: declining prospects at home combined with the promise of a better life.[19]

The Atlantic voyage to North America was often perilous and risky and initially not regulated by the British government. While often travelling on ordinary cargo ships that could take as many as 10 weeks to arrive in America, the "overcrowding, bad provisioning, and sanitation problems were complicated by the rise of diseases such as smallpox and cholera in the impoverished areas from where many emigrants originated." A shift to steam vessels with steerage quarters, and increased government regulation beginning in the 1860s, gradually improved the journeys and shortened many of the passage trips to one week.[20]

Between 1815 and 1870, more than 170,000 Scottish immigrants came to Canada.[21] While most were from the working class of Scottish society, a sizable number in the middle and upper classes moved, as well: schoolteachers, religious leaders, some doctors and lawyers, most largely Protestant. This period "witnessed the establishment of the Scots as one of the major ethnic components of the Canadian population,[22] and "according to the Canadian Census of 1871, 157 out of every thousand Canadians were of Scottish origin," with a provincial distribution of 20 percent of that total in Ontario.[23] From 1871 to 1901, the flow of Scottish immigrants to Canada remained constant, with roughly 80,000 entering the country.

During a further immigration boom between 1901 and 1914, nearly 1.2 million people from England, Scotland, and Ireland immigrated to Canada, 240,000 (or 20 percent) of these newcomers from Scotland. Of these thousands of displaced agricultural labourers, industrial workers, craftsmen, tradesmen, and in numerous cases their families, many found their way to Toronto. By 1901, Toronto had a population of 208,040, including 6,464 (or 3.1 percent) who were Scottish-born or born of Scottish-born residents; by 1921, 29,402 were of Scottish heritage, or 5.6 percent.[24] As with their English cousins, many Scottish immigrants to Toronto lived in Modest Hope house types that reflected and maintained a connection to the cottages they had known back home, reflecting the British imperial roots of the city.

Irish Immigration to Canada

As Patrick Dunae and George Woodcock write, "By 1851 [the most recent British] immigration had settled down, and after a considerable outflow to the US, some 93,000 people born in England remained in Canada West (Ontario), constituting about one-tenth of the population. They were almost matched in number by the Scottish-born (90,000) and greatly outnumbered by the 227,000 Irish-born."[25]

Fig. 3.5 *Irish Emigrants Leaving Queenstown Harbour,* in *Illustrated London News,* September 5, 1874.

Since the 1790s, close to 450,000 Irish immigrants had arrived in British North America.[26] They "settled Upper Canada's rich farmlands, built canals, established businesses in cities, and helped create the social and economic foundations of everyday life."[27]

Before 1846, Protestant Irish emigration outnumbered that of Irish Catholics by a margin of almost three to one until the late 1830s,[28] a "perplexing anomaly, considering that Catholics comprised 70 to 80 percent of Ireland's population"[29] at that time. The Irish were arguably the single largest ethnic group in English Canada from the 1830s to the late 1880s.

In *Death or Canada*, Dr. Mark McGowan, professor of history and Celtic studies at the University of St. Michael's College, states: "The repeated failure of the potato crop in the 1840s was the worst trauma to afflict Ireland in modern history."[30] An unparalleled combination of interwoven events created a perfect storm in Ireland: an outmoded landholding system, falling agricultural prices, a population explosion, and at the storm's centre, the failure of the country's potato staple between 1845 and 1851.[31] An unprecedented, unimaginable poverty ensued for the Irish people. In just 20 years, from 1841 to 1861, the population in Ireland dropped from more than eight million to just over five million.[32] The famine and other related elements claimed nearly a million lives, while two million were lost to emigration. Whole villages and farms were abandoned, others disappeared entirely, and the "many sounds of the lively pre-Famine world were replaced by the 'eerie silence' brought on by depopulation."[33] Ireland had become a land "scavenged by famine deaths, deprivation, and dispersion."[34]

The poorest in Ireland died of starvation, while those who could fled to England, Scotland, or where possible farther afield to Australia, the United States, or British North America. "The Irish who came to Canada in the late 1840s and 1850s, however, were leaving behind a society and a landscape in a state of distress,"[35] writes William Jenkins in "Poverty and Place: Documenting and Representing Toronto's Catholic Irish, 1845–1890." The vast majority of emigrants paid for their own passage (if they had any money) or relied on charity or the system of remittances — prepaid tickets paid for by family members already settled overseas. Since Canada was the cheapest destination and the quickest way to reach North America, it was attractive to potential Irish migrants. Emigration from Ireland to Canada was made all the easier because the Irish were British citizens and as such could not be refused entry to Canada.[36]

From 1845 to 1855, ships brought two million Irish immigrants to ports in Boston, New York City, and Toronto. These were typically packet vessels making regularly scheduled voyages between Britain, the United States, and Canada. The ships were mostly brigs, two-masted vessels "low between decks, badly ventilated, and small...."[37] The law required that there be a minimum of five feet between decks, but this rule was often broken. The slow-moving ships took weeks to reach their destinations. While steamships were faster, their cost was typically out of reach for many Irish emigrants.[38]

Of the 97,492 Irish Famine migrants bound for Canada in 1847, one-fifth did not survive the six-week journey on cramped, disease-infested "coffin ships," or they succumbed to outbreaks of typhus upon arrival.[39] Sharks were said to follow these ships because so many bodies were thrown overboard. The *Times* of London described the ships as akin to "the worst horrors of the slave-trade." The year 1847 became notorious in history as "Black '47" when a flood of Irish immigrants came to Canada, marking the apex of their arrival in Toronto and altering the city's urban landscape.

Brian Murphy, in *Adrift: A True Story of Tragedy on the Icy Atlantic and the One Who Lived to Tell About It*, offers an account of the conditions on the famine ships:

> The stench quickly grew overpowering. The unmistakable acid-sweet smell of vomit infused every corner. If you couldn't get to the deck, the only place to retch was in your berth or into the floor. Washing up was out of the question. The only way to do that was on deck with a bucket and some fat-and-lye soap. The two latrines — for more than 120 people — were simple holes that emptied into the bilge water, a horrific concoction of waste and runoff that sloshed in the hold below the steerage compartment. Rags soaked in vinegar were provided for common use as stand-ins for toilet paper.[40]

This large group of immigrants had a profound impact on all aspects of Toronto at that time. One of the legacies, and a somewhat historically dismissive reminder of this "out-group" phenomena today, are the vibrant neighbourhoods in the city still called Cabbagetown and Corktown, whose names have a strong relationship to the Irish who first lived there.

The conditions many Irish left behind, followed by their difficult journeys to get to Canada and the early reactions of Torontonians to them when they first arrived, reinforces our understanding of the tremendous trajectory of improvement represented by their lives and the Modest Hope houses some were able to live in.

The residual effect of Black '47 on Toronto was an "indelible set of images regarding the nature and character of 'the Irish'" that led locals to "thereafter view all Irish through the single lens of this tragic moment." Toronto's Victorian Protestant middle class saw the arrival of the Irish as an "impediment to progress,"[41] a blight on its colonial city, and met their arrival with fear and hostility that soon replaced any fragments of pity and sympathy. Newspaper accounts contained "lurid mixes of unsavoury people, animals, and alcohol,"[42] and enhanced the Protestant belief that poverty was a penalty for immoral and irresponsible behaviour. This growing ethno-religious approach divided the city spatially, economically, and culturally. Irish Catholics were "the city's original immigrant underclass, and faced frank, bitter discrimination for decades."[43]

Continental European Immigration to Canada

Eastern Europeans were the first large wave of immigrants to Canada not from England, Scotland, Ireland, or France. Tens of thousands of rural European workers arrived in the middle to late 19th and early 20th centuries, lured to Canada by the promise of cheap land, especially in the prairies. Ukrainians were the most prominent Eastern European community to arrive, but there were other significant waves, as well, during this time:

- **1830 and 1858:** Polish refugees begin to come to Canada in 1830 to escape Russian oppression. The year 1858 marks the first significant mass migration of Poles fleeing the Russian occupation of northern Poland.[44]
- **1880–1914:** Many Italians immigrate to Canada to evade hardships experienced during Italy's unification and new state reforms. Large numbers of farmers are driven off their land and left jobless and homeless.[45] Many hoped to find work in railways,

mining, and industry in Canada. As the economic situation worsens in Italy, the migration numbers escalate. In 1906, and then again in 1913, close to a million Italians leave each year for other nations. From 1896 to 1915, about 16 million depart in total, though about a third of these later return to Italy.[46]

*   **1880–1914**: Thousands of persecuted Jews, fleeing pogroms in the Pale of Settlement, seek refuge in Canada.[47]
*   **1891:** The emigration of 170,000 Ukrainians begins, mainly to flee oppression from areas under Austro-Hungarian rule, marking the first wave of these people seeking refuge in Canada.[48]

Romania, for example, was a turbulent place for Jews dating back more than three centuries, since they were an endless target of religious persecution in Romanian society. Under Peter VI the Lame, the Prince of Moldavia (reigned 1574–79 and 1583–91), many Jewish traders were taxed and ultimately expelled. In 1650, and again in 1741, Jews were required to wear clothing displaying their status and ethnicity. During the Russo-Turkish War (1768–74), they endured persecution in almost every town and village, and later, during the Greek War of Independence (1821–30), they were the victims of pogroms, violent riots, massacres, and oppression, whereupon many synagogues were burned. Anti-Semitism was enforced under the leadership of Ion C. Brătianu from 1875 to 1888, who prohibited Jews from settling in the countryside and relocated them to urban centres, then subsequently declared city inhabitants to be vagrants and expelled them from the nation altogether. By 1878, emigration of Romanian Jews commenced on a large scale.

Also, in this period, "more than two million Russian Jews journeyed across the Atlantic to North America. The vast majority wound up on New York City's Lower East Side and in other large American cities. About 100,000 made their way to Canada; of those, approximately 30,000 settled in Toronto, increasing the city's Jewish population from 500 in 1881 to 35,000 by 1921."[49]

Toronto's population of 208,000 in 1901 jumped to 380,000 by 1911. At that time and among that number, 3,000 were Italians, 18,000 were Jews, 9,800 were Germans, 1,000 were Chinese, and there was also an assortment of Poles, Macedonians, and Ukrainians.[50]

African and Caribbean Immigration to Canada

In 1608, the first Black person believed to have set foot on what became Canadian soil was Mathieu Da Costa, who had been hired by the French to serve as an interpreter of the Mi'kmaq language to the governor of Acadia. Eleven years later, 350 Africans were kidnapped from their villages in present-day Angola and forced onto the Portuguese slave ship *São João Bautista* bound for the New World. The journey was full of terror, hunger, and death, with about half of the Africans perishing on board. En route, English pirates intercepted the ship and forced 50 Africans aboard their two vessels, the *White Lion* and the *Treasurer*.

On August 20, 1619, the *White Lion* arrived at Point Comfort in present-day Virginia, where the captain sold his African cargo of 20 slaves in exchange for food. This trade marked one of the earliest documented sale of slaves in America; however, the first people of direct African descent were slaves in a Spanish colony in 1526 in South Carolina.

In 1685, Louis XIV's *Code Noir* permitted limited slavery of Black people and Indigenous Peoples for economic purposes only for the colonists of New France. And while he established strict guidelines for their ownership, it was formally authorized by 1709. When New France was conquered by the British in 1760, the Articles of Capitulation stated that Black people and Indigenous Peoples were to remain slaves. Yet the American Revolutionary War saw a shift in the roles and contributions of Black people to the nation. Many actively aided the British side in the Revolutionary War, serving as boatmen, general labourers, buglers, and musicians. For the British, General Henry Clinton formed a corps of free Black people called the Black Pioneers and encouraged enslaved Black people to desert their American masters, promising them freedom and shelter. The commander-in-chief of the British, Guy Carlton, guaranteed freedom to all slaves who formally requested protection. As a result, an estimated 100,000 Black slaves fled to the British side during the American Revolution.[51]

However, the transition to freedom was not smooth or without controversy. Following the Revolutionary War, the Black Pioneers were among the first settlers in Shelburne, Nova Scotia, forming the community of Birchtown in 1784. The district was met with hostility from hundreds of white decommissioned soldiers angry at having to compete for work and wages with their Black neighbours, with Canada experiencing its first race riot there. Meanwhile, white societal discomfort with Black fellow citizens saw signs such as NEGRO FROLICS PROHIBITED posted by officials.

Despite promises made by the British at the end of the American War of Independence, the North-West Ordinance Law and the Imperial Statute of 1790 made freedom for Black slaves elusive. In the early 1790s, about 1,200 Black slaves accepted the opportunity to leave Halifax to relocate to Sierra Leone, convinced they would never find freedom and equality in Nova Scotia.

In Upper Canada, the 1793 beating and subsequent sale of Chloe Cooley, an enslaved American, convinced Lieutenant Governor John Graves Simcoe that the abolition of slavery was necessary, prompting the passage of the Act to Limit Slavery, also known as the Act Against Slavery. His legislation made it illegal for anyone coming into the colony to enslave others and ruled that those currently enslaved, or born to a mother who was enslaved, would be freed at the age of 25.

The War of 1812 united Black and white people in Upper and Lower Canada in their fear of American conquest. Under the Union Jack, thousands of Black volunteers served heroically, inspired by the British promise of freedom and land. In 1813, 4,000 former U.S. slaves desert-ed to the British and were transported to Britain's colonies north of the border. The Imperial Act of 1833 officially abolished slavery in most British colonies, formally freeing 800,000 slaves, but there were fewer than 50 actually living in British North America at that time.[52]

Canada's reputation as a safe haven for Black slaves was widely cir-culated while the United States maintained its slavery laws. Between 1815 and 1865, tens of thousands of African Americans sought refuge in Canada via the legendary Underground Railroad. Among those travellers was Josiah Henson and his family, who escaped from Kentucky. In his own words, he recalls his time while enslaved and living in a slave cabin:

> Wooden floors were an unknown luxury. In a single room were huddled, like cattle, ten or a dozen persons, men, women, and children. All ideas of refinement and decency were, of course, out of the question. We had neither bedsteads, nor furniture of any description. Our beds were collections of straw and old rags, thrown down in the corners and boxed in with boards; a single blanket the only covering.[53]

Harriet Beecher Stowe's famous novel *Uncle Tom's Cabin* is believed to be a depiction of Josiah's life. Born in 1789, he served his master for many years before escaping to Southern Ontario. As a free man, he helped found the Dawn Settlement, a colony where Black people lived free and could study. In his new life in Canada, Henson spoke publicly about his experi-ences and helped other slaves escape and adapt to new lives in Canada.

By the mid-19th century, Great Lake steamers actively transported Black people to Canada, and their population in Toronto continued to rise steadily. In 1853, Mary Ann Shadd founded the *Provincial Freeman* newspaper to promote Black immigration to Canada. She became the first North American Black woman to publish a paper and was one of the first female journalists in Canada.

When the American Civil War began in April 1861, there were about 30,000 to 40,000 Black people living in Canada. The lifting of the ban on Black soldiers in the Union Army prompted nearly 1,000 Black Canadian men to join various regiments. In January 1863, the Emancipation Proclamation declared that slaves under U.S. federal law were free. By June 1865, the Thirteenth Amendment to the U.S. Constitution had officially abolished slavery throughout the United States, including all members of the former Confederacy. This action motivated a number of Black Americans to go back to the United States to live freely, to find loved ones left behind or stolen from them, or to search for those lost along the way.[54] It is estimated that as many as two-thirds of Canada's Black population returned to the United States after the Civil War; Black people in Canada declined so much that they did not reach similar numbers until 1961, when they totalled 32,100, accounting for 0.2 percent of the country's population then.[55]

Chinese Immigration to Canada

As Arlene Chan relates in *The Chinese in Toronto from 1878*, the first documented Chinese immigrants to Canada were "recorded in 1788 by Captain John Meares, who left from the Portuguese colony of Macau with 50 Chinese labourers, carpenters, and shipwrights aboard the ship *Felice*. They landed at Nootka Sound on Vancouver Island to build a trading post and a small schooner ... for use in the trade of sea otter pelts to China."[56]

For generations in China, a tradition existed of men seeking financial opportunities overseas and sending money back home to help their wives, their children, or a network of related families left behind. The majority of migrants came from four districts in China: Taishan, Xinhui, Kaiping, and Enping in the Pearl River delta of Guangdong Province. In the 19th century, floods, droughts, wars, scarcity of good farmland, and rural poverty were driving forces that motivated emigration from China.

Fig. 3.6 Chinese workers on the Canadian Pacific Railway, circa 1884.

Political upheaval stemming from the First Opium War (1839–42), the Taiping Rebellion (1850–64), and the Second Opium War (1856–60) caused widespread Chinese emigration. After losing the Opium Wars to Great Britain, a condition of China's surrender was a massive payment to the victors amounting to a third of the annual intake of China's treasury. The cost in turn was passed on to Chinese citizens, whose taxes rose steeply.[57]

In April 1858, gold was discovered on British Columbia's Fraser River. Thousands of prospectors, by boat or land, travelled to the future Canadian province "on the hunt for dazzling riches." Three hundred Chinese men made the dangerous journey from their villages to Guangdong's port of Guangzhou where they crossed the Pacific Ocean, "which tossed them at sea for four to eight weeks." Upon arriving on the Fraser River, they worked tirelessly among thousands of fellow prospectors, driven by the possibility of fortune. The Fraser River Gold Rush (1858–60) was followed by the Cariboo Gold Rush (1860–63), and by 1863, 4,000 Chinese were panning for gold. Sadly, the dreams of riches were only realized by a few Chinese while "most faced failure and disappointment."[58]

The second major wave of Chinese immigrants to Canada consisted of labourers to build the transcontinental Canadian Pacific Railway, the essential link to connect the country from coast to coast. Since British

Columbia was largely cut off from the rest of the nation, "it was easier, cheaper, and faster to get to British Columbia from Hong Kong than from Halifax."[59] Ten thousand workers were needed to construct the railway line in British Columbia, yet only an estimated 400 white males were available. The Workingman's Protection Association (later known as the Anti-Chinese Association) objected strongly to the hiring of Chinese labourers, but Prime Minister John A. Macdonald informed the people of British Columbia: "If you wish to have the railway finished within any reasonable time, there must be no such step against Chinese labour ... it is simply a question of alternative — either you must have this labour or you cannot have the railway."[60]

By the end of 1882, there were 9,000 railway workers in British Columbia, 6,500 of them Chinese.[61] They endured accidents, illness, death, frostbite, and malnutrition and were largely left out of the archival record of railway construction. Initially, British Columbia had the strongest anti-Chinese movement, but such sentiments soon spread across the country.[62] When the railway was completed, many Chinese workers decided to stay in Canada. Alarmed, the Canadian government imposed a head tax of $50 to deter immigration, which soon rose to $100 and then $500. In search of employment and a less hostile environment, the Chinese workers walked on the very track they had just built in search of railway towns, cities eastward, and for many, Toronto.

Toronto's cultural landscape developed and evolved continuously throughout the early 19th to early 20th centuries. It became home to Loyalists as well as to English, Irish, Scottish, Italian, Eastern European, Jewish, African American, Caribbean, and Chinese immigrants. Through an understanding of their various realities on how they got to Canada and what they left behind, it becomes clear how important the rental or even ownership of a Modest Hope was for those able to make one their home. What these little houses meant in terms of the improvement in the quality of their day-to-day existence should be reflected in the heritage value and preservation of these Modest Hopes today.

Fig. 4.1 Osgoode Hall.

4

TORONTO

1820–1920

Before the real city could be seen it
had to be imagined …
— Michael Ondaatje,
In the Skin of a Lion

W orkers' cottages in which so many new immigrants eventually settled in Toronto represent a thematic arc connecting housing and hope. Whether from Scotland, England, Ireland,
Continental Europe, the United States, or elsewhere, these people had
collective journeys to Toronto that were often epic, yet they arrived
with so little. The stories of these people gravitating to Canada in hope
of better lives are varied: displaced peasants from small lots on a lord's
estate; farmers forced off their land by the nationwide failure of the
potato crop; transient labourers from villages, towns, and cities seeking
jobs; victims of racism and cultural genocide searching for acceptance
and freedom.

Fig. 4.2 Toronto from the top of the Rossin Hotel, 1856 or 1857.

What these many immigrants brought with them to Canada was an architectural memory of "home," perhaps memories of rural stone or urban wood-framed cottages with thatched or shingled roofs, or compact one- to two-storey rowhouses or workers' factory cottages on crowded urban streets, or overcrowded tenements in converted townhouses and apartment blocks.

These architectural memories of workers' housing from abroad became Modest Hope prototypes and were heavily influenced by the place of origin of Toronto's early immigrants. The city once had thousands of workers' cottages, particularly in areas such as Corktown, Cabbagetown, Leslieville, Riverside, Macaulaytown, The Junction, and on streets like Lombard and Niagara. Today, relatively few survive, except in small pockets scattered throughout the city. Yet for working-class immigrants arriving in Toronto between 1820 and 1920, the city was a sea of such housing, with many more built by immigrants who came later. That was what Toronto's streetscapes looked like; this was their Toronto.

Toronto, City of Cottages

Toronto was once a city of cottages.[1] For many newcomers to the municipality whose lives might have begun in neighbourhoods such as The Ward or Corktown, or on streets like March[2] or Dummer,[3] or one of the various shantytowns, renting or owning one of their own cottages without sharing with multiple tenants or other families was a magnificent

accomplishment. It marked a
transition from despair to hope,
from house to home. To have
a home with its own address,
front door, running water, and
proper windows with appropri-
ate ventilation provided a tremendous pride of place. Today,
only broken rows of these houses
remain, unexpected treasures on
streetscapes, the gaps resulting
from their demolition now filled
with newer, larger buildings.

Fig. 4.3 Gilead Place, Corktown, 1912.

As mentioned in Chapter One, the workers' cottage designs reflected
Nathaniel Kent's revolutionary housing theories, John Wood's British pattern books, and James Avon Smith's "Small Gothic Cottage" or "A Cheap
Farm House" plans in the *Canada Farmer*. Many displayed aesthetic expressions of larger homes on a smaller scale, with Second Empire, Georgian,
or Gothic motifs, or a combination of styles and references. Regardless
of their architectural influences, their aesthetic was often pleasing. What
linked so many of these cottages was their intention to be simple, efficient,
economical, and for the most part, beautiful.[4] They raised the spiritual
lives of their inhabitants by improving the aesthetics of their experiences.

By the 1820s, there was a shift in how the urban middle class viewed
their dwellings, "coming to see households as more than just lodgings,"
as Christine Stansell writes in *City of Women*. The idea of "home" to
describe a domestic setting symbolized their own "pillar of civilization,
an incubator of morals and family affections, a critical alternative to the
harsh and competitive world of trade and politics." In its "psychological
form," the idea of home symbolized the difference between the public
and private life — home was the "embellished inner space cut off from
the public world."[5] Stansell further notes that:

In this sense, the home was absent from the lives of urban laboring women, who observed no sharp distinctions between public and private. Rather, their domestic lives spread out to the hallways of their tenements, to adjoining apartments and to the streets below. Household work involved them constantly with the milieu outside their own four walls; lodgers, neighbors, peddlers and shopkeepers figured as prominently in their domestic routines and dramas as did husbands and children. It was in the urban neighborhoods, not the home, that the identity of working-class wives and mothers was rooted.[6]

Compared to the homelands of so many of Toronto's early immigrants, Toronto was a young city. In just over a few centuries, "Toronto has grown from a tiny outpost of the British empire to a world-class city,"[7] and the largest one in Canada.

Toronto: Early History

Toronto is young, but settlement stretches back before the first Europeans carved out the city's landscape. Along the waterways of the city — the Don, Humber, and Rouge Rivers — First Nations fishing camps, largely Algonquin-speaking, were established as early as 1000 CE.[8] The introduction of maize to the region about 1,400 years ago led to a shift in diet and population patterns that saw the Iroquoian-speaking Huron-Wyandot move into the present region of Toronto between 1200 and 1600.[9]

In the early 17th century, First Nations people made contact with European settlers for the first time. Some records claim Étienne Brûlé to be the original European explorer to reach the northern shore of Lake Ontario. Brûlé became a guide and interpreter for Samuel de Champlain when he arrived at the Great Lakes.

The coming of Europeans brought battles, territorial conflict, disease, and death for First Nations people. As a growing fur trade industry developed, the Haudenosaunee moved into the Toronto region, while many Huron-Wyandot fled the area. The Haudenosaunee founded several settlements on the north shore of Lake Ontario, such as Teiaiagon, near the Humber River, and Ganatsekwyagon, close to the Rouge River,[10] before they, too, shifted slowly north, while the Mississaugas replaced them in the Toronto area, dominating there until the end of the 18th century.[11]

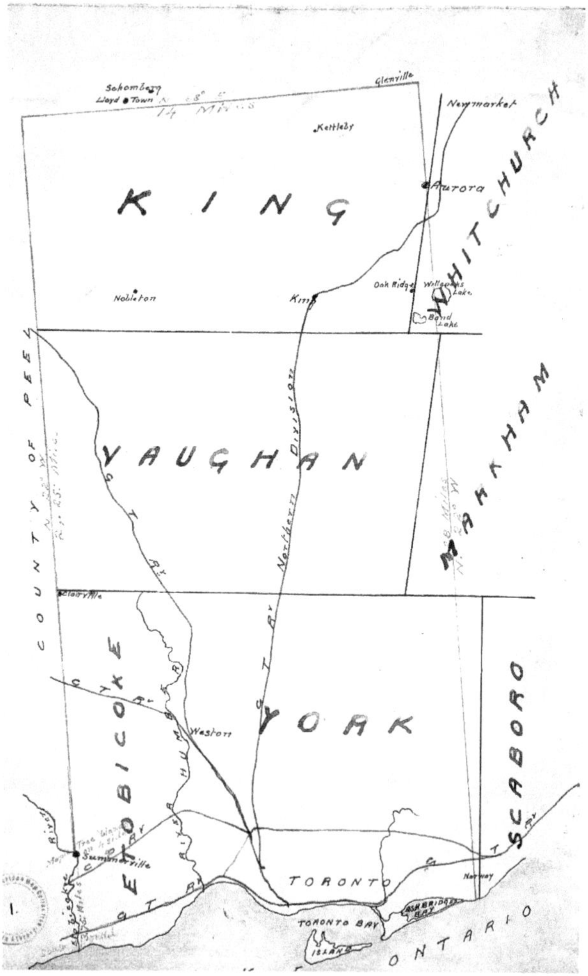

The Toronto region became a significant centre for fur trading. The French built Fort Douville in 1720, which the British responded to by establishing a larger competing post in Oswego, New York, in 1726. The French soon abandoned Fort Douville and erected Fort Rouillé (or Fort Toronto) on the grounds of Toronto's current Exhibition Place. In 1759, Fort Rouillé was burned down by the French, and the British took possession of the Toronto area.[12]

Fig. 4.4 The controversial "purchase" of 250,880 acres from the Mississaugas.

Now that the region was under British control, the controversial Toronto Purchase was implemented in 1781. In exchange for a small monetary amount and European goods, the Mississaugas surrendered their land to the British Crown. The land in the purchase constituted 250,880 acres, which today encompasses Lake Ontario to the south, Highway 27 as the approximate west border, Ashbridges Bay/Woodbine Avenue/Highway 404 as the approximate eastern border, and Sideroad 15/Bloomington Road as the approximate northern border. The price was 10 shillings (roughly $60), 2,000 gun flints, 24 brass kettles, 120 mirrors, 24 laced hats, a bale of flowered flannel, and 96 gallons of rum.[13] While the British thought they had "bought" the land, the Indigenous interpretation differed: "[O]ur understanding in 1787 was that this land was to be made freely available to the settlers, that these 'gifts' would be given in perpetuity, and that no one, in fact, can own the earth …"[14,15]

A year after the Toronto Purchase, a short-lived townsite was laid out in a gridiron, with government and military buildings planned around a central square.[16] Soon, more than 10,000 United Empire Loyalists arrived after the American Revolution. Their appearance was followed by the Constitutional Act of 1791, effectively splitting the Province of Quebec to form the Provinces of Lower and Upper Canada, the latter including Toronto.

The Establishment of the Town of York, 1793–1814

In May 1793, Lieutenant Governor John Graves Simcoe, along with his wife, Elizabeth, and their entourage made their first trip to Toronto in search of a provincial capital. In a climate of rising hostilities between Britain and the United States, Simcoe had decided against capital contender Newark (today's Niagara-on-the-Lake) due to its location on the American border. Simcoe's preferred choice, London, failed to get approval, so he set sail for the future Toronto. Upon arriving, he was taken with its natural harbour, suitable situation for trade, distance from the American border, and enclosed location, which made it well suited to defend against the looming threat of U.S. attacks.

Landforms of the Toronto site, such as the low east-to-west rise of the escarpment, later separated the more affluent neighbourhoods from industries and workers' housing. The mouth of the Don River became the natural division between the industrial east end and the city centre reaching to the west, but in the beginning there was only a gap in the forested shore. The prevailing wind from west to east eventually carried noise, wood and coal smoke, and the noxious smells of animal and human waste eastward, but when Simcoe and his wife reached the roughly mapped townsite of Toronto, there was only a gentle breeze.

Favouring a British name over the Indigenous *Tkaronto*, Simcoe quickly declared the developing townsite York in honour of Prince Frederick, Duke of York. He authorized the construction of Fort York to guard the entrance to the harbour, while the town centre and first Parliament Buildings were planned near the foot of Parliament Street. Little of this early development is evident today.

Simcoe "opted to reinvent the wheel."[17] In 1793, he hired his own surveyor, Alexander Aitken, to come up with a new plan for the town. Aitken devised a gridiron blueprint with 10 square blocks "bounded by George, Berkeley, Adelaide, and Front streets, with the areas from Parliament to the Don and from Peter to the Humber set aside for government and military purposes."[18]

The blocks between those defining streets is where the town started to proliferate with businesses centred along muddy Yonge and King Streets. To the east and west of Yonge, and south along the lake, the working city slowly expanded — barns, stables, blacksmiths, and fabricating and processing industries, as well as housing for the people who worked in them.

Simcoe's time in Toronto was short-lived. Poor health forced him to return to England by 1796. In his brief but effective stint, he instituted law courts, played a significant role in the gradual abolition of slavery in Upper Canada,[19] and transformed the Town of York from a military outpost with a few log houses to a busy, industrious place of 240 people.[20] He also helped establish the settlement's distinctive British and Anglican character that came to define it.[21]

York continued to develop, transform, and flourish. Its first jail was set up in 1798, followed by the first St. Lawrence Market in 1803 and the first wooden Anglican church in 1807, which eventually became today's Cathedral Church of St. James. York began to expand east of the Don River, then westward and northward. The steadily burgeoning community's largely one- and two-storey log-and-frame buildings were under constant threat of fire and were later replaced by brick and stone structures. As the town's population grew denser, the sanitation became poorer, while outbreaks of malaria were frequent; wood-planked sidewalks with dirt roads were problematic when it rained, bringing "seas of mud" and a nickname, "Muddy York."[22] By 1809, the town's population was 500, more than double since Simcoe's departure.[23] There were now 14 round-long cottages, 11 one-storey and 27 two-storey houses with squared timbers, and 55 houses with clapboard.[24]

By 1812, Muddy York had a population of 700, comprised mostly of American Loyalists and free Black slaves, English, Scottish, and Irish. Its garrison, harbour, and roads gave it an economic advantage, attracting merchants, craftsmen, and labourers alike.[25] Early York streets were filled with thick clouds of wood and later coal smoke, while the mechanical grinding of industry, clatter of horse-drawn carriages, and shouts of carters and merchants in the streets advertising their wares or town criers belting out morning and evening news assaulted the ears. And then there was the ever-pervasive stench of horse dung and backyard privies.

The War of 1812: The 1813 Battle of York and the Second and Third Incursions

While the War of 1812 was a military conflict between the United States and Great Britain, Canada, as a colony of the latter, was swept up in the hostilities.[26] On April 27, 1813, American forces attacked York. The British, unable to defend against the U.S. landings, withdrew from York, killing the leader of the Yankee forces in retaliation upon their retreat. The Americans responded by plundering, ransacking, and burning many York properties, including the Parliament Buildings, and occupied the town until May 8, then departed. In July 1813 and August 1814, there were Second and Third Incursions of Americans that left still more destruction in their wake.

The American destruction of Upper Canada's settlements saw Canadian public opinions concerning Americans shift. The U.S. transgressions during the war had a significant impact on Canadian identity: they helped inspire a national narrative that ultimately influenced the birth of Canada as a nation.[27] As Allan Levine notes in *Toronto: Biography of a City*:

Nonetheless, a decided anti-Americanism gripped the 720 people now living in York as it did the rest of Upper Canada, a collective mindset that was to shape the political battles, economic progress,

Fig. 4.5 Toronto Harbour (northeast view from Parkside Drive) and the arrival of the American fleet prior to the capture of York, April 27, 1813.

and social cultural scene in the tumultuous decades ahead. But this much was clear: there was no going back, and the separation from the Americans was permanent.[28]

Expansion, Growth, and Prosperity and the Great Migration, 1815–1850

As a British Columbia website indicates, "From 1783 until 1812 the most important source of immigrants to British North America was the United States.... That ended with the War of 1812. After 1815 British North America became much more British than it had ever been before."[29]

Before the War of 1812, the roughly 110,000 people of Upper Canada consisted of about 80,000 Loyalists, while the remainder was comprised largely of immigrants from the United Kingdom. After the Napoleonic Wars in 1815, a large influx of English immigrants to British North America seeking relief from high unemployment caused by technology replacing them, bad harvests, and low wages in their homeland. Poverty, slums, and crime had become the hallmarks of cities such as London and Birmingham where petty crime ruled the streets by day and "unruly ruffians" controlled the night.[30] As British immigrants poured into Canada, Anglocentrism became predominant in York. The explosion of immigrants from England, Scotland, and Ireland in the early and mid-19th century came to be known as the Great Migration, utterly transforming York as it developed and stretched westward and eastward.[31]

In the 1830s, a large number of Irish immigrants arrived in York, carrying on their ships a cholera epidemic that swept through the town in 1832 and killed hundreds upon arrival as well as the many who perished en route. The epidemic called into question the state of public health in the province and was a catalyst for the formation of York's first Board of Health to help care for the "indigent sick and destitute immigrants and to secure legal power to enforce sanitary measures deemed essential to preserve the health of the community."[32]

Between 1820 and 1834, the population of York jumped from 1,240 to 9,252.[33] The British majority made York "decidedly British." English Anglicans, Scottish Presbyterians, Irish Catholics, and Protestant Orangemen "all brought their distinctive religious, cultural, and political baggage with them," shaping York. "They were proud, principled, passionate, and somewhat tainted by the economic and social turmoil that had engulfed their lives."[34] As diversity grew in York, so, too, did economic disparity. The town's first slums became part of the urban landscape in the form of small cabins in the community's centre and in the east end near the Don River.

Muddy York, or Little York, was not a name synonymous with pride and grandeur, nor did it match York's "weighty aspirations."[35] The cholera crisis confirmed that the administration was not strong enough to serve York's expanding population. On March 6, 1834, after heated debate,

Fig. 4.6 Plan of the Town of York, J.G. Chewett, 1827.

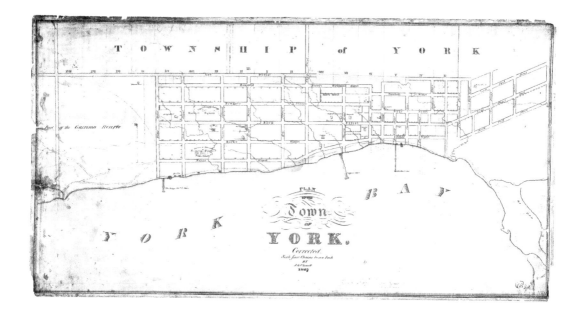

Muddy York reverted to its original Indigenous name and was incorporated as the City of Toronto. It stretched from Parliament to Bathurst Streets, Queen Street to the lake, with five wards soon dividing the city: St. Andrew's, St. David's, St. George's, St. Lawrence's and St. Patrick's.

While Torontonians were becoming accustomed to waves of immigration, nothing prepared them for Black '47.

Black '47

As Dr. Mark McGowan states in "Famine, Facts and Fabrication," 1847 "marked an extraordinary moment in both Irish and Canadian history."[36] In *Death or Canada*, he further writes:

> By the time the Famine refugees had made their way to Lake Ontario in June 1847, they had already experienced more than their share of tragedy. Behind them they had left an unpredictable and unforgiving rural existence, marred by the repeated failure of their food staple, the potato. They had witnessed the destitution and death of loved ones, friends and neighbours who could not salvage enough food and were weakened and thus made vulnerable to disease.... In Toronto, they would soon encounter a host community frantically trying to cope with the mass migration and with the limits of contemporary medical science.[37]

As already mentioned in Chapter Three, of the 97,492 Irish Famine migrants bound for Canada in 1847, one-fifth did not survive the six-week journey on cramped, disease-infested "coffin ships," or they succumbed to outbreaks of typhus upon arrival.[38] The *Times* of London described the ships as akin to "the worst horrors of [the] slave-trade." Black '47 "unleashed a virtual flood" of Irish immigrants to Canada, marking the apex of their immigration to Toronto and altering the city's urban landscape.

In the summer of 1847, the Toronto waterfront witnessed one of the greatest human tragedies in the history of the city. From May to October of that year, 38,560 refugees, most of them from Ireland and predominately Catholic, arrived in Toronto, which at that time was a young, largely Protestant city of under 20,000 people.[39] "The sight of haggard, vermin-infested, and diseased travellers disembarking after their harrowing trans-Atlantic voyage undertaken in sub-human conditions left indelible images on the society that hesitatingly received them."[40] Upon landing, the sick were triaged to fever sheds to contain further spread, while an anxious local bureaucracy quickly moved as many as possible outside the city.[41] Those without family connections in Toronto were sent away. However, many made their way back to the city.

Sickness and death tolls were unprecedented. Of the 38,560 Irish migrants, 1,186 died and were buried in the city by the end of 1847.[42] In *Death or Canada*, Dr. Mark McGowan writes that "the memory of 'Black '47' would leave an indelible set of images on the minds of the local population regarding the nature and character of 'the Irish.'"[43]

This overwhelmingly working-class group of Catholics became the first significant, recognized minority in Toronto and was the city's initial "out-group."[44] Prior to 1847, Toronto saw itself as law-abiding, relatively affluent, and Protestant. Irish Catholics arriving in the city met widespread intolerance and discrimination and were frequently shut out of Toronto society. Signs such as NO IRISH NEED APPLY were often found outside the city's shops and factories in the 19th century, frequent tensions arose between the Protestant Orange Order and Catholics, and Protestant-leaning newspapers fervently depicted the Irish in a disproportionately negative light, highlighting their poverty and supposed weaknesses for crime and alcohol. The *Globe* pontificated that the Irish were "unaccustomed to the habits and occupations of Canadians" and would "sink down into the sloth to which they had been accustomed at home."[45]

As the largest immigrant group to come to Canada in the 19th century,[46] by 1851, there were 227,000 Irish born residents in Upper Canada, representing 24.4 percent of the population of 930,000.[47] The 1871 Canada Census recorded that close to half a million people, or 83.6 percent of the foreign-born population of Canada, came from the British Isles, while 24.3 percent of all Canadians were of Irish ethnicity, in comparison to the English with 20.3 percent and the Scottish with 15.8 percent.[48]

Against great adversity, the Black '47 Irish eventually settled and put down roots in Toronto. Many initially congregated in pockets throughout the downtown area, often in small wooden cottages or boarding houses, usually sharing with multiple families or boarders. The most popular neighbourhood came to be called Corktown, which had previously been settled by Irish Protestants but was close to St. Paul's Basilica, a Catholic church near Queen and Parliament Streets. Irish Catholics and working-class Protestants also settled in Cabbagetown, again living side by side. They also gravitated to Dummer and Stanley Streets, which quickly descended into horrendous poverty and crime. The Irish newcomers were attracted, as well, to Macaulaytown or The Ward, fated to become the most well-known impoverished immigrant quarter in the city for more than a century. For many, these areas were merely launching pads for subsequent settlements in Toronto.

The Catholic Church slowly and steadily built a network of charitable organizations such as hospitals, schools, boarding homes, and orphanages that strengthened the Irish identity and transformed the Irish presence in the city. By 1851, the Irish-born population became the largest single ethnic group in Toronto.

As Allan Levine relates in *Toronto: Biography of a City*:

The impact of the Irish Catholic migration on Toronto's collective psyche was demographic, emotional, and, for some residents, worrisome. By 1851, one in four Torontonians (7,940) was Catholic, and nearly all of these were Irish. Ten years later, the city's population had increased to 44,821, and 12,135 or 27 percent of that total was Irish Catholic, the highest number they reached.[49]

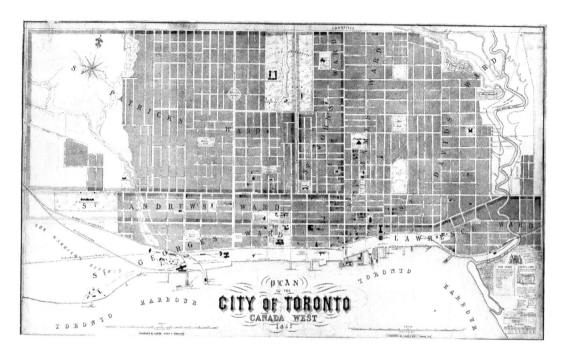

The Boom, 1850–1862

Decade by decade, Toronto grew in leaps and bounds. Between 1842 and 1860, the city expanded exponentially from a modest size of 14,250 people to an industrial powerhouse of 45,000 and over 50,000 at Confederation in 1867.[50]

From the 1830s and 1860s, a small Black population had found freedom from slavery in British North America. Many arrived in Toronto by the Underground Railroad and lived side by side with Irish Catholics and were tolerated almost to the same degree. By 1858, the city's Black population numbered fewer than 2,000 in a population of 50,000, a small portion, but their "stories of bravery and resourcefulness in the face of bigotry and injustice" had a profound impact in the local newspapers and throughout Toronto.[51] The *Globe*'s George Brown "found slavery a stain on civilization that had to be blotted away"[52] and was instrumental in

Fig. 4.7 Plan of the City of Toronto, Canada West, Fleming Ridout & Schreiber, 1857.

establishing the Anti-Slavery Society of Canada in 1851. Toronto became more tolerant of Black people than elsewhere in Canada, and the Black community grew steadily, forming connections and the confidence to assert itself politically and socially.

However, acceptance was far from widespread. Segregation in schools, public society, restaurants, and real estate were frequently encountered by the Black population. As quoted by Allan Levine in *Toronto: Biography of a City*, Samuel Thompson, writing in an editorial in the *Daily Colonist* in April 1855, stated, "We fear that they are coming rather too fast for the good of the Province. People may talk about the horrors of slavery as much as they choose; but the fugitive slaves are by no means a desirable class of immigrants for Canada, especially when they come in large numbers."[53]

It has been argued that "despite the mythology that later accrued around the Underground Railroad and Canada as a kind of promised land of freedom, the Black refugees who arrived in places like Chatham, Oro, or other small [Ontario] towns experienced significant hostility and overt racism from white settlers."[54] Initially, the Black community suffered a very constrained freedom, with unequal access to land and employment and segregation in schools, churches, and society associations.[55]

Seemingly, Toronto was an exception and perhaps "the one place where segregation in public education was never the norm."[56] The city had become accustomed to large influxes of very poor newcomers, notably its experience with Irish migration during Black '47.[57] There was an integration of the Black community in Toronto unmatched in other areas of North America. While Black people were only a fraction of the population, their numbers grew quickly as U.S. tensions over slavery raged on. By 1840, there were reportedly 525 Black people living in Toronto;[58] within 15 years, that figure had almost doubled to 973.[59]

William Howard, an escaped slave living in Toronto in the 1840s as a free man, wrote eloquently about his new home and his fellow Black immigrants:

I expected to work for a living, go where I would. I could not be stopped from working. Canada is the best place that ever I saw: I can make more money here than anywhere else I know of. The colored people, taken as a whole, are as industrious as any people you will find. They have a good deal of ambition to go forward and take a good stand in the community. I know several who own houses and lands. They are a very temperate people.[60]

The Railway Comes to Town

The railway changed the urban landscape and transformed Toronto in the 1850s. Three railway companies built tracks to Toronto, coming in along the harbour as right-of-way lines: the Grand Trunk Railway, the Great Western Railway, and the Northern Railway of Canada. New wharves were built to accommodate the expanding industrial waterfront, forever altering the potential of a unified harbour and planned "Esplanade," as Eric Arthur notes in *Toronto, No Mean City*:

> Since 1852, when the railways were allowed to ravage the waterfront and leave on their flanks an unplanned mess of roundhouses, warehouses, factories, and slums, Toronto has turned its back on the lake. We still have the Esplanade, but no longer is it a place for promenade, for seeing ships at anchor, or for Easter parades. Today the pedestrian is rare on the Esplanade. Trucks and trains have taken his place, and the lakefront has receded beyond sight.[61]

The railways made Toronto an industrial heartland,[62] shaping banking and leading to the building of numerous factories. The demand for factory workers greatly increased the population of the city, while thousands of new immigrants continued to flood into Toronto, arriving at the new Union Station. By 1871, Toronto's population was 56,000; by 1901, 208,000.

The development of railways in Toronto had an enormous impact on the Gooderham & Worts mill and distillery. William Gooderham was a businessman with a social conscience. He was instrumental in the construction of Little Trinity Church on King Street East, where members did not have to pay for their pews as they did at St. James Cathedral. Gooderham also financed the construction of small cottages near his distillery so that his workers did not have to travel far to work and had affordable, well-situated housing. These small cottages were on streets such as Trinity and Sackville and demonstrated the benefit of keeping workers near their employment while providing well-built homes for increased productivity.

In 1861, the Toronto Street Railway Company was launched and was hailed as a significant milestone for the city.[63] Toronto soon became a leader in exporting farm products — largely, pigs, earning the unfortunate nickname of "Hogtown." From the 1850s, the slaughtering and curing of hogs' flesh became a major industry in the city. By the beginning of the 20th century, the William Davies Company was shipping over 400,000 hog carcasses to Britain, becoming the largest pork-packing firm under the Union Jack and making Toronto the hog butcher of the empire.[64]

Hogtown now "stood in the centre of so much of the growth, and itself grew with dazzling speed."[65] Toronto was the Canadian entry point, manufacturing capital, and centre of the colony and then the country. Its harbour and railways made it so, inputting goods from Montreal and the North and outputting to Buffalo and New York City in the United States. The city's population grew in leaps and bounds: 86,000 in 1881, 208,000 in 1901, and 380,000 in 1911, becoming "cleanly, godly, and very, very prosperous."[66]

Besides giving birth to new neighbourhoods around Gooderham & Worts, this growth spawned workers' cottages close to the William Davies Company, the Railway Lands, the brickyards of Todmorden (in the upper Don River Valley) and Leslieville, and the stockyards. They were compact, plentiful, and largely aesthetically pleasing to the eye.

As brick became more plentiful, fired from local clay at brickyards around the city, it became a more desirable, safer option instead of wood for buildings. The Great Fire of Toronto in 1849 was the first major one in the city's history, destroying much of the business core, including damaging an earlier version of St. James Cathedral, the 1831 City Hall, and the first St. Lawrence Market.

This was the community in which some of the first Modest Hopes were built: simple, small, one- or two-storey, easy-to-construct cottages made from local materials by and for the city's earliest workers.

The Emerging Metropolis, 1862–1920

By the 1860s, Toronto had become a vibrant, industrial, multicultural, multi-faith, multi-class society. The arrival of railways in the 1850s had transformed the waterfront and cut off the city from Lake Ontario. Established neighbourhoods had formed often connected to industry. Working-class districts, such as The Ward, Corktown, Cabbagetown, and Leslieville, were closer to factories, while middle- and upper-class neighbourhoods had the luxury of being removed from them and farther away. The arrival of horse-drawn cars and streetcars in the 1860s and electric streetcars in the 1890s encouraged a middle-class movement to roomier suburban fringes such as Yorkville, Rosedale, and eventually North Toronto.[67]

On midnight, June 30, 1867, the bells of St. James Cathedral rang, marking the beginning of the Dominion of Canada. Fifty thousand citizens of Toronto — English Anglicans, Scottish Presbyterians, Irish Protestants and Roman Catholics, roughly 2,000 Black people, a couple of hundred Jews and Quakers, among others — gathered to celebrate Confederation on July 1, 1867. The *Globe*'s George Brown had this to say about the occasion: "We hail the birthday of a new nationality. A United British America, with its four millions of people, takes its place this day among the nations of the world."[68]

Many of those assembled Torontonians worked for a living by 1867. The occupations listed in a census taken in 1871 reveal much about the city's population. In *Toronto Remembered*, William Kilbourn itemizes the many occupations: 2,872 servants, 2,184 common labourers, 232 blacksmiths, 1,414 clerks, 70 booksellers, 381 printers and publishers, 1,100 carpenters, 56 carvers and gilders, 86 saddlers, 41 photographers, 48 brewers and distillers, 40 engravers, 302 hotelkeepers, 31 architects, and 683 shoemakers.[69]

As Toronto expanded, public services were forced to modernize, professionalize, and catch up to the emerging needs of the city. After the Great Fire of 1849, Toronto improved its fire code and enhanced its ability to fight fires with the formation of the Toronto Fire Services in 1874. The Toronto Police Service, which had been founded in 1834, eventually introduced "emergency telephone call boxes linked to a central dispatcher, plus bicycles, motorcycles, and automobiles shifted the patrolman's duties from passively walking the beat to fast reaction to reported incidents, as well as handling automobile traffic."[70]

Beginning in the 1880s, electric elevators, taller iron-framed buildings, and telephones facilitated greater business concentration in the downtown core. Steel skyscrapers soon rose in the early 1900s. The downtown was roughly mapped out and divided into wholesaling around Yonge Street below King Street, with major retailing along the former near Queen Street and finance centred on Bay and King Streets.[71]

In 1873, the Grand Trunk Railway built a second Union Station at the same location as earlier incarnations in time to welcome another British wave of immigration. Still, the city continued to be a remarkably homogenous place, known for its strong churchgoing populace and strict measures for shutting down almost everything on the Sabbath Sunday.

The economic turmoil and depression of the 1870s profoundly affected the lives of Toronto's workers and their families, and there was little job security during that decade. At the end of the 1870s, according to the Ontario Bureau of Industries, Toronto workers averaged only 44 weeks of employment a year. For many, being out of work for large portions of the year was the norm. In *Toronto's Poor*, Bryan D. Palmer and Gaétan Héroux write: "By the end of the [19th century], at least one out of five urban Canadian workers was wageless at some point in the year regardless."[72] Given these conditions, for workers and their families to rent or own housing, especially a Modest Hope, was a life-changing achievement.

According to Dr. Mark McGowan, the years 1890 to 1920 were significant for the city's Irish Catholic population. Since the arrival in Toronto of the Irish earlier in the 19th century, especially in the summer of 1847, they experienced a major social, ideological, and economic shift between 1890 and 1920 that allowed them to integrate into Toronto's society and finally shake off their second-class status.[73]

The Irish were no longer the latest immigration wave to Toronto, and the traumatic memory of Black '47 had begun to fade in the city's memory. Their hard landing and societal prejudices were softened as they settled into their new city and helped equally to shape it. As the 19th century drew to a close, Germans, Italians, Jews, Ukrainians, and later, Chinese, Russians, Finns, Poles, and others from Eastern Europe arrived in Canada.

Toronto did not see a major surge in Chinese immigrants until the late 1870s. In Canada's West, though, they began to arrive in 1858, attracted by the gold rush on the Fraser River in British Columbia. By 1863, 3,000 Chinese people were in British Columbia to search for life-changing riches. Sadly, very few were successful, and unfortunately, they were not welcomed by white fellow fortune seekers, who used violence to scare and drive them away. They were treated harshly because of their "large numbers, physical differences, incomprehensible language, and eating habits with chopsticks that made them easy targets to spot."[74]

The second major wave of Chinese immigrants was lured to Canada to be labourers on the last westerly portion of the Canadian Pacific Railway in British Columbia. Andrew Onderdonk, an American engineer, bid successfully on the right to build the B.C. section and was determined to acquire "cheap labour to come within budget." He favoured Chinese labourers, who worked hard at wages 30 to 50 percent lower than their white counterparts. From 1881 to 1884, 15,701 Chinese workers came to Canada to build the railway, yet their hard labour and contributions were largely ignored in Canadian history for many years.

When the railway was completed, many decided to stay in Canada. Alarmed, the federal government, as described in the previous chapter, implemented a head tax of $50 to dissuade further immigration, raising it to $100, then $500 by 1903. In search of new employment and a less hostile environment, numerous Chinese railway workers migrated eastward, settling in towns and cities along the tracks, while others eventually travelled farther to make Toronto their home.

The first Chinese immigrants found a niche and business opportunity in Toronto, initially established by Sam Ching, and later Wo Kee, in 1877: the hand laundry business. Already the city had steam laundries operated mostly by white men who handled large orders from restaurants, hotels, and hospitals, but their expensive machinery made for high start-up costs. On the contrary, all that was needed for a hand laundry were kettles, washtubs, scrubbing boards, soap, and elbow grease, plus a stove to heat the water and dry the clothes and a space large enough to hang laundry in the winter. Hand laundry was considered "women's work" and no white men wanted to do it. Chinese hand laundries did not originate in China. They were largely an invention by circumstance that "filled the demand of a rapidly growing urban economy by providing quality, low-cost laundry service to a workforce of single men who lived in boarding houses or apartment hotels, men who needed their clothes washed."[75] Moreover, the space could double as a residence.[76]

By 1885, there were 100 Chinese people living in Toronto; by 1911, the population had reached 1,000. As the population grew, so did the number of Chinese laundries. A 1907 *Globe* editorial entitled "Asiatic Peril to National Life" contended that Asian immigrants were not good citizenry material, and accepting them would lead to "national decay."

The fear of the "Yellow Peril," the idea that Chinese "blood" would swamp the so-called superior Anglo-Saxon population, was rampant in the early 20th century. Fearing the West would be flooded by Chinese and Japanese immigrants unless it was "fully occupied," Canada developed an immigration policy to lure white Eastern Europeans to the prairies.

In the late 19th and early 20th centuries, high taxes, low wages, unemployment, poor farmland, pests, and disease drove millions of Italians out of their homeland. Many came to Toronto with trades and skills to build and shape the city and enhance its character and flavour. The Italians in Toronto grew from almost 4,900 in 1911 to over 9,000 in 1921. By the 1931 Canada Census, they had expanded to 15,600.[77]

Each new immigrant group followed a similar journey, settling first in Toronto's poor inner-city areas, then moving outward throughout the city.[78] Toronto's population was around 380,000 in 1911, still Anglo-Celtic and largely Protestant, with an increasingly growing diversity that included 4,900 Italians, 18,000 Jews, 9,800 Germans, and 1,000 Chinese, along with small groups of Poles, Macedonians, and Ukrainians. The city continued to grow, diversify, reidentify, and evolve.

A third influx of English immigrants arrived in Canada as part of a nationwide campaign in the early 20th century. However, this steady stream of new immigrants stayed in Toronto, something no one imagined they would do. The city had no effective system to deal with this large migration and was soon engulfed in a "house famine."

Through resourcefulness, these new English immigrants found jobs and homes in working-class neighbourhoods all over Toronto, especially in The Ward, Cabbagetown, Corktown, and east of the Don River. They brought to the city an enormous pride in and respect for the British Empire as well as a tradition of trade unionism whose roots ran deep.

Fig. 5.1 Alpha Avenue,
Cabbagetown.

THE NEIGHBOURHOODS

A Selection of Historic Toronto Areas Where Modest Hopes Were Concentrated

Home is where one starts from.
— T.S. Eliot, "East Coker," *Four Quartets*

The socio-economic structure in Toronto in the 19th century, and how the location of residential areas related to it, followed certain patterns. The areas with the greatest amenities, such as high ground with views, clean air, and proximity to municipal and religious institutions, attracted the wealthy and powerful. Those parts of the city where land and housing were inexpensive, such as low, wet areas choked by the smoke of burning coal and wood, or next to industry, railways, and the harbour, were where lower-income workers and newcomers found community. In Toronto, the less-desirable areas were either west of Yonge Street and north and south of Bloor Street or in the east end of the city.

When immigrants to Toronto first arrived, they gravitated to the neighbourhoods they could afford. Those lucky enough to have family or friends in the city could be temporarily lodged with them until other housing was found. For those with no connections in the city, low-rent rooming houses and other shared housing options in areas such as Lombard Street, The Junction, The Ward, Cabbagetown, Corktown, and Leslieville were available. People without resources, such as the jobless, the incapacitated, and seasonal workers, built shelters and camped in wooded areas along the Don River or in the ravines twisting throughout the city.

Toronto did provide some temporary housing for the homeless in the Toronto House of Industry, set up in January 1837 in an unused courthouse downtown on Richmond Street until a permanent home, designed by architect William Thomas, was built in 1848 at Elizabeth and Elm Streets.[1] However, the quality of early housing in the city varied greatly. In the shadow of a report from a royal commission on the state of working-class housing in the United Kingdom, an article in the *Globe* on May 27, 1885, entitled "Workingmen's Houses," clearly expresses the hope that Toronto would provide safe and sanitary accommodation for the city's poor. It insists that on

no consideration shall we allow in our towns or cities, houses to be either built or rented that are unfit for decent human habitation. Things are tending in that direction among us already, and unless very strict measures are taken, overcrowding in places scarcely fit for pig styes will be a fact greatly nearer to Canadians than anything taking place in the United Kingdom.

Lombard Street (Formerly March and Stanley Streets)

Before it was Lombard Street, it was Stanley Street, and before that, March Street. What is left of Lombard today reflects very little of the notorious thoroughfare it once was. There is an evocative and engaging old fire hall at the eastern end of the street, a former city morgue, a Victorian-Era industrial building, and a well-appointed three-storey former hotel at the corner of Victoria and Lombard Streets. Slotted in between are glassy condominiums, nondescript low-rise office buildings, and parking lots. It is hard to believe that this unassuming two-block street once had a rich history and notorious reputation.

First appearing on the Town of York map in the 1820s, March Street did not always have a bad name and was once a pleasant, quiet "downtown" street. A few dozen residents lived in modest wooden cottages, while services such as grocery stores, provision shops, a children's day school, a boarding house, the Roman Catholic Chapel of Ease, and Toronto's first Baptist church were their neighbours.

Fig. 5.2 (left) Lombard Street Fire Hall.

Fig. 5.3 (right) The former Lombard Street City Morgue.

In the summer of 1847, Black '47 rattled Toronto to its core. The large influx of Irish Famine immigrants who arrived in the city more than doubled its population. Many of these new refugees were attracted to March Street for its cheap, available housing, and the street soon tripled with a predominately Irish population. Overcrowding in wooden cottages, flats, and rooms quickly became common as dozens of tenants boarded together, while families doubled and tripled up to share rents and spaces as they tried desperately to begin new lives in Toronto.

Two summers later, in 1849, March Street and its Irish occupants entered the news and spotlight once again. Toronto was hit with a cholera epidemic, and the street's large Irish contingent had a disproportionate number of cases. John Townsend, chairman of the Toronto Board of Health, reported in 1849:

> March Street (as you are well aware) is for the most part composed of low, undrained, ill-ventilated wooden buildings, chiefly occupied by the poorest classes of society to be found in this City, and taking into consideration the habits of many of its people, and the crowded and filthy state in which many of them live, it is a matter of no surprise that more than double the number fell victim to the Cholera there than in any other portion of the city.[2]

Two-block-long March Street had 107 cholera cases and 68 deaths, making it the hardest-hit location in the city. For many Toronto residents, the cholera epidemic of 1832 brought on a ship from Ireland was still a recent memory, and with the subsequent crisis of Black '47, Irish Catholic immigrants to Toronto were quickly branded as disease carriers as well as sufferers.[3]

March Street once housed many labourers packed into two blocks of crowded, shoddy frame cottages with "an impressive number of taverns."[4] Public drinking and brawls on the street, with its seven taverns and several brothels, gave it plenty of colour and a worsening reputation.

So the street's name was changed in April 1850 to Stanley. The switch did not fix March Street,[5] though, and the problems remained; in fact, they ramped up[6] as the old wooden houses grew increasingly decrepit.

Newspapers were fond of reporting the street's crimes, "horrendous" poverty, and "muck and filth" squalor. The words *idle* and *wretched* were used repeatedly in the press to depict the street's occupants, as well as other stereotypes to describe their depravity. The papers also wrote of the street's overflowing sewers, cottages with stagnant water in the basements "rotting the floors and breeding disease," backyards with putrid garbage breeding the "plague," and "miserable hovels which in themselves are better fitted for pig-styes and cow-pens than residences for human beings."[7] An 1858 *Globe* article had this to say about the street's inhabitants: "Irish beggars are to be met everywhere, and they are as ignorant and vicious as they are poor. They are lazy, improvident, and unthankful; they fill our poorhouses and our prisons and are as brutish in their superstitions as Hindus."

So once more the street's name was changed, this time to Lombard, with the hope of shedding its ghosts and stigma. Not surprisingly, the new designation failed to fix the problems, not at first, anyway. In 1886, a fire hall was erected near the corner of Lombard and Jarvis. As Toronto became an increasingly industrial city, Lombard Street began to figure as prime real estate. Many of the poorly constructed, dangerously over-crowded wooden cottages that lined the street were demolished. The vacant lots were then sold to companies such as Ontario Lead and Barb Wire, R.G. McLean Printers, and Dunlop Tires.[8]

Toward the late 19th century, "the city was discovering it had a new troubled area, and several new groups of immigrants, on which to focus its concern," so it turned its attention to The Ward. Lombard Street, "finally freed from the ghosts of its March and Stanley Streets past, slowly took on a new life."[9]

Today, there are few historic remnants of Lombard Street left. The fire hall became the home of The Second City in 1977, where Dan Aykroyd, Gilda Radner, John Candy, and many other popular comedians got their

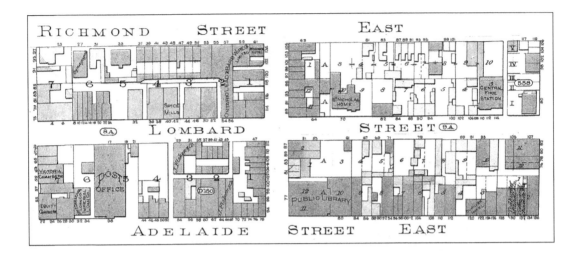

Fig. 5.4 Lombard Street, 1890, showing several large new brick buildings and factories, with just a few wooden structures (in light grey) remaining.

start. It is now the College of Makeup Art & Design. The former city morgue became the Women's Cultural Centre in 1975. Today, it is the Fred Victor Women's Hostel, a shelter for homeless women.

The Ward

Before it was "The Ward," it was Macaulaytown, named for James Macaulay, who once owned a 100-acre plot on this site before it was subdivided into streets and housing. This new "subdivision" was one of Toronto's first suburbs,[10] a "pleasant working-class neighbourhood"[11] that housed early settlers to Toronto who were largely from the British Isles. The modest working-class suburb soon became the best-known impoverished immigrant quarter in the city for the next century.

The Ward's boundaries were Yonge Street to the east, University Avenue to the west, College Street to the north, and Queen Street to the south, and its roads were once lined with small, mostly one-storey cottages in rows or singles, reflective of workers' housing in Britain, many of the designs taken from the pages of John Wood's pattern books. They were also inspired by the housing movement ideals espoused by Nathaniel Kent, who sought to improve the conditions and aesthetics of workers' homes. The early Ward housed taverns, shops, churches, and even a few bowling alleys.[12]

As Toronto expanded, Macaulaytown soon became engulfed by that growth. Soon, five city wards were created, with Macaulaytown becoming part of St. John's Ward. Shortly, though,

Fig. 5.5 A view of The Ward from the top of the T. Eaton factory in 1910.

it was simply called The Ward. Inexpensive housing and proximity to Union Station made The Ward a popular place to reside for each successive wave of new immigrants. Land parcels were small but were soon made smaller as landlords carved them up to generate even more rent. On a single plot, front and rear cottages were often built, with multiple families or tenants pooling their resources to share rent. Such overcrowding in tiny, filthy rooms or compact cottages soon became common, as did lack of sanitation from overflowing outdoor privies and garbage. The House of Industry at 87 Elm Street (now the Young Women's Christian Association), colloquially called "The Poor House," symbolized a shift in The Ward, which by 1850 was considered a slum. Thousands of Irish Famine refugees sought refuge there in the 1840s and afterward, settling on streets such as Centre, Chestnut, Elizabeth, and Agnes. Perhaps the shacks, small cottages, and tenements reminded them of home.

But, as Allan Levine writes in *Toronto: Biography of a City*, other immigrants flocked to The Ward: "Living side by side with Irish Catholics in the shacks and cottages of Macaulay Town and tolerated to about the same degree by Toronto's upstanding citizens, was another smaller group of newcomers, black refugees from the United States."[13] Toronto's first Black community found homes here. Among its earliest settlers were Lucie and Thornton Blackburn, fugitive slaves from Kentucky, who arrived in the 1830s. The story of another Black immigrant, the widowed Ann Maria Jackson, also a fugitive slave from the United States, is featured in Chapter Six. Ann Maria and her seven children first lived with Lucie and Thornton Blackburn upon arriving in Toronto in the 1850s before settling in the Ward. Although Black people lived throughout The Ward, many eventually moved out and settled around Bloor and Bathurst Streets to the west. By the 1850s, the Blackburns had acquired several properties throughout The Ward and had assisted many recently arrived fugitive slaves to find housing, as did John Meriwether Tinsley, a free Black carpenter who came to Toronto from Virginia in 1843 with his wife, Douglass. They initially opened a grocery store at the corner of Albert and Elizabeth Streets, but it failed abruptly upon Douglass's early death. Bereaved, Tinsley shuttered the shop and built a pair of attached workers' cottages near the corner of Terauley (Bay) and Agnes (Dundas) Streets and started his own construction company, possibly the first Black Canadian to do so. Tinsley became a very prosperous building contractor and property owner in downtown Toronto and helped many new fugitive slaves find their first jobs and build their own homes. As his obituary in the *Globe* on October 6, 1892, put it, he became the "celebrated patriarch of the coloured community," with friends among all classes and in many cities. Tinsley died in Toronto, at the age of 109, outliving all eight of his children.

With war looming between the states south of the border, freedom seekers flowed into Canada in ever-greater numbers. By 1861, there were about 1,000 Black people in Toronto, more than half of whom lived in The Ward.[14] At the beginning of the 1870s, 10,868 people of all kinds resided in The Ward.[15] As the Irish and Black immigrants moved out of the neighbourhood, many relocating to their first Modest Hopes elsewhere in the city, a large wave of Italian labourers began immigrating to Toronto in the 1880s. For many, The Ward became their place of first landing, settling largely around Edward and Chestnut Streets, which became the city's first Little

Italy before Italians moved west and north to College Street.[16]

Beginning in the 1890s, thousands of Eastern European Jews fleeing pogroms arrived in The Ward. The story of Murray Buchman and his grandparents, as an example of this immigrant wave, is featured in the next chapter. Murray's grandparents first settled in The Ward after escaping from Romania in 1902. They lived in several houses on Edward Street before buying their first house in the city's west end. Between the 1890s and 1920s, though, as wave upon wave of immigration arrived in Toronto, The Ward faced a serious housing shortage.

Fig. 5.6 Slum housing interior, 1913.

The small cottages of Macaulaytown, originally built for one family, now increasingly housed multiple families or tenants, while many more houses were erected in backyards and laneways to increase occupancy, making the future Ward one of the densest neighbourhoods in the city, if not the country.[17]

As more people moved into The Ward, its colourful, noisy, unsanitary conditions became a source of anxiety and fascination for Anglo Toronto,[18] which was largely unfamiliar with the sights, sounds, and smells of a crowded but vibrant multicultural community. As a city "that saw itself as more British than the British," Toronto viewed the foreign languages, customs, commercial practices, and cultural and religious habits in The Ward as "intolerably alien."[19]

The Ward became a subject of great interest in the local press, as well. The *Christian Guardian* reported that it was a "festering sore of our city life … The lanes, alleyways and backyards are strewn with refuse, houses behind houses, and in the yards between unsightly piles of ramshackle out-houses that are supposed to provide sanitary conveniences."[20]

In his essay "Before the Ward: Macaulaytown," Stephen A. Otto writes:

> As the new century dawned, the population of St. John's Ward had nosed well above 13,000, with many of the residents packed into hundreds of wood cottages located just steps from E.J. Lennox's majestic new city hall and the hulking Eaton's factory next door. By that point, civic officials could no longer ignore the poverty on their doorstep.[21]

The infamous "slum report" written by Dr. Charles Hastings in 1911 documented the living conditions of The Ward. He reported on the "overflowing outdoor 'privies' and filthy, unventilated apartments [that] could be implicated in high levels of infectious diseases including typhoid, cholera and tuberculosis,"[22] or as the *Toronto Daily Star* summed it up in the heading of an article: "Enough Filth in One Block to Turn a Whole City Sick."[23]

For many Torontonians, The Ward became associated with immigrant housing, disease, and epidemics. But Anglo Torontonians' implicit bias was ultimately proven wrong. The succession of immigrants who first

Fig. 5.7 Slum housing interior, 1914.

lived in The Ward "built and paved Toronto's streets, sweated in its garment-manufacturing industry, did the dirty work at the Keele Street stockyards, and gradually made the city more cosmopolitan," and in time created their own neighbourhoods and built institutions such as "schools, shops, synagogues, churches, ethnic-language newspapers, social clubs, and benefit societies."[24]

By 1918, there were 17,000 people living in The Ward.[25] In the 1920s, the Jewish community largely left The Ward for Kensington Market to the west, but the former soon became home to Toronto's first Chinatown as Chinese immigrants moved into the area.

The Ward became a microcosm of the multicultural settlements throughout Toronto. As wave upon wave arrived in the city, new communities were founded and new houses of worship were erected. Anglican, Catholic, African Episcopalian, and Methodist churches, and later, synagogues and more churches, were established.

Fig. 5.8 Two children in the backyard of a home on Centre Avenue in Toronto's Ward, 1912.

After the Second World War, city officials voted to demolish most of The Ward to make way for the New City Hall, various hospitals, and new office towers and hotels. Today, very little is left of the neighbourhood, and all of the area's first cottages and Modest Hopes are gone. A short strip along Dundas Street West, the YWCA on Elm Street, along with a small group of rowhouses, are all that remain to remind us of its former character.

Corktown

The historic boundaries of the Corktown neighbourhood are Shuter Street to the north, Front Street East to the south, Berkeley Street to the west, and the Don River to the east. While once a working-class neighbourhood full of workers' cottages, only vestiges — short streets and broken rows — remind us of what Corktown originally looked like. Today, amid architectural vestiges of its past, Corktown has several vacant lots,

Fig. 5.9 Housing at 9–15 Power Street in Corktown, 1936.

industrial buildings, and new condos, while the redevelopment of the neighbouring West Don Lands area has re-created an entirely new residential and mixed-use community. Corktown is now a thriving, gentrified, prosperous neighbourhood, but again, its roots tell a different story.

One of Toronto's first neighbourhoods, Corktown became home to Irish Protestant and Catholic immigrants who began arriving in appreciable numbers in 1820. They were drawn to live in this area where they were close to the wharves, warehouses, mills, and factories rising along the lakefront in which they worked. Canadian author and clergyman Henry Scadding dismissed the neighbourhood as "a row of dilapidated wooden buildings inhabited for the most part by a thriftless and noisy set of people."[26] The growing residential area earned the nickname "Corktown," since many of its residents came from County Cork in Ireland.

Housing conditions east of Berkeley Street were often less than ideal. Closeness to the marshy Don River made the area undesirable, increasingly inferior, and unsanitary. According to an 1829 petition signed by 69 Town of York residents, many of the residences around the marshlands were "untenanted" due to the area's unhealthy conditions.[27]

While many of the cottages that once lined Corktown's streets have been demolished, small collections of them still stand, as well as some of the community's institutions. Although Corktown was settled by a large Irish Protestant contingent, there was also a sizable Irish Catholic community in the early 19th century, as well. In 1822, the first Roman Catholic church, St. Paul's Basilica, was established on Power Street in Corktown, then replaced with the current building in 1887–89. St. Paul

Catholic School, the oldest Catholic elementary school in the city, was founded in 1842 and is now behind the basilica on Sackville Street. The school was rebuilt in 1959 and is the third building on the site. Under the concrete playground and parking lot of the school lie the remains of the basilica's old burial ground where thousands of Irish Catholic immigrants were buried, victims of cholera and typhus in the late 1840s and 1850s. The cemetery was decommissioned in 1857.[28]

Fig. 5.10 Gilead Place, Corktown, 1936.

Working-class Irish Protestants in Corktown could not afford the steep pew rentals at nearby St. James Cathedral, so they created their own religious institution: Little Trinity Anglican Church, built in 1843–44 on King Street East, the oldest surviving church building in Toronto. Corktown is also home to Toronto's first "free school." In 1848, the Enoch Turner Schoolhouse, the oldest still-standing school in Toronto, was established on Trinity Street, funded by its namesake, a prominent Corktown brewer and philanthropist.

The population of Corktown grew exponentially in 1847 after the immense flood of Irish immigrants fleeing Ireland during the Potato Famine. That year, forever known as Black '47, almost 40,000 famine immigrants arrived in Toronto, which had a population of about 20,000 at the time. In the mid-19th century, Irish Catholics and Protestants lived side by side in densely populated Corktown where conditions were often harsh, poverty was widespread, and newspaper reports chronicled rampant alcoholism and crime. Hundreds of workers' cottages were built in Corktown then, and many of the original ones can still be seen on side streets such as Bright, Trinity, Wilkins, Ashby Place, St. Paul, and Sackville.

In Chapter Six the life of world-champion rower William O'Connor, who learned his sport on the Don River, steps from his Corktown worker's cottage, is recounted. His teacher was the even more famous rower Ned Hanlan. Chapter Six also reveals the mystery of the lone cottage on Bright Street, and its connection to the home of widowed dairywoman Anne O'Rourke, who raised her large family on this street.

A significant part of Corktown was demolished in the early 1960s for the Don Valley Parkway, the Eastern Avenue Overpass, and the Richmond Street off-ramp, erasing much of the area's history.

Cabbagetown

Today's Cabbagetown is a neighbourhood bounded by Sherbourne Street to the west, the Don River to the east, Wellesley Street to the north, and Shuter and Gerrard Streets to the south. It is now a thriving gentrified, prosperous east-end neighbourhood, but its roots tell a different story.[29]

Lieutenant Governor John Graves Simcoe and his entourage arrived in Toronto in 1793, yet "easterly expansion into what would someday become Cabbagetown was very slow in coming."[30] The division and creation of 100-acre "park lots," which had been set aside as estates for government officials, limited expansion, while the eastern lots, roughly Parliament Street to the Don River, today's Cabbagetown, was covered with enormous pines and was earmarked for public institutions. As the Town of York and then the City of Toronto expanded steadily, land near the Don River remained undeveloped, largely encumbered by fears that the marshy waterway was a breeding ground for cholera and typhus. Although Simcoe purchased his own lot in this area and built his summer retreat, named Castle Frank after his son, the lands bordering the Don River "remained virtually uninhabited until well into the 1800s."[31]

It was industry that brought residential development to the area, beginning in the 1830s. With the establishment of the Gooderham & Worts

mill and distillery, the building of homes and boarding houses soon followed. As Colleen Kelly writes in
Cabbagetown in Pictures, "What had once been an
unhealthy living environment was now considered an
essential working environment … with no means of
transportation, the workers had little choice but to live
within walking distance of their jobs."[32] Slowly, the region developed further.

The original Cabbagetown was located south of
Gerrard Street to Queen Street, from Sherbourne
Street to the Don River, while the area we call
"Cabbagetown" today was originally the Village of
Don Vale. Don Vale grew up around Playter's Bridge
(later Winchester Street Bridge),[33] the main northern
bridge crossing the Don River and connecting the
areas east of it to the City of Toronto. The Don Vale
Tavern and Fox's Inn near the bridge welcomed and
catered to travellers, while the village "stayed little more than a fringe of
humble cottages and vegetable plots"[34] surrounded by farmland. In 1844
and 1850, respectively, St. James Cemetery and the Necropolis opened,
for a time the city's main cemeteries.

In the late 1840s and early 1850s, many of the Irish Potato Famine
immigrants settled in Don Vale and Cabbagetown, which became popular first entry points for them, and later, other immigrants from Poland
and Macedonia, all attracted to the area's local industry, its need for
unskilled labour, and the availability of cheap, unsettled land. They were
drawn together by their common suffering and arduous journeys to
forge strong communities.[35]

The name "Cabbagetown" had its origin with Toronto's prosperous
British residents who assigned the degrading moniker to the neighbourhood's impoverished residents who often dug up their front lawns and
planted cabbages, along with potatoes and turnips, as sources of food.[36]

Fig. 5.11 Cabbages
growing in a
Cabbagetown garden,
273 Sackville Street,
between Dundas Street
East and Oak Street.

The numerous immigrants, the advent of the railway, and the subsequent expansion of manufacturing in Toronto created perfect conditions for development in the area. Many small workers' cottages were built south of Gerrard Street, providing homes for workers in the industries established along the river, such as Gooderham & Worts, the William Davies Company, Sheet Metal Products, and several breweries. In Cabbagetown, the Lamb's Glue and Blacking Manufactory, as well as Toronto General Hospital, opened, providing other sources of employment. North of Gerrard Street, the area was more mixed, with houses belonging to both blue- and white-collar workers and company owners. Among workers' cottages, some larger brick Victorian homes were built along streets such as Carlton.

Many homes were built in what is now considered the quintessential Cabbagetown style. Tall, thin, asymmetrical, and often semi-detached, these Gothic Revival houses featured protruding bay windows, finials, and pointed front gables with carved and ornamented plank "gingerbread" bargeboards or roof trim.

Homes were rented or owned, but some residents were able to purchase professionally built houses, while others had small plots of land to build homes. For most houses, the designs came from "pattern books and vernacular precedents, not from architectural drawings. Due to this, the aesthetic of Cabbagetown is unique."[37] Many Cabbagetown homes are attributed to the carpenter William Hooker, who built the Wellesley Cottages, a row of seven houses constructed in 1886–87. In the 1800s, the most common form of small house in Ontario was the worker's cottage. The rough template for this design was influenced by British architects trying to reduce the unsanitary and crowded conditions of working-class housing. The award-winning Prince Albert Model Cottage designed by Henry Roberts, as noted in Chapter One, was showcased at the 1851 Crystal Palace Exhibition in London, giving momentum to its appearance in construction pattern books throughout the British Isles and overseas and in magazines (e.g., the *Canada Farmer* in the 1860s and 1870s). Innovations included running water, internal sanitation, fresh air, better insulation, and separate bedrooms for parents and children.[38]

In Ontario, besides Gothic Revival, Second Empire and Georgian styles or a mix of many of their elements were combined to produce usually pleasing aesthetics. The "early developers of the cottage designs were also trying to raise the spiritual lives" of the working class by improving the aesthetics of their home life. "These houses were intended to be simple, efficient, economical and beautiful."[39]

Fig. 5.12 Housing at 56–58 Oak Street, Cabbagetown, 1949.

By the end of the 19th century, Cabbagetown and Don Vale were incorporated into the City of Toronto. The Winchester Bridge had to be rebuilt several times because the currents of the Don River consistently broke it down; eventually, it was replaced by the Prince of Wales Viaduct in 1910. What prosperity Cabbagetown experienced peaked at the turn of the century, but the First World War had a crushing impact on the area, causing it to slide into decline even before the Great Depression, which further devasted it.

Unemployment rose while the quality of people's lives sagged. Many were forced to leave their homes, while an even poorer population moved into many of the houses, which were subdivided into apartments and rooming houses, leading to further deterioration and increasing disrepair. Cabbagetown soon became, as expressed by prominent author Hugh Garner, "the largest Anglo-Saxon slum in North America."[40]

The slums of Cabbagetown, south of Gerrard Street, were demolished in the late 1940s to make way for Regent Park. Don Vale managed to miss destruction and largely remains intact today. In the 1960s, there

Fig. 5.13 Parliament Street, west side, north of Shuter Street, 1908.

was a shift in the neighbourhood, and as Cabbagetown became more gentrified, Regent Park deteriorated. In time, Don Vale eventually assumed the name of its former neighbour and became Cabbagetown.[41]

The neighbourhood that was originally the home of working-class people has evolved over time and adapted to Toronto's booming housing market. Since the 1960s, more affluent Toronto families have made Cabbagetown their home. Yet the social fabric of the neighbourhood continues to be varied. Near the intersections of both Gerrard and Parliament and Dundas and Sherbourne Streets are some of the highest concentrations of homeless shelters, drop-in centres, rooming houses, and low-income housing in Canada.[42]

Leslieville

Leslieville is located east of the Don River and is bounded on the north by the Canadian National Railway line and Gerrard Street East, on the west by Empire Avenue, on the south by Eastern Avenue, and on the east by Coxwell Avenue. Today, it is a thriving, gentrified east-end neighbourhood, but it has come a long way since its beginning as a tiny village in the countryside, centred around a former tollbooth near Leslie Street and Kingston Road (Queen Street). In the beginning, this village was named Ashport, and it had only a steam sawmill, a barrel-making shop, a blacksmith, a tavern, and a scattering of log cabins.[43]

In 1842, George Leslie, a horticulturist and businessman from Ross-shire, Scotland, established a nursery in the Ashport area, which became one of Canada's largest, eventually covering more than 150 acres in the vicinity of Leslie Street. Toronto had just under 15,000 people in 1841, but a decade later, the population had more than doubled, due to the massive influx of Irish immigrants escaping their native land's potato famine While many of these immigrants stayed in Toronto, others moved on to the United States or rural Ontario, especially in the case of the latter, places such as Ashport, providing a cheap pool of labour for jobs no one else wanted. They soon found themselves working alongside African Americans who had escaped slavery south of the border.[44] The passage of the 1850 Fugitive Slave Act in the United States saw "the trickle of African Americans into Ontario [become] a flood."[45]

While Toronto was notably more tolerant of Black immigrants than the rest of Canada, some felt Ontario had too many already, as the *Daily Colonist* stated: "Already we have a far greater number of negroes in the Province than the good of the Country requires" and "our country is overrun by Blacks."[46] George Leslie, however, much like his close friend, newspaper publisher George Brown, was very vocal in his support of abolition. Ashport, and subsequently Leslieville, soon developed a reputation for tolerance. A number of Black, as well as Irish, immigrants moved onto small plots in the growing village to begin their lives in Canada. In 1861, about 20 percent of Ashport's (Leslieville's) population were Black men, women, and children.[47]

The Irish Famine immigrants who arrived in the summer of 1847 in Toronto were not the first of their kind in the city. In the early 19th century, almost half a million Irish came to British North America, along with Scottish and English immigrants. These, for the most part by contrast, arrived on sound, relatively comfortable ships, were well educated, practised trades, possessed savings, and helped form a middle class of entrepreneurs who contributed to the shaping of Toronto.

The Ashport Post Office opened in 1860 to serve the burgeoning village, with market gardener William Lambert as the first postmaster, but the community was already being called Leslieville after George Leslie's thriving nursery, the village's largest employer. Two years later, the new

Fig. 5.14 Leslieville, Ashdale Avenue, east side, 1910.

name became official and George Leslie Jr. was its postmaster.

By 1866, Leslieville had a population of about 400, and the George Leslie & Company nurseries continued to be a principal employer in the village.[48] However, as Leslieville grew, so, too, did its Irish Catholic contingent of butchers and piggeries. The discovery of clay and sand deposits along the banks of local creeks and streams led to a thriving brickmaking industry. The deposits were burnt to manufacture red, white, or yellow bricks, which were used in thousands of buildings throughout Toronto. Several brickyards were established in Leslieville, employing numerous residents in the neighbourhood. The business was lucrative, since labour, largely Irish Catholic, was cheap. Whole families, including women and children, made bricks.

Ice-cutting was another form of employment in Leslieville, and as Joanne Doucette writes in *Pigs, Flowers and Bricks*, the crews that did it were "the poorest of the poor, mostly Irish and refugees from slavery."[49] The work was cold, miserable, and dangerous with abysmal pay.[50] Doucette goes on to say:

Leslieville was something of a Wild Wild West; a roughly predominately Irish village with a substantial black population and a Scots/Irish Protestant Middle Class. Most of it lay north of Kingston Road, outside of the City of Toronto. Policing was virtually non-existent and there were many drinking holes, both legal and not. Irish "shebeens" attracted not only Leslieville drinkers but Torontonians. Gambling, cockfighting, and bare-knuckle boxing seemed to be as popular as church-going, strawberry socials and the reciting of Robbie Burns' poems, but with different people. The "Good Old Days" were not so good.[51]

In the mid-1850s and onward in Leslieville, developers and land speculators created subdivisions with more market gardens, brickyards, industries, churches, country estates, and plenty of small urban lots with workers' cottages. George Leslie built one of the first of these subdivisions around Jones and Hastings Avenues, which became a largely Irish Catholic and Black refugee enclave. "Throughout his life, discrimination on the basis of creed was abhorrent to Leslie…. In a racist society, he worked towards providing a safe place for refugees from slavery and from the Irish Potato Famine."[52] Both the Black community and the Irish thrived in Leslieville in a city dominated by the Protestant Orange Lodge.

Other Leslieville subdivisions had pockets of Protestant Irish, English, or Scottish immigrants, largely forming the village's middle class. Along with working-class people, the upper class developed an intricate fabric in Leslieville, where with a few exceptions, as Doucette relates:

> Scots and Ulster Presbyterians owned the businesses and Irish Catholics worked for them…. For working-class people, and in Leslieville that usually meant Irish Catholics, it was different [from the middle class]. Men and women usually worked side by side in the fields, hoeing rows of cabbages, or making bricks. Shopkeepers, tavern keepers and other small family-owned business relied on both the men and women of the family to make their places successful.[53]

Although Irish Catholics were welcome, just as Black men and women were, as menial labourers, neither was entirely accepted in society. Mid- to late-19th-century Toronto was "hierarchical, patriarchal and racist — people were expected to know their place."[54] The city was easier on ambitious Protestants, but it was much harder for Irish Catholics to climb the social ladder and even more difficult for Black men and women.

In the late 1800s, Leslieville's subdivisions stretched south of Queen Street to the shoreline, where brickmakers joined fishermen. They also

Fig. 5.15 A coal wagon stuck on muddy Ashdale Avenue, 1908.

reached north of Queen, mapped out with varying lot sizes for different classes and aligned with railway tracks that soon filled up with workers' cottages — first log, then frame, then brick, for rail and factory workers. Rendering plants, market gardens, factories, churches, train tracks, and housing were all in proximity to one another, some closer than others. In 1855, the village even had its own public school at Queen Street East (Kingston Road) and Curzon Street.

Toronto's population increased from just over 9,000 in 1834 to more than 200,000 by 1901. The 1901 Canada Census notes that 90 percent of the city's citizens were either English, Scottish, Welsh, or Irish.[55] The turn of the century brought thousands of European immigrants to Toronto, including Germans, Italians, Austro-Hungarians, Jews, and others. However, Leslieville saw the Scots-Irish Protestant middle class and Irish Catholic labouring class grow.

In Chapter Six, the story of the Moore family, who arrived from England in the early 20th century and settled on Erie Terrace (Craven Road) in Leslieville, is told. As the street developed, the family multiplied and had a long history on the well-known "Street with the Fence." Mrs. Moore saw her four sons and husband enlist in the First World War, but not all returned.

Chapter Six also recounts the story of Riverside and Leslieville resident Thomas Ferguson, who arrived in Toronto at the age of six months with his mother and met his Scottish father for the first time at Union Station. The large Ferguson family lived at various places in Leslieville and Riverside while Thomas attended local schools and worked in the village's factories. Sadly, his young life was cut short.

As the 20th century dawned, many more factories sprang up along Carlaw and Eastern Avenues. By 1909, Leslieville was annexed by

the City of Toronto; however, it maintained a distinct identity, as did Riverside. While Riverdale became the umbrella neighbourhood designation, Leslieville and Riverside quietly lived on. In the 1980s, a community group successfully lobbied the City of Toronto for new street signs identifying Leslieville as a unique historic community. Today, Leslieville continues, albeit transformed, gentrified, and more affluent, but with its nature as a village intact.

Fig. 5.16 (left) Row of cottages on Munro Street, 1880.

Fig. 5.17 (right) The same Munro Street cottage row in Fig. 5.16 in Riverside in 2019.

* * *

Decades of prosperity and growth provided employment for the thousands of immigrants who came to Toronto in the 19th and early 20th centuries. Many of them started their lives in the new land in the fever sheds near modern-day John and King Streets, in tenements in The Ward, in cottages or rooms crowded with multiple families, in men's lodgings or flophouses, or in the shacktowns on the fringes of the city and along the Don River. But with hard work and a deep willingness to thrive in the various neighbourhoods in their new city, many of these people eventually came to live in Modest Hopes of their own.

Fig. 6 208 Claremont Street.

6

THE STORIES

Portraits of the People and
Their Modest Hopes Homes

Architecture is really about well-being. I think that
people want to feel good in a space.… On one hand,
it's about shelter, but it's also about pleasure.
— Zaha Hadid, architect, artist, and designer

Chapter Six is the beating heart of *Modest Hopes*. Chronicled here are eight stories out of hundreds more that showcase the individuals and their families who lived in workers' cottages — Modest Hopes — the "vessels" that contained these lives and helped them to flourish. Their lives and their stories are part of the fabric of Toronto's history.

BRIDGET ANN TREACY McTAGUE (1840–1924)[1]

88½ Victoria Street, 78 Richmond Street East, 36 Bond Street, 70 Richmond Street West, 27 Widmer Street, 69 Cameron Street

Bridget Ann Treacy McTague was born in Ireland and once lived in many workers' cottages and Modest Hopes throughout Toronto. The homes she lived in offer insight into hopes once realized, that once sheltered, nurtured, and supported an incredible journey to a life and future in Canada.

From the 1790s to the mid-1800s, upward of 450,000 Irish immigrants had already arrived in British North America.[2] They "settled Upper Canada's rich farmland, built canals, established businesses in cities, and helped create the social and economic foundations of everyday life."[2] Before 1846, although it varied from region to region, often Protestant Irish migrants outnumbered Irish Catholics by a ratio of two to one.[3]

As we have seen, 1847 "marked an extraordinary moment in both Irish and Canadian history."[4] In Ireland, years of an outmoded landholding system, falling agricultural prices, an unprecedented population explosion, and a catastrophic failure of the potato crop from 1845 to 1849 culminated in disastrous, unprecedented poverty among the Irish.[5] The poorest in the country died of starvation, while those who could fled to England, Scotland, or farther afield to Canada, the United States, or Australia.

As mentioned previously in Chapter Four, in 1847, in particular, Toronto witnessed one of the greatest human tragedies in the history of the city. "The sight of haggard, vermin-infested, and diseased travellers disembarking after their harrowing trans-Atlantic voyage undertaken in sub-human conditions left indelible images on the society that hesitatingly received them."[6] For Torontonians, the massive flood of Irish Famine refugees that year in which three in every four were Roman Catholic challenged their collective Protestant identity, haunted public officials, and strained local resources, becoming the greatest civic crisis in the young city's history.[7]

Bridget Ann Treacy was one of these famine refugees. Born in Ireland in Newry, County Wicklow,
on February 2, 1840, to parents, Martin Tracy and
Honora (Norry) Ryan, Bridget Ann and her siblings
had become orphans by 1847. Forced to leave Ireland,
Bridget (age about seven) and Thomas (age about
five) accompanied their aunt, Peggy Ryan Clancy, to
Liverpool, England, to board the infamous *Jane Black*,
one of the first ships with Irish immigrants to leave
that port for Canada. However, in the chaos of boarding, Thomas was separated from his family. Bridget
Ann and her aunt were forced to get on the ship without him. It is not known what became of Thomas.

The passage across the Atlantic Ocean on the
Jane Black was perilous and horrific. With little food
or water, sickness soon became rampant. The "coffin ship," as these vessels were soon called, became a
nightmare of death, disease, and starvation. Bridget's hunger became so
intense that she chewed on her leather laces for comfort. As the ship made
its way to Canada, Bridget Ann clutched a treasure from her homeland:
a small gold-painted creamer jug, which travelled with her to Toronto.[8]
Their ship was one of the first to enter Toronto's waterfront, with many
more to follow. Numerous immigrants survived the passage but just barely,
and some succumbed to sickness upon arrival as typhus became epidemic
in Toronto. As soon as they landed, the sick were triaged to fever sheds
to contain the diseases, while the healthy without family connections in
Toronto were sent out of the city. As mentioned earlier in Chapter Four, of
the almost 40,000 immigrants, 1,186 died and were buried in Toronto by
the end of 1847.[9]

Bridget Ann and her aunt Peggy settled in Whitby, Ontario. Peggy
found work as a cook, and Bridget Ann grew into a beautiful young
woman who earned the title "The Belle of Whitby" one year. Bridget Ann

Fig. 6.1a Bridget Ann
Treacy, around age 25,
became a nurse when
she moved to Canada.

met a fellow Irish immigrant named Michael John McTague, a shoemaker, whom she married on November 14, 1865. Less than a year later, their first child, Edward James McTague, was born in Whitby on July 1, 1866.

In 1867, the young family moved to Toronto, where they settled at 88½ Victoria Street amid a row of workers' cottages (80–90 Victoria Street) between Queen and Shuter Streets. Insurance maps suggest that 88½ was likely a one-storey Modest Hope (see Chapter Two), the ½ hinting it was either an upper floor of the house or a rear apartment. They shared the residence with another shoemaker named David Strachan and likely others. This row eventually became a neighbour of Massey Music Hall, which opened in 1894, but 80–90 Victoria Street was demolished in 1913 for the construction of Loew's Theatre, now the Elgin and Winter Garden Theatre.

Bridget Ann and Michael had their second child, Annie, in 1879. Likely timed with Annie's birth, the growing family moved to 78 Richmond Street East between Church and Jarvis Streets amid a row of six workers' townhouses, 68–78 Richmond East, which were later renumbered 76–86 Richmond East. The McTague family shared this rowhouse with fellow shoemaker Vincent Cozens and his family. By 1912, only numbers 82–84 (formerly 74–76) Richmond East continued to survive, and still does. Bridget Ann's house was just to the right (east) of the remaining rowhouse.

In 1882, the family relocated with Vincent Cozens to 36 Bond Street (see Fig. 6.1c), just north of Queen Street, amid a row of seven two-and-half-storey brick workers' cottages, numbered 34–46 Bond. Across the street from their home was the majestic Metropolitan Methodist Church (now the Metropolitan United Church), while next to their row to the south was Notre-Dame-des-Anges, a refuge for girls run by the Sisters of St. Joseph. In 1892, the sisters turned part of their property into a hospital to treat patients during a diphtheria outbreak. That institution became St. Michael's Hospital, which soon expanded to encompass the entire city block, resulting in the demolition of 34–46 Bond.

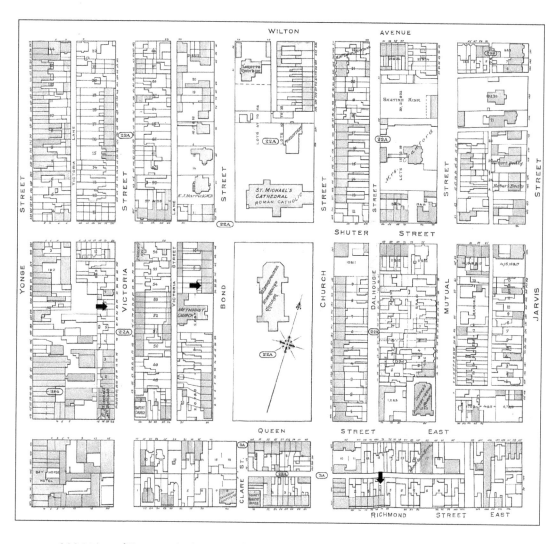

Fig. 6.1b 1884 Map of Toronto. The location of Bridget Ann Treacy's houses at 88½ Victoria Street (see black arrow, Victoria), 36 Bond Street (see black arrow, Bond), and 78 Richmond Street East (see black arrow, Richmond East). Buildings in dark grey are brick; buildings in light grey are wood.

Fig. 6.1c Bond Street, circa 1890. Although 34–46 Bond is obscured by trees, this was the streetscape Bridget Ann and her family lived on.

From 1884 to 1887, the family resided at 70 Richmond Street West between Yonge and York Streets, likely a small frame house. It has since been torn down to make way for more towers in the financial district. They also lived at 27 Widmer Street (1887–1890), where their third child, Norah Matilda, was born. That house has long since been razed for condominiums.

In 1890, the family of five, Bridget Ann (age 49), Michael (age 49), Edward (age 23), Annie (age 11), and Norah (age 3) moved to 69 Cameron Street near Queen Street and Spadina Avenue, a modest house on the end of a long row of workers' cottages. Having moved so frequently, sharing

Fig. 6.1d The McTague house at 69 Cameron Street, circa 1966, just before demolition of houses on Cameron Street.

Fig. 6.1e 82–84 Richmond Street East (originally a row of six houses). Number 86, which is demolished, was Bridget Ann Treacy's house (in front of the fire hydrant).

households often with other families, the McTagues likely owned and lived in 69 Cameron Street as their sole residence, their first true Modest Hope.

Their household grew again as the McTagues' son, Edward, married Alice and started their own family in 1892, with the birth of their first child, Bridget, and then Mary Ida Madelaine. Eventually, Edward and Alice had two more children.

In 1895, Michael John McTague, who had spent his entire working life as a shoemaker, died. Bridget Ann's son, Edward, became the principal breadwinner, making $600 per year as a varnisher, while her daughter Annie worked as a hairdresser, earning $225 per year.

Widowed Bridget Ann Treacy McTague continued to live at 69 Cameron Street until 1910, at which time she moved to Port Credit. In 1967, Cameron Street in its entirety, including 69, was demolished for the Alexandra Park Public Housing complex. Bridget Ann died in Port Credit in 1924, age 84. Her aunt Peggy lived to age 103.

Bridget's youngest daughter, Norah, got married and had nine children. Norah's granddaughter, Terry Smith, is a former Ontario deputy minister of culture who now runs a Toronto-based company called Philanthropic Partnerships, which matches donors with charities. Terry has traced more than 200 of her great-grandmother Bridget Ann's descendants in Canada and the United States, and she is the only famine descendant sitting on the board of the Ireland Park Foundation. Terry's older sister has inherited the small gold creamer from their great-grandmother Bridget, which she keeps in the china cabinet of Norah, her grandmother.

Every single Toronto home that Bridget Ann Treacy McTague lived in has been demolished, replaced by theatres, hospitals, financial district office buildings, housing complexes, and condominiums. For this long and important piece of Canadian and Irish history, there are few Modest Hope houses that exist today to remind us of Bridget Ann's remarkable immigration journey to Toronto. We only have the stories of her hopes and a creamer jug. The workers' homes that once contained her and her family's lives have been torn down, but their history has been reconstructed.

MURRAY BUCHMAN (1923–)

208 Claremont Street

The story of Murray Buchman and 208 Claremont Street in the west end of Toronto is drawn from a long interview with Murray in 2019 and the recollections of his time at 208 Claremont in the 1920s and 1930s, plus additional research. Murray lived in many houses over the course of his life, but he talks most vividly and fondly about 208 Claremont, the first house he ever lived in and the first his family owned, which they did from 1915 to the early 1950s.

The house at 208 Claremont Street, just north of Dundas Street West between Manning and Bellwoods Avenues, was built circa 1888. The first occupants were Andrew Williams, an American teamster, with his wife and five children, followed by Herbert Baker, a British clerk at Massey Manufacturing Company, then William Griffin, an Irish barber. In 1915, 208 Claremont was purchased by Murray's grandparents, Hannah and Harry Haimovitch,[1] Jewish immigrants from Romania. Hannah and Harry arrived in Canada around 1902 but did not buy 208 Claremont for another 13 years. Their journey to this Modest Hope was slow and steady.

Harry Haimovitch and Hannah Grupar were born in Romania in 1874 and 1877, respectively. For centuries, Romania was a turbulent place for Jews, who were targets of religious persecution. By 1878, emigration of Romanian Jews had commenced on a large scale.

During this tumultuous time in Brăila, Romania, Harry and Hannah brought their first child, Mary Haimovitch, into the world in May 1898. Exactly three years later, their second daughter, Pearl Haimovitch (Murray Buchman's mother), was born. But the young family did not stay in Romania much longer. Around 1902, Harry and Hannah, with daughters Mary and Pearl, left Romania for Canada in search of and with hopes for a better life. While discrimination continued in the new

Fig. 6.2a Murray Buchman, age three.

country and they had to work harder for every dollar earned, life was better.

By 1904, Harry and Hannah Haimovitch's first address in Toronto was 40 Edward Street (see Fig. 6.2b) between Terauley (Bay) and Yonge Streets in The Ward. Directories suggest they shared this address with Ida Groper, a widow, who might have been Hannah's mother (her name was Chaia Sarah Grupar) and likely came with them to Canada. They also shared the home with a boarder named Lucin Cohn, a furniture finisher at Jones Bros. & Company. Harry found factory work as a presser for T. Eaton and Company, with additional work as a tailor. On April 12, 1904, Hannah gave birth to daughter Tilly Haimovitch, her first child born in Canada.

By 1907, the growing family had moved to 63 Edward Street (see Figs. 6.2b and 6.2c) at the corner of Terauley (Bay) Street. It was here where they had their fourth child and first son, Samuel Aaron Haimovitch, on September 10, 1907. Later, Samuel changed his last name to Haimes. And the family just kept growing and moving.

In 1909, Harry, Hannah, and their four children, Mary, Pearl, Tilly, and Samuel, moved to 15 Edward Street (see Fig. 6.2b) near Yonge Street, likely in preparation for their fifth child, Molly, born May 24, 1910. The house at 15 Edward was slightly larger, though narrower and longer, with a bay window. By 1911, Harry was making $500 per year as a presser for

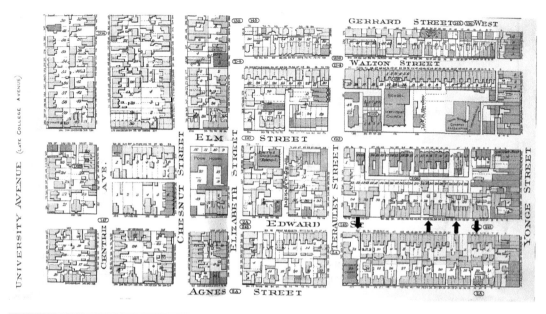

Fig. 6.2b (top) The four residences — 63, 40, 26, and 15 — that Murray's family lived at on Edward Street in The Ward.

Fig. 6.2c (left) 63 Edward Street at the corner of Terauley (Bay) Street where the Haimovitch family lived from 1907 to 1909.

Fig. 6.2d (right) The house at 26 Edward Street where the Haimovitch family lived from 1913 to 1915.

T. Eaton and Company, while the eldest daughter, Mary, now 13, contributed to the family income, earning $150 per year as a tailor in a factory. The house was lively and full. Along with Harry and Hannah and their five children, there was another couple, Sarah and Jacob Greenspoon (a furrier at Canadian Fur Company), as well as Levi and Leroy Harris (jewellers at T. Eaton and Company), who lived in the rear of the home.

The Haimovitch family moved once more to 26 Edward Street (see Fig. 6.2d) in 1913. Harry continued to work as a presser, Mary as a tailor in a factory, and by 1915, 15-year-old Pearl, Murray's mother, was working at the Empire Flower and Fancy Feather Company. Three incomes now contributed to the family finances, and they soon achieved their dream of buying a first house in 1915.

The house at 208 Claremont Street was small, but to the Haimovitches it felt spacious; for the first time they did not have to share it with boarders or renters. It was all theirs, and the bank's! Here, a sixth child, Clara, was born in 1919.

Part of a Second Empire–style row of six houses, 208 Claremont was 14 feet wide and approximately 28 feet long, with a living room in the front, dining room in the middle, and a kitchen in the rear, each separate rooms. The front porch was their outdoor living room; the backyard was tiny. The front entrance opened into a long hall leading to a staircase to the second floor. Off the front hall was a doorway into the dining room that led to the parlour in the front of the house. The basement was low, with a dirt floor and a coal furnace. A coalman dumped sacks of coal through a window into a bin in the basement. On the second floor, there were three bedrooms and a small bathroom. Harry and Hannah initially slept in the larger front bedroom; the middle and back ones were divided among the children and eventually grandchildren.

In 1917, Hannah and Harry's eldest daughter, Mary, age 19, married David Siegel, age 20, a Russian film projectionist who operated projectors in downtown theatres such as the Mary Pickford at Queen Street and Spadina Avenue and the Broadway Burlesque House

Fig. 6.2e The residences at 206–212 Claremont Street (208 is second from the left).

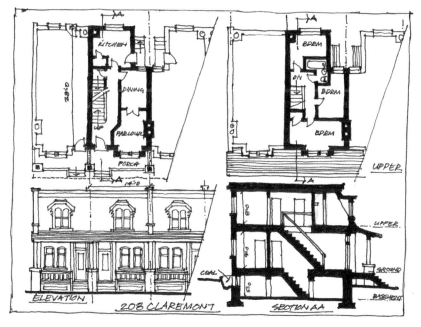

Fig. 6.2f Floor plan, elevation, and section of 208 Claremont Street.

Fig. 6.2g Pearl (née Haimovitch) and James Buchman, Murray's parents.

(formerly the Globe Theatre and The Roxy) on Queen Street across from where the New City Hall now stands. It was likely at the Broadway that 17-year-old Murray saw his first "striptease" when his uncle David let him watch from the projection booth, something Murray says "nearly traumatized him." David was in charge of projection installations in small northern towns and eventually became the president of the projectionists' union. He appears to have moved into 208 Claremont, as well, for a short time.

The oldest three daughters, Mary, Tilly, and Pearl, contributed to the family income by working as telephone operators and machine operators in local factories such as the Sweater Factory (Scotland Woollen Mills Company) and the Dominion Ostrich Feather Company. Between a young baby and four or five working adults, the household was a multi-generational hub of activity.

On May 6, 1920, Pearl Haimovitch married James Buchman. It was likely an arranged marriage with a broker, or *shadchan* in Yiddish. James had been sent to Toronto when he was 15 to establish himself and send money back to his family to help bring them to Canada. This was a tradition in Jewish families: dispatching the eldest son to America to lay the foundation for the rest of the family to follow. James came to Toronto alone, could not speak English, and knew only one cousin. He was in the Canadian Army during the First World War, secured work with the Toronto Transportation (now Transit) Commission (TTC), and found a wife, Pearl. Apparently, they moved into 208 Claremont, as well.

Murray Buchman was born on January 20, 1923, to Pearl and James at 208 Claremont, now a full and hectic household with babies, cousins, aunts, uncles, husbands, wives, parents, and grandparents. Murray's Aunt Clara was only four years old when he was born.

Two years later, after five years of marriage, Murray's parents divorced. Murray has no knowledge of the circumstances of his parents' divorce, nor does he recall a time when his father lived with them. Except for one meeting in 1950, right after Murray was married himself, he never saw his father again. In 1969, his father's cousin, Jack Buchman, told Murray that his father had died. Murray went to the funeral, where he met much of his paternal family for the first time.

For two-year-old Murray, his mother, grandparents, aunts, uncles, and cousins became his village, his collective parents. He remembers his childhood with great fondness:

> My attachment to my grandmother and grandfather was very strong. My grandmother was very kind and soft, my mother was the disciplinarian. For the first seven years, before my mother remarried, it was my grandmother who raised me, since my mother was working. I always remember sitting on my grandfather's lap, on the veranda outside, or going to the synagogue with him.

Murray's grandmother was the matriarch of the family, while his grandfather, mother, aunts, and uncles went to work. His mother, Pearl, worked in a sweater factory doing cover seaming, while his aunt Mary worked as a sewing machine operator.

On the Sabbath Saturday, Murray recalls walking hand in hand with his grandfather to the Adath Israel Synagogue on Centre Avenue, also known as "The Romanian Shul," where the congregation was largely from Romania. He walked by himself around the corner to Treford Place to learn the Hebrew alphabet at a young age from a *melamed* (Hebrew teacher).

The house at 208 Claremont was furnished with a collection of pieces gathered over the family's years of renting on Edward Street. But in the front room was a prized possession: an upright piano upon which Aunt Molly took lessons and Murray plunked out "God Save the King," the only song he was able to play.

Their home had one bathroom, but it was a luxury then to have indoor plumbing. Everyone — Murray's grandparents, mother, aunts, uncles, cousins, and himself — got a bath once a week. It was an ordeal to heat the water, which involved the lengthy task of going to the basement and warming the water over a wood burner. They all took baths on the same day.

In the winter, the house was freezing, since there was often not enough coal to get them through the night. Grown-ups and older cousins took turns sifting through the spent coal in the basement to reuse pieces. If Murray woke in the night and needed to use the washroom, it was too cold to get out from under the covers, so he waited uncomfortably until morning when the house heated up again, choosing warmth over discomfort.

Milk and bread were delivered by horse and wagon, while peddlers came by with carts to sell vegetables. The service cost a few cents more but was worth it for the convenience.

One Friday night the Shabbat candles were lit on the icebox too close to the curtains while Murray and his grandfather sat on the front porch enjoying a mild evening. Murray happened to go inside and was shocked to discover the curtains on fire. On impulse, he threw water on them and put out the flames. There might not be a 208 Claremont today (or 206, 210, 212, 214, or 216) had Murray not gone inside when he did.

To grow up on Claremont was to live in a community rich with a mélange of immigrants. At 206, there was a Lithuanian family who did not speak much English. At 212, the Barnardis, Italians, only spoke their native language. The Barnardi grandmother and Murray's grandmother were friends but neither spoke a word of English, communicating with gestures instead. The Barnardis were kind to Murray, though he "didn't think they cared for Jews much." Yet the two older Barnardi boys came to Murray's aid several times when he was "at the end of a fist" in a street brawl. While the community had a Jewish presence then, perhaps five or six families, it also had a sizable Italian Catholic population, including a Catholic school across the street and a Catholic church on the corner.

While Murray's experience with anti-Semitism was a far cry from his mother's and grandparents' in Romania, it was still very much felt. Mostly, kids from different backgrounds stuck to themselves and did not play together much. When Murray was four, though, an older kid pinned him against a fence, yelling, "You killed Jesus!" to which Murray responded, "But I didn't even know him!"

A few years later, when he walked the two short blocks to Grace Street School by himself, Murray never took the direct route. Instead, he used a secret way, ducking down back alleys to avoid being beaten up by waiting gangs of boys. Several times he was rescued by the neighbouring Barnardi boys. Once, Murray had to fight back, punching a kid while tears ran down his face. "I wasn't a fighter," he admits today.

PRANK MAY COST BOY HIS LEFT EYE

Playfellow   Shot   Screw-Nail
Into Face

Murray Bookman, aged 9, of 208 Claremont St. may lose the sight of his left eye through the prank of a seven-year-old playfellow yesterday, who, with a catapult shot a screw-nail into his eye. Murray was on his way to the store to buy himself some candy. Police took the catapult away from the child. Murray, crying with the pain, ran and told his mother that he could not see anything and explained what had occurred. A doctor, after treatment, sent him to Mount Sinai hospital.

Murray Bookman

When Murray was nine, a Polish kid who lived down the street toward Dundas shot Murray in the eye with a catapulted screw nail, causing Murray to lose sight in his eye for a while. The incident was reported in the *Globe* and *Toronto Star* newspapers, though he was called "Murray Bookman."

In 1930, when Murray was seven, his mother married Harry Steinberg at the beginning of the Great Depression, a second marriage for both of them. Harry moved into 208 Claremont with his two children, Sidney and Ruth. As an only child, Murray was elated to have siblings and a father figure, whom he grew very close to. Of Harry, Murray recalls that he was a "very decent man who was very proud of me." Pearl's second

Fig. 6.2h Newspaper clipping about Murray Buchman's injury, *Toronto Star*, 1932.

marriage changed Murray's life from an only-child, single-parent dynamic to an immediate family of five.

The new blended family moved into the front bedroom of 208 Claremont: Pearl and Harry in one bed, Murray and his stepbrother, Sidney, in another, with stepsister, Ruth, in her own bed. Murray's grandparents moved into the smaller middle bedroom, while Aunt Clara shifted into the tiny back bedroom. Clara "did some cooking and most of the cleaning and complained bitterly," Murray says, though Murray's grandmother, Hannah, did most of the cooking. Pearl continued her employment at the factory doing cover seaming for sweaters, while Harry worked as a tailor making alterations for Tip Top Tailors at its Yonge Street store. Unfortunately, Harry lost his job shortly after they married, but Murray's mother kept working.

Murray lived at 208 Claremont at the start of the Great Depression but does not remember life being that different before or after it: "We were very, very poor, but as a kid, I didn't know we were poor. I thought everyone lived like that. I didn't even think about it. I didn't know that my grandmother put a little more water in the soup." He had a house and friends, was part of street life, and was content in the world. "I didn't even think about it until I got older and then realized there were differences and that everyone I knew was pretty much in the same boat."

Money was tight. Murray's grandfather could no longer work as a presser because he had injured his hand in the T. Eaton factory. Murray was sent on errands to Dundas Street to pick up groceries at Mrs. Toon's Grocery. The family kept a tab at the store and sometimes were unable to make payments. In the early 1930s, a newspaper was two cents, and Murray recalls going to the Duchess Theatre on Dundas Street near Bathurst Street, getting a hot dog and drink at the Jewish delicatessen next door, and only paying 25 cents for the whole outing, including the film. His favourite summertime activity was heading to Sunnyside Beach, riding the free streetcar, and going to the free beach beside the Sunnyside tank, which cost a dime to enter. He rarely had that dime, but on occasions

that he did he still remembers the diving tower. However, with a smile, he says, "I didn't dive. I jumped!"

Although money was scarce, fun was plentiful. Claremont was Murray's universe. He played outside in summer and winter from morning until night and recalls a magazine he had delivered from England with stories about young boys in Britain. Impatiently, he waited for its delivery so he could pore over the tales. But fun was not always that wholesome:

> [I once] got an awful beating from my mother.... I went into the laneway with a whole bunch of dried-up leaves and a package of

Fig. 6.2i (left) Murray and his mother, Pearl, circa 1930.

Fig. 6.2j (right) Murray and stepbrother, Sidney, on Claremont Street, circa 1930.

cigarette papers and tried rolling them to try and smoke them … and she found matches in my pocket and I got punished really badly. It must have worked because I never did it again.

Around 1932, Pearl, Harry, Murray, Sidney, and Ruth moved from 208 Claremont to an apartment above a store at 1414 Dundas Street West. Murray's grandparents, Uncle Sam and his wife, Sally, and Aunts Molly and Clara continued to live at 208 Claremont. Murray's stepfather, Harry, opened a dry cleaner's shop below where he did alterations. He also initiated a clever side business of buying old suits at the Salvation Army, spending four or five hours altering them, and then reselling them for $4 or $5, good money back then. Unfortunately, neither the shop nor the side business was very successful.

Murray vividly recalls the Christie Pits Riot, which occurred in August 1933: "I was 10 years old when they came around and picked me up in the back of a truck to take me there. It was 1933 … they just picked me up to fight with the Jewish kids. They were looking for Jewish people to fight with them, to support them."

At about age 12, Murray got a job, his first, as a delivery boy for a pharmacy at Bathurst and Queen Streets, working after school and all day Sunday. He was paid $3.50 per week and delivered three-cent stamps in the depths of winter on his bicycle. When he got his first paycheque, he kept 50 cents for himself and gave $3 to his grandmother because he knew she needed it.

In 1936, Pearl and Harry bought a house at 4 Lakeview Avenue near Ossington Avenue and Dundas Street West for $25,000. They had a huge mortgage, paid in $45 installments three times annually, which took them 25 years to pay off.

Fig. 6.2k Murray on the front porch of 208 Claremont Street, circa 1930.

It took the outbreak of the Second World War in 1939 to pull Canada out of the Depression. An increased demand in Europe for materials and ramped-up spending by the Canadian government boosted the economy, and as unemployed men enlisted in the military, prosperity began returning to Canada.

Before the war, though, in the late 1930s, Murray attended high school at Harbord Collegiate. He worked hard and reaped the benefits of being a model student. In 1940, he earned an employment scholarship from Simpson's department store. Upon graduation from high school, Murray worked at Simpson's for a while, followed by a stint as a chartered accountant, but he was "bored to death."

Murray applied to the Faculty of Dentistry at the University of Toronto and took the aptitude test with little hope. Then he decided to try the Royal Canadian Air Force (RCAF) as a backup plan. The first response came from the RCAF, which accepted him, so he wrote the air force, taking it up on its offer. The next day, Murray received a letter from the Faculty of Dentistry, which also approved him, so he retracted his acceptance with the RCAF and enrolled at the University of Toronto. During Murray's time in the dentistry faculty, he heard about a conversation in the admissions department that intimated "Jews are smart, but they don't have dexterity." When Murray applied to the dentistry program, 25 Jews applied but only four were accepted, Murray being one of them.

University was expensive. Murray's next dilemma was how to pay for it. He found out about an insurance policy his mother had taken out for him when he was a baby, putting aside 50 cents per week until he turned 18. It was now worth $600. Dental school was $300 per year, so the policy paid for two years. Murray then worked every summer to pay his way through the rest of school. He worked as an "ice man" for Belle Ewart Ice and Fuel, driving a truck to deliver ice to people and carrying the huge blocks up many long stairwells. It was a hard job, but he learned to drive thanks to it! After graduation, Murray's first job was at the Red Cross driving a dental bus in 1947.

Murray's family continued to own 208 Claremont. His uncle Sam still lived there with his wife, Sally, along with Murray's grandparents, Harry and Hannah, and his aunt Clara, who now worked as a stenographer.

In January 1947, three days before Murray's 24th birthday, his grandmother, Hannah, died at the age of 70. His grandfather passed away three years later in 1950, at the age of 76. Upon the death of Murray's grandfather, Uncle Sam sold 208 Claremont for $7,000, dividing the sum six ways. It was the end of a long chapter at that house for the Haimovitch family.

A few months after his grandfather died, Murray spotted Faygie Weingarten, a nursery schoolteacher, at a Purim Ball and was instantly smitten. He asked a mutual friend to make an introduction. On March 11, 1950, they went on their first date, with Murray going all out to impress her: dinner and dancing at the Royal York Hotel's Imperial Room. He knew she was the one from the moment he met her, proposed to her 10 days later, and she accepted. On October 31, 1950, Faygie and Murray were married at Beth Sholom Synagogue.

Fig. 6.2l (left) Murray's grandparents, Hannah and Harry, on their 50th wedding anniversary.

Fig. 6.2m (right) Faygie and Murray, 1950.

Faygie and Murray's first apartment was in The Warwick on Bathurst Street, where they lived for two years. It was here that their first child, Ellen Joy, was born. Faygie became quite active in the local synagogue, while Murray opened his first dental practice on Kingston Road near Midland Avenue. Later, he started a practice on St. Clair West near Yonge Street.

In the early 1950s, Faygie and Murray moved to Forest Hill, where their family grew to three children — Ellen Joy, Sandy, and Lorne — who gave them an abundance of happiness. What Murray lacked from his own biological father, he invested 100 times over as a dad to his three children. He was loving, supportive, and ever-present as a father to his children and a husband to Faygie. They raised beautiful, confident human beings in the rich family life Murray created with Faygie.

Clearly, Murray has good genes. His mother, Pearl, lived to 102, dying in 2003. In the 1990s, Faygie and Murray moved to a condo in Forest Hill Village, where they still live today, age 93 and 98, respectively. The couple recently celebrated their 70th wedding anniversary.

Fig. 6.2n (left) Murray with his first born daughter, Ellen Joy Buchman.

Fig. 6.2o (right) Faygie and Murray's three children: Sandy, Lorne, and Ellen Joy.

Fig. 6.2p Faygie and Murray on their 67th wedding anniversary.

Faygie and Murray prioritized education with their children and the importance of hard work. As a result, their children and grandchildren are high achievers, with a list of accomplishments that is staggering. Their daughter, Ellen Joy, became a popular, award-winning family doctor, mental health practitioner, and meditation teacher. Their son Sandy, also a doctor, is a trailblazer in palliative care, was the president of the Canadian Medical Association from 2019 to 2020, and is currently the medical director of North York General Hospital's Freeman Centre for the Advancement of Palliative Care. Their youngest son, Lorne, is an author, scholar, theatre director, and president of the Art Center College of Design in Pasadena, California.

The Buchmans' three children have given them seven grandchildren, five step-grandchildren, seven great-grandchildren, and five step-great-grandchildren. Murray has embraced each into his life with all the love he has to give, welcoming his extended family as if they were his own blood and deeply understanding and appreciating their value, much as his stepfather did for him. He delights in the legacy he has fashioned with such a large family tree that now extends to well over 39 people and counting! Not bad for an only child.

At 98, Murray's memory is as sharp as a whip. He says today: "I remember things so well because I tell the truth. If you lie, you can't tell the same story twice." Murray deeply cherishes the life he has made because he came from so little. When he talks about his childhood, 208 Claremont still figures prominently, and to know Murray is to know about that house. He speaks of it more than any other place he has lived. When you ask him why, he smiles and says: "Because it was my first inkling of being alive."

SAM CHING AND DENNIS CHOW

9 Adelaide Street East and 176 Avenue Road

Early Chinese immigrants to Toronto went into the laundry and restaurant businesses. But with a severity arguably unmatched by other ethnic groups, they faced anti-Chinese laws that ensured they lived and worked alone without their families, returning briefly to their impoverished villages in China to visit or start families, the women raising the children on their own in their native land.[1]

Initially, British Columbia had the strongest anti-Chinese movement. The 1857 discovery of gold on Canada's West Coast in the Fraser Valley saw one of the first groups of Chinese immigrants arrive by boat from San Francisco to Victoria in June 1858. They were soon followed by Chinese labourers arriving directly from Hong Kong to take up the back-breaking work of clearing land, building trails and roads, and digging ditches. The prosperous period of the gold rush was over in 1865, and job loss and an economic crash ensued. White workers blamed the Chinese for taking away their jobs and livelihood, and by the early 1870s, hostility and tension had reached a fever pitch. When British Columbia entered Confederation in 1871, the province's Legislative Assembly passed an act to disenfranchise Indigenous Peoples and Chinese people.[2]

The 1881 Canada Census listed 4,383 Chinese in Canada of which 4,350 resided in British Columbia, four in Manitoba, seven in Quebec, and only 22 in Ontario. A first record of a man named Sam Ching appears in Toronto in 1877. His arrival was ahead of the wave of immigration that hit Toronto by the mid-1880s.

Toronto's initial surge of Chinese immigration was largely connected to the construction of the Canadian Pacific Railway, the essential link to bind the new country from coast to coast. British Columbia was largely cut off from the rest of the nation, and it was often said that "It was easier, cheaper, and faster to get to British Columbia from Hong Kong than from Halifax."[3]

Fig. 6.3a (left) Dennis Chow, owner of Chow Keong Hand Laundry.

Fig. 6.3b (right) Chow Keong Hand Laundry, one of the last remaining in Toronto.

It was determined that 10,000 workers were needed to construct the railway line in British Columbia, yet only an estimated 400 white males were available for employment. There was strong opposition from the Workingmen's Protection Association, later known as the Anti-Chinese Association, against employing Chinese labour, but Prime Minister John A. Macdonald told the people of British Columbia they had a choice between that or no railway.[4]

By the end of 1882, there were 9,000 railway workers in British Columbia, 6,500 of them Chinese.[5] Enduring accidents, illness, frostbite, malnutrition, and death, the Chinese were largely left out of the archival record of the railway's construction. An iconic photograph shows only white men in the visual record as the last spike was hammered in, even though Chinese labourers made up three-quarters of the workforce.[6] While

Canada had "tolerated" the employment of the Chinese, when the railway was completed in 1885, it wanted them to return home. Nevertheless, many stayed, enticed by the financial opportunities the country presented.

As mentioned in Chapter Three, the federal government imposed a "head tax" in 1885 of $50 on every Chinese immigrant to dissuade further immigration. The average Chinese labourer only made $225 per year, and after deducting food, clothing, rent, medicine, and other expenses, he could perhaps save $43 annually. The head tax was increased to $100 in 1901 and then to $500 in 1903,[7] "making it prohibitively expensive" for Chinese men "to bring their wives and children to Canada" and effectively sundering families.[8] Despite the high tax, Chinese men could earn upward of 10 times the amount they could at home, so immigration continued. Many who were already in British Columbia headed eastward along the very railway they had built, seeking new jobs in towns and cities across Canada, with some ultimately ending up in Toronto.

A predominantly male population, single or married with wives back home, began to rise in Toronto by the late 1880s. Sam Ching came to Canada just ahead of the railway wave and the head tax. In the 1870s, the *Globe* noted that a "mysterious" group of Chinese men arrived in Toronto — Sam Ching, along with fellow countrymen Ah Saum, Ah Lung, Wah Lee, and Chu Heng. Whether they knew one another beforehand has been difficult to determine, but it is possible they were part of the same community with connections in the United States.

By the 1870s, Chinese immigration was already on the rise south of the border. Upward of 40 Chinese laundries were operating in Chicago, as well as many in New York City and San Francisco.[9] A soured U.S. economy in the 1870s and 1880s influenced some Chinese immigrants to move north of the border to escape discrimination and being scapegoated when jobs became scarce for Americans.[10]

Sam Ching appears to have come to Toronto from the United States,[11] while Ah Saum likely arrived in Toronto from China with two brothers from St. Louis, Missouri, one a laundryman, the other a tobacconist. By the late 1870s, Sam Ching and Ah Saum were in business together and made quite an impression on Toronto.

Ah Saum, 25 years old, was featured in the *Globe* in 1873 and was possibly one of the earliest Chinese immigrants to Toronto. Formerly a tea tester for the governor of Beijing, Ah Saum earned an assistant position at the Pekin Tea Company at Yonge and Albert Streets and anticipated attracting "no inconsiderable number of customers."

By 1877,[12] Sam Ching, Ah Lung, Wah Lee, Chu Heng, and possibly Ah Saum had gone into business together, creating Sam Ching and Company, Toronto's first Chinese hand laundry, located at 9 Adelaide Street East in a two-storey building owned by barrister Thomas Ince. Sam Ching both lived and worked at 9 Adelaide; it was his first residential listing in the city.

Sam saw a business opportunity in the Toronto market for hand laundries. Already the city had steam laundries operated mostly by white men, which handled large orders from restaurants, hotels, and hospitals, but their expensive machinery made for exorbitant start-up costs. All that was needed for a hand laundry, however, were kettles, washtubs, scrubbing boards, soap, and elbow grease, plus a stove to heat the water and dry the clothes and a space large enough to hang laundry in the winter. Chinese hand laundries, as previously mentioned, were largely an invention by circumstance and "filled the demand of a rapidly growing urban economy by providing quality, low cost laundry service to a workforce of single men who lived in boarding houses or apartment hotels, men who needed their clothes washed."[13] Plus, the space could double as a residence.[14]

Not all laundry owners had the luxury of an upstairs residence; many had to live as frugally as possible and sleep in the shop at night. Whether Sam resided above the shop or within it is unknown. Since he did not own the building, he would have had to pay rent.

Shortly after Sam Ching's laundry opened, his partner, Ah Lung, died of tuberculosis at age 30. Born in Hong Kong, Ah Lung had resided in St. Louis, Missouri, since 1867 before coming to Toronto in 1875. On October 22, 1877, his funeral procession wove through Toronto streets to

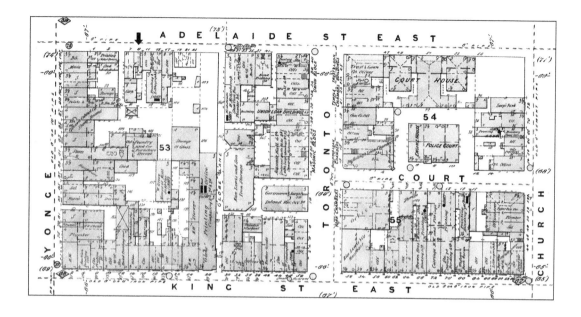

the Necropolis, with the hearse in the lead followed by two cabs. The first contained all of Ah Lung's personal effects, including bedding and furniture, along with a satchel full of trinkets and valuables. In the second cab rode Sam Ching, Wah Lee, Chi Heng, and "another of their countrymen."[15] The friends of Ah Lung placed the clothing and satchel of valuables in the coffin, then refused the services of a clergyman at the interment while they solemnly watched the coffin lowered into the ground.[16] Upon the lowered coffin, they placed additional personal effects of Ah Lung, which would not fit in the coffin. No speech was made at the graveside, yet a service was held at Wah Lee's house, with a promise that Ah Lung's remains would be returned to his homeland, which they were in April 1891.

The initial reception of Torontonians to Chinese immigrants such as Sam Ching and his countrymen appears to have been mild curiosity. But by the early 1880s, attitudes hardened and became increasingly hostile as tensions rose. Just six years after Sam opened his laundry on Adelaide East, the Chinese industry was condemned as a "curse" by several union

Fig. 6.3c Insurance plan for 1884. The arrow shows the location of Sam Ching and Company Laundry at 9 Adelaide Street East.

leaders, who viewed it as a threat to existing laundries and a real estate hindrance to any streetscape it occupied.[17]

By 1881, Sam was living with an "Au Sam" at his laundry and residence. Both men were listed as married yet lived together alone, most likely with wives back home in China. Sam's foothold in the Toronto market changed in the mid-1880s as the Chinese hand laundry industry expanded in the city and across the country. During the 1886 civic election, Vancouver politicians called on all candidates to denounce Chinese laundries as a nuisance. Two months later, an anti-Chinese riot saw arsonists burn down several laundries in Vancouver to drive them out of town. Recently unemployed Chinese railway workers began migrating eastward "on the very railway they had built to unite the country,"[18] and the number of Chinese-operated restaurants and laundries soon mushroomed in towns and cities across Canada. By the early 1890s, there were at least 24 Chinese laundries in Toronto.[19]

The Chinese immigrants in Toronto initially settled around York and Wellington Streets, moving into former residences of Jewish and Black people as they in turn relocated to other areas in the city. Owners of new Chinese laundries did all the work themselves, toiling six to seven days a week, often from 6:00 a.m. to 1:00 a.m. the next morning.[20] As business picked up, they hired help, typically family or friends, at comparatively low wages. At the beginning of the 20th century, the average Chinese laundry worker earned $8 to $18 per month, with room and board, while white laundry workers got $10 to $18 a week.[21] They also charged less than their white competitors: a laundered shirt cost 12 cents compared to 15 to 18 cents at white laundries, while a bedsheet cost 15 cents and a handkerchief three cents.[22]

The physical layout of a typical Chinese laundry in Toronto and across the nation became a familiar sight. It featured a small space set up in a nondescript building in a working-class neighbourhood with a simple HAND LAUNDRY shingle or painted words on the front window. Inside, a wall-to-wall counter divided the shop into reception area and working place. Behind the counter, brown packages of clean laundry waiting for pickup were tucked into several shelves with Chinese labels to identify the customers. On the other side of the shelves was the working area with stoves to warm up the irons and dry the clothes, as well as wash troughs, pressers, ironing boards, a hanging area, and the living quarters.[23] "The absence of family life and the priority to save money led to living conditions that reflected little concern for personal health and well-being." Many laundry owners "ate, slept, and worked in these small and crowded workplaces, which often reached temperatures upwards of 38°C (100°F)."[24]

By 1901, there were 96 Chinese laundries in Toronto compared to 66 operated by other ethnic groups. The Chinese laundry business continued to thrive. Between 1900 and 1925, even in the face of restrictions and bigotry, they numbered 374 in 1921. By that year, the population of Chinese Canadians in Toronto was 2,134, and "assuming an average Chinese laundry employed four persons, including the owner himself, then over 50 percent of the Chinese Canadian population in Toronto was related to the laundry business in the early 1920s."[25]

Chinese laundries were opened all over the city, yet slowly communities were formed in specific areas. Typically, owners and their families lived in their shops or above them, which were largely found on main streets or thoroughfares. Initially, rarely were Chinese found living on side streets, due to restrictive covenants and outright racial discrimination.[26]

Fig. 6.3d An interior of a Chinese laundry, circa 1920s.

By 1910, the Chinese population in Toronto had reached 1,000; that same year, the redevelopment of the York-Wellington area forced many Chinese to relocate to The Ward on Queen Street West between Elizabeth and York Streets.[27] Redevelopment of Queen Street West less than ten years later compelled them to move again, this time to Elizabeth Street, recently vacated by Toronto's Jewish community. Elizabeth Street became a bustling epicentre for a stable Chinese community. It "served as Chinatown's spine, lined with businesses, restaurants and [grocery and import stores]," and became a refuge the Chinese felt accepted in — the first organized Chinatown in Toronto.[28]

The Chinese communities were predominantly male — bachelor societies of men, most of whom were married with wives in China. Men who saved enough money temporarily returned home to get married, visit wives, and father children.[29] Too often the cost was simply prohibitive to bring wives and children to Canada, so many Chinese children were raised fatherless.

Such was the narrative for Chow Chew Kam's family. He was born in China in 1887 in Kaiping, a village in southern China. In 1905, at just 18 years old, he left behind his pregnant wife and immigrated to the West Coast of Canada. He paid the $500 head tax and found work in the coal mines around Kamloops, British Columbia, making $1 per day. Later, he worked as a farmer.

In 1906, Chow Chew Kam's wife gave birth to their first son, Chow Keong, in China; *keong* means "strong." He was raised by his mother, fatherless, in China. Chow Chew Kam eventually made his way to Toronto, where he learned the hand laundry business and worked for others. After 15 years in Canada, he was finally able to send for his son and wife to come to Canada, paying a large head tax. In 1921, Chow Keong arrived in Canada, age 15.[30]

The son had come just in time. On July 1, 1923, the Dominion of Canada passed Bill 45, later known as the Chinese Exclusion Act, which prohibited Chinese immigration to the country. Chow Keong did not

Fig. 6.3e Chong Yee Laundry, 48 Elizabeth Street, 1912. Elizabeth Street became the site of the first organized Chinatown, where the many laundries helped foster the first true sense of community for the Chinese in Toronto. The laundries typically had commercial space on the ground floor with residential above. These could be considered commercial Modest Hopes.

become a Canadian citizen until March 15, 1955. In the early 1930s, though, he returned home for a short visit to marry and father a child. Dennis Chow was born in 1933 and grew up fatherless in Kaiping while his dad returned to Toronto.

Working hard, Chow Keong was able to save money. In 1946, after toiling 25 years for other people, he opened his own laundry at 176 Avenue Road, just north of Davenport Road, proudly naming it after himself. A year later, the Chinese Exclusion Act was revoked. By now, the number of Chinese laundries in Toronto had shrunk to 258.

Fig. 6.3f (left) Shops at 88–98 Elizabeth Street, 1937.

Fig. 6.3g (right) Avenue Road, circa 1950s, showing the Chow Keong Laundry around the time that it opened.

Fig. 6.3h Dennis Chow's hand laundry at 176 Avenue Road today.

In 1950, Chow Keong sent for his son, Dennis, and Dennis's mother, who were now 17 and 40, respectively. Dennis remembers his first trip to Chinatown, where "there were no young kids, all old men … when they see me, they're very, very happy." He lived above the shop with his parents and attended school in Chinatown, but only for a year. His father needed help in the laundry and asked Dennis to leave school and work with him. Dennis was sad to end his education but felt he had no choice: "He's father, you do what your father say." Dennis worked long hours, sometimes from 6:30 a.m. to 1:00 a.m. the next morning. He has worked in the laundry ever since.[31]

Dennis never returned to China. The closest he came was Hong Kong to court his wife, Fung Chew Chow, in 1957, whom he married and brought to Canada.[32] They raised three children together, one girl and two boys, living as a family above the laundry on Avenue Road. Dennis's life is very different from the generations that preceded him: he got to see his children grow up.

Now in their late fifties and early sixties, Dennis's children are well educated, successful in their careers, and extremely proud of what their parents have accomplished. Dennis and his wife also have two grandchildren: the grandson is a social worker; the granddaughter is a lawyer in Ottawa.

Jan Wong, in an article she published in the *Globe and Mail* in 2001, describes what Dennis's laundry is like:

The hand-painted name still graces the shop window, which is crammed with jade plants and bonsai. Customers pass through a red door into a living museum, frozen in time. Beyond the counter are three high-ceilinged rooms, each just 9½ feet wide, joined one to another like railway cars. Chow uses an ancient cash register with pop-up cards showing sums from five cents to $1....

In the first room, Chow irons side by side with his wife at a broad counter called in Chinese an "ironing bed." ... Chow's consists of a wooden counter with ventilation holes drilled through, padded with four layers of wool blankets bound with a clean white sheet.

The second room is the washing room. Against one wall is a wooden trough, lined with galvanized steel. His father once scrubbed laundry in it, using a washboard. In the late 1950s, Chow Keong acquired a wooden washing tub with a hand wringer. But the most important day in the laundry's history was May 18, 1966, when a professional, stainless-steel, front-loading washing machine arrived from Chicago....[33]

Dennis still does hand laundry, though, and in a third room, garments are air-dried.

Upon his arrival in Canada in 1906, Dennis's grandfather probably lived where he worked in rented quarters attached to his employment. Dennis's father appears to have done the same until he opened his own laundry at 176 Avenue Road and then lived above the shop. Even after he got married and had three children, Dennis continued this tradition. However, by the late 1960s, the space above the store was too small to raise three children, and with great pride, he bought a house for his family. Just a short walk from their laundry, Dennis and his wife purchased their first Modest Hope, a semi-detached Victorian that nurtured the lives of his growing family, provided a welcome separation from endlessly long days of work, and helped improve their quality of life.

Dennis has now worked and owned Chow Keong Hand Laundry & Cleaners for 70 years. As Jan Wong has written, his business "marks an era that began in discrimination and is ending in diversity." Once scrubbing socks for customers too poor to own a washing machine, he now caters to Toronto's carriage trade. The shirts he cleans with care have labels such as Gucci, Pierre Cardin, and Dolce & Gabbana, and cost hundreds of dollars. His multicultural customers are lawyers, doctors, and stock-brokers, and his regular clientele has included Lincoln Alexander, Izzie Sharp, Dave Nichol, and Harry Rosen. Often the smell of perfume, aftershave, cologne, or expensive cigars is too much for Dennis to take in his small shop, where almost 100 shirts per day are ironed.[34]

Now, in 2021, at 88 years old, Dennis is tired. His wife is 83. Covid-19 deeply impacted their business, since fewer people have been working in offices or attending events and do not need the same volume of shirts anymore. So finances are tight now, and extras are the first thing to go. On a chilly day toward the end of September 2020, he made only $25 and decided to shut down and go home early, something he almost never does.

The sale of Dennis's business and retirement are close now. He thinks about it all the time. His hand laundry is one of the last of its kind in Toronto. In an era of "permanent-press shirts, paper napkins and casual Fridays, not to mention automatic washing machines,"[35] its shuttering will mark the end of an era in Canadian history.

* * *

Sam Ching was a trailblazer — the first Chinese immigrant to have his business listed in a Toronto directory. His Chinese laundry was the first of its kind in Toronto and inspired many of his countrymen to establish their own businesses and realize their own hopes and dreams.

The building that housed Sam Ching's first laundry at 9 Adelaide Street East has long since been demolished. In 2012, a laneway tucked beside the Ontario Heritage Trust at 8 Adelaide Street East officially adopted the name "Ching Lane," a fitting acknowledgement of a legacy that began across the street.

WILLIAM JOSEPH O'CONNOR (1862–1892)

Tate Street

Future champion oarsman William Joseph O'Connor had his humble beginnings in a worker's cottage in Corktown, eventually rising to adoration and fame and "a tremendous set of accomplishments"[1] in a life cut short. The accolades he received initiated a turning point in his family's history, propelling it toward prosperity.[2]

William came from "extremely poor Irish-Catholic roots."[3] His parents, Michael O'Connor Sr. (born 1814), a labourer, and Ellen O'Connor (née Grace, born 1826), hailed from County Clare, Ireland. They immigrated to Canada in the late 1840s or early 1850s, and given the time, were likely impacted by the Irish Potato Famine.

Michael and Ellen arrived in Canada with three young children, Patrick, Michael Jr., and Bridget. Soon after, in 1852, they had John,

Fig. 6.4a William Joseph O'Connor in his element.

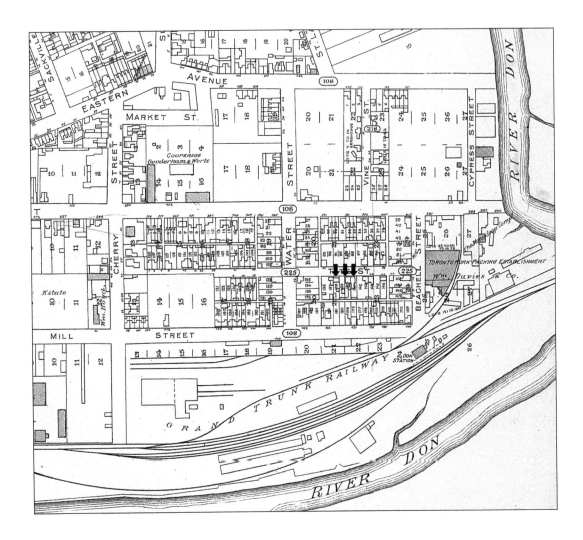

Fig. 6.4b The O'Connor family lived at several addresses along Tate Street, starting at 34 Tate (Lot 138), then spreading out to 38 Tate (Lot 141) and then 36 Tate Street (Lot 140).

then Ellen around 1855, both probably in Toronto. Next were Thomas in 1857, followed by Henry in 1859.

While records of the family's early life in Toronto have proven difficult to track down, we can determine that by 1861 Michael and Ellen had settled on East Street, just east of Cherry Street and north of Mill Street, then called Front Street. By 1862, Michael and Ellen and their seven children had moved around the corner to Tate Street to one of the first three houses on the street.[4, 5] It was here that their youngest child, William, was born on May 4, 1862, into a large and loving family.

Tate Street first shows up on Toronto maps in the late 1850s, running two blocks east from Cherry Street, just north of Mill Street (the former Front Street). Tate was in a neighbourhood surrounded by industries: Gooderham & Worts Distillery to the southwest; the William Davies meat-packing plant at the east end of Tate, which became the largest pork packer in Canada; and the railway, which slowly expanded into the area, eventually bisecting Tate by 1890, then consuming it.[6, 7] Cherry, Front, Water, and Tate Streets originally encompassed a bustling neighbourhood, with rows and rows of workers' cottages as well as large and small factories. It is hard to imagine such a scene in what is today's West Don Lands.

Examination and comparison of an 1884 fire insurance plan suggests the O'Connors' first home on Tate Street, number 34, was a small detached worker's cottage built in the early 1860s. Upward of two adults, and at times eight O'Connor children, lived in these compact quarters at once.

On July 30, 1863, 14 months after the birth of William, his mother, Ellen, died at age 37, leaving her youngest son to be raised by his father and older siblings at 34 Tate Street. Sadly, Ellen never saw William become a worldwide sensation.

William's older brother, Michael Jr., married Maria Walsh at St. Paul's Basilica on November 24, 1870. They soon started a small grocery at 363 Front Street East near the corner of Trinity Street. Over the next 18 years, they had nine children. Within a few years, Michael Jr., Maria, and their three young children, Thomas, John, and Henry, moved back into 34 Tate and resumed their grocery business, joining Michael Sr., and siblings John, Ellen, Thomas, Henry, and William. The younger children, including William, went to school, likely at the Palace Street School at the corner of Cherry and Palace (Front) Streets, while the older kids worked.[8] The 34 Tate home was a crowded, lively, multi-generational household and likely a confusing place with all the double names!

Fig. 6.4c The Don Rowing Club on Cherry Street.

By 1878, the O'Connor family had spread out along Tate Street. With the birth of Michael Jr. and Maria's fourth child, 34 Tate was bursting at the seams. A larger house was built down the street at 38 Tate, and Michael Jr., Maria, and their four children, Thomas, John, Henry, and baby Ellen, relocated their family and grocery business to it. Michael Sr., Thomas, now a Grand Trunk Railway switchman, John, now a railway agent, and William continued to live at 34 Tate.

Meanwhile, William took an interest in water sports at a young age. Although surrounded by factories and the railway, the latter which some of his brothers worked for, William found his future life and work inspired by his closeness to Lake Ontario and the Don River.

Historian and *Toronto Sun* columnist Mike Filey says in a 1992 article for the *Catholic Register*: "There was a time in our country's history when the sport of rowing was as popular as ice hockey is today. And it was to this sport that the City of Toronto contributed as fine a group of rowers as ever pulled an oar."[9] In Toronto in the late 19th century, aquatic sports along the harbour were popular draws. Rowing and competitive regattas were favourites with spectators, and William's proximity to the waterfront gave him a front-row seat. It is also where he first saw the sculler Ned Hanlan race, motivating him to follow in the champion's footsteps.

Hanlan became a professional rower in 1876 and was arguably "the biggest sports star this country ever produced, the first professional athlete in Canadian history." As many as 100,000 spectators attended Hanlan's races, and betting pools ran into the tens of millions of dollars in today's money, with Hanlan routinely winning $5,000 purses. Hanlan and William soon developed a lifelong friendship, and William's passion for rowing led him to the Irish Catholic Don Rowing Club on Vine Street, just steps from his house.[10]

The Christie brothers established the Don Rowing Club in 1878 at a time when Toronto was becoming a rowing capital of the world. Regattas were held on Saturday afternoons, and the Don was one of many such small clubs in and around the city. A vacant house on Vine Street at the edge of the Don River just south of the now-defunct Eastern Avenue Bridge became its clubhouse. With three other friends, Andrew McFarlane, T. Hogarth, and J. Swanson, the Christies formed the nucleus of what was to become the Don Rowing Club, which still exists. Today, the club continues to thrive, and contrary to its name, is now on the Credit River.[11]

William was one of the founding members of the Don Rowing Club. It was not the "high-end" club of the city — that distinction belonged to the Argonaut Rowing Club — but the Don, in its early days, was no more than an informal place for Irish Catholic friends to meet, talk about rowing, row, and store their equipment. William Laing (Laing Street's namesake), a boat builder in Leslieville, sold the rowing club skiffs or rowing shells (single rowboats) and clinker boats.[12]

Captain Thomas Blackwell, writing in the magazine *Outing*, had this to say about the young rower William: "At the commencement he was unusually awkward in his boat, and the old hands advised him to give over attempting to row, for he would never make an oarsman, they said. But not daunted, he persevered and has met his well-merited award."[13]

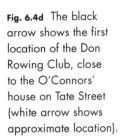

Fig. 6.4d The black arrow shows the first location of the Don Rowing Club, close to the O'Connors' house on Tate Street (white arrow shows approximate location).

Throughout the late 19th century, the popularity of rowing remained high. The Don Rowing Club continued to attract more rowers, and soon memberships increased to 60 and larger quarters were needed. In 1880, a new boathouse was constructed on Eastern Avenue near the Don River, but the overflowing of the river forced the club to relocate again, and a new building was erected near the Queen Street Bridge.[14] That same year the Canadian Association of Amateur Oarsmen (CAAO) was formed by existing rowing clubs to coordinate and regulate the amateur sport.

By 1880, William, now 18, was still living in the O'Connor family home at 34 Tate with his father and four of his adult siblings: John (age 28), Ellen (age 24), Thomas (age 23), and Henry (age 20). Around 1882, John and his wife, Annie, moved downtown to live and work at a saloon on the corner of Adelaide and Simcoe Streets. William, his other siblings, and his father moved one door down to 36 Tate, next to Michael Jr. and an ever-expanding family of five kids: Thomas (age nine), John (age six), Henry (age five), Ellen (age four), and William (age two). Side by side on Tate, the two O'Connor families and their matching sets of names likely had a significant presence on the street. The O'Connors were active members of St. Paul's Basilica on Power

Street, and a priest there referred to William as one of a "large family of brawny, powerful men." Sports and athletics were a passion for St. Paul's younger congregation members, who were active year-round in summer and winter sports, which were encouraged by the teachers and clergy as a means of physical and moral development.[15]

In 1882, William raced for the first time with Cornelius T. Enright in the In-Rigged Double Sculls Championship at Lachine, Quebec, but they lost. The following year they won the CAAO Double Sculls, and William triumphed in the CAAO Junior Singles. He was hooked and wanted more.

Also in 1883, William's brother Thomas married Bridgit Finn, and they eventually had 12 children in 19 years. Although Thomas and Bridgit left the family street for a few years, they, too, moved back into 36 Tate with their first two children. Both 36 and 38 Tate continued to be a multi-generational revolving door for the O'Connor family.

The victories of William and Enright brought fame to the Don Rowing Club as well as their departure from the organization. In 1884, they joined the more established Toronto Rowing Club. That same year the pair won the CAAO Double Scull Championship as well as the National Association of Amateur Oarsmen (NAAO) Double Scull and the North Western Amateur Rowing Association Double Scull in the United States. Clearly, they had hit their stride.

In 1885, Enright and William were Double Scull CAAO champions again, while William won Senior Singles with "the tactic that would become his trademark, a rapid, explosive stroke at the start." Their repeated successes and reports of wagering on them brought charges of professionalism against William and Enright. Although they were exonerated by the CAAO, the NAAO would not budge. So, in 1886, they turned professional, backed by Toronto businessman Joseph Rogers.[16]

As Goca Lebl writes in *Don Rowing Club*, "Unlike the average professional athlete, William was of a modest and unassuming character and on that account, he made a large number of friends."[17] He was also a handsome man, "possessing an immense head topped by jet black hair, a massive body well-browned by the suns of many climes, and well-stocked limbs set off by a perfect exhibition of herculean muscles."[18] Not surprisingly, William attracted many admirers.

In his first year as a professional, William won $1,000 in a single-scull race in Minneapolis.[19] Now in his early twenties, he moved off Tate Street, leaving behind his father, brother Henry and family at 36 Tate, and brother Michael and family at 38 Tate. William moved downtown to keep bar for extra money and board at brother John's hotel, the Sherman House at Adelaide and Simcoe Streets.

William decided in 1887 to focus on the single scull, which served him well. He won regatta after regatta with ease and grace, prizes and prestige each greater than the next. Soon, William found it hard to find suitable opponents to race against. His strokes were so powerful that few oarsmen accepted the challenge of racing him. He once famously rowed alone when prominent professional Wallace Ross of Saint John, New Brunswick, backed out at the last minute. As William's popularity grew, so did his fan base.[20]

The best year ever for William proved to be 1888. In March of that year, he defeated the Pacific coast champion Henry Peterson, winning a prize of $2,000. In August, his race time of 19 minutes and 43 seconds for three miles was considered a world record. In November 1888, on the Potomac River in Washington, D.C., William defeated the American champion John Teemer, who had twice taken the title from Ned Hanlan. More than 10,000 fans lined the Potomac to witness that race. William's robust strokes gained him a 10-length lead over Teemer, earning him the title "Champion Oarsman of America."[21]

Crowds of Torontonians and the Royal Grenadier Marching Band playing "See, the Conqu'ring Hero Comes!" met William's train at Union Station upon his return home. Mounted police led the procession, with scores of torchbearers and more than 50 carriages filled with supporters travelling up York Street and along Carlton Street to the Horticultural Pavilion at Allan Gardens. There, William was rewarded with a gala reception and a $1,000 cheque from Toronto fans presented by the city's mayor, Edward Frederick Clarke, plus $300 in gold. William gave a speech to the crowd, pledging his commitment to bring the world championship title back to Toronto, last held by Ned Hanlan in 1884.[22]

Fig. 6.4e Sherman (later O'Connor) House, circa 1890, at Adelaide and Simcoe Streets, run by William O'Connor's brother John.

William continued to win regattas with such ease that except for one race against fellow Canadian Jacob Gill Gaudaur in San Francisco on March 2, 1889, no one challenged him. He remained the U.S. champion until his death.

While William tried desperately to make good on his promise to Torontonians, he could not bring the world championship crown back to his hometown. In September 1889 in London, England, a fated race took place on the Thames for the championship of the world and £1,000. William famously lost his challenge to world champion Henry Ernest Searle of Australia. Yet he lost the title gracefully. On his time in England, William remarked that he was treated splendidly and was accorded fair play in every respect:

As regards to the contest in England, I have no fault to find. I was beaten on my merits. But I was out of condition and weighed only 159 pounds, dressed in street costume the day of the race, when I should have scaled 165 pounds stripped. Then, again, I had never rowed a race on a river before and was handicapped in that respect. All my rowing has been done on lakes and bodies of smooth water. Searle has done all his work on rivers and was accustomed to the work. He is a clever oarsman, a perfect gentleman, and a fit man to lead the world's championship.[23]

Fig. 6.4f William O'Connor trading card for World Champion Series to promote Allen & Ginter Cigarettes. Issued in 1888 in a set of 50 cards, the 50 athletes in the series included cyclists, baseball players, lawn tennis players, wrestlers, skaters, pole vaulters, pedestrian walkers, pedestrian runners, high jumpers, weightlifters, hammer throwers, club swingers, swimmers, and oarsmen.

Upon William's return to Toronto after his world championship loss, he was given a warm reception and a banquet from his friends, fans, and loved ones in Toronto. Such a scene as that was "the best proof of his position in the hearts of his fellows." The welcome could not have been more gracious if he had come back victorious."[24]

Ned Hanlan did not let the title and defeat go with the same grace. In a crowded New York City hotel, he boldly challenged Henry Searle to a rematch with William, saying:

To prove what I think of [O'Connor], I am prepared to back the youngster against Searle for any amount from $5,000 upward. I will give Searle $5,000 to come here and row O'Connor on any fair course and guarantee him $10,000 if he wins. Searle can make $5,000 if he loses. This amount will be given to him as an inducement to come here. With O'Connor as a partner I will make a double-scull match against any two men in the world for any amount of money. If anybody wants to accept that offer, I am prepared to make a deposit for a match between Searle and O'Connor.[25]

Unfortunately, this rematch never happened. The world championship race in London was Henry Searle's last race. On the sea voyage home from England, he contracted typhoid fever and died in Melbourne on December 10, 1889, at the age of 23. William then travelled to Australia in search of the title, but his attempts failed. He lost twice to James Stanbury, who subsequently became world champion.[26]

In the 1890 *Toronto Directory*, William is listed for the first time as "oarsman," no longer as barkeeper or boarder. While William was making a name for himself as a professional athlete, his two brothers were

Fig. 6.4g Engraving printed in the *Illustrated London News* in September 1889 for the match between Henry Searle of Australia and William O'Connor.

forging reputations for themselves in the hotel business. John's Sherman House, where William still lived, was a landmark establishment. By 1888–89, Michael Jr. was also running a hotel, the Standard at 252 King Street East. By 1892, both hotels were called O'Connor House; fame had made William's last name highly marketable.

By 1890, the railway near the O'Connors' Tate Street home had expanded. Houses were demolished on their street to make room for tracks that soon bisected the thoroughfare. The first O'Connor residence at 34 Tate was torn down, as was 36, while 38 remained but was renumbered 77. Just Michael Sr. and brother Henry and family remained, but not for long. Thomas moved to 17 Broadview Avenue close to the corner of Eastern Avenue, where he was near his job as a Grand Trunk Railway yardmaster at Don Station.

The construction of the Don Valley Parkway and the resulting Eastern Avenue Flyover in the 1960s forever changed the intersection of Broadview and Eastern, as well as Corktown east of Cherry Street and south of Queen Street. The flyover created a new Eastern Avenue that crossed farther north on Broadview. Numbers 1 to 33 Broadview were wiped off the map and the street now starts at 35. But not for long: a derelict row of houses at the bottom of Broadview, 35–49, are slated for demolition (see Fig. 7.1). While Thomas O'Connor's house at 17 Broadview is long gone, it is a fair assumption that it might have looked like one of the houses that remain.

In 1890, tragedy struck William. After his failed attempts to capture the world championship, his sister-in-law, Annie, brother John's wife, whom he lived with at the hotel, died suddenly in June.[27] Only four months later, brother John died, too.

William shouldered running Sherman House by himself, stepping back from rowing while he cared for his now-orphaned nephew, John, age 11, as well. These new responsibilities might have reduced his rowing appearances, but they did not diminish the quality of his performances.[28] He continued his training with full force, even famously walking from Hamilton to Toronto in December 1891 and setting a new record of nine hours and 26 minutes.[29]

By 1891, 77 Tate Street was vacant. For the first time since 1862, no O'Connors were living on the street. After nearly three decades of vibrant life there, Michael Sr. and Henry and family moved to 482 Front Street near the corner of Cherry Street. Henry's wife, Annie, continued the grocery business, while Henry worked as a foreman.

That same year, William and Ned Hanlan won the world championship in double sculls before 30,000 spectators at Burlington Beach. The following year, the two won a double-scull race in Hamilton. They had no idea that would be William's last victory.[30]

Throughout the summer of 1892, William complained of depression that he was unable to shake off, though he continued his full training and devotion to participation in the sport. In the fall of 1892, while training with Hanlan, William became ill and was instructed to remain indoors and rest. Never one to sit still for long, he ventured out to conduct some business for O'Connor House. The next day, "a relapse brought on typhoid fever."[31] On November 23, 1892, William passed away in a small corner room of his hotel. He was only 29. The *Globe* reported: "Few men have held the love and the regard of their followers as O'Connor did, even in defeat, and there [was] many a sad heart over the sudden loss of a bright young life."[32]

William was widely mourned.[33] At his funeral at St. Patrick's Catholic Church, floral tributes from various rowing clubs surrounded his red cedar casket topped with a pair of crossed oars from Ned Hanlan, who was a pallbearer along with William's brothers. Hundreds turned out to witness the solemn procession of his horse-drawn casket pulled by four black horses. In addition to his large family and wide-ranging friends, the mayor, the local alderman, and provincial representatives were at his funeral.[34]

The hotel torch was passed again by the O'Connor brothers. Once John's hotel, then William's, O'Connor House at Adelaide and Simcoe Streets was taken over by Michael Jr. upon William's death. He now ran two establishments, the second at the corner of Parliament and King Streets.

On April 14, 1893, Michael Jr. died, just months after assuming responsibility for both O'Connor hotels. William's father, Michael Sr., passed away at the end of that year at the house of his son Henry. He had outlived his wife and three of his sons.

William is not officially recognized by Canada's Sports Hall of Fame due to inaccurate records kept during the very first days of rowing. In the early 1980s, William's family presented a heavily documented file to a Hall of Fame committee for consideration. It remains in the hall's archives and is open to researchers.[35]

In 1913, the last house on Tate Street was demolished for railway expansion. Today, the neighbourhood is a shadow of its former self; the newly developed area looks nothing like the Corktown where the O'Connors once lived. The neighbourhood is now called the Canary District or West Don Lands. Block after block, street after street, Modest Hopes were torn down and forgotten, including the O'Connor homes at 34, 36, and 38 Tate. Henry O'Connor's house at 482 Front Street East is now a parking lot, while Thomas O'Connor's home at 17 Broadview Avenue is currently a traffic island and sister Bridget's at 72 Eastern Avenue is buried under the concrete playground of the Inglenook Community High School at 19 Sackville Street. Inglenook is the oldest continuous school operated by the Toronto District School Board. It first opened its doors in 1887 as the Sackville Public School.[36]

William's legacy comes in forms other than Tate Street. The Don Rowing Club still exists, albeit in Port Credit. The building that once hosted the Sherman House and O'Connor House hotels still remains at Adelaide and Simcoe Streets, as does the building that was once Michael O'Connor's Standard Hotel at 252 King Street East near the corner of Parliament Street. William's rowing career and championship "appeared to be the turning point to help position the O'Connor family for greater prosperity. It also became the great symbol of hope — later

Fig. 6.4h The O'Connor House building at Simcoe and Adelaide Streets, extensively restored, still stands. It is now the exclusive Soho House.

almost eclipsed by JFK as an Irish Catholic getting into the White House, but not quite."[37]

Thomas O'Connor purchased a very large plot, still in use today, for the O'Connor and O'Neill families at Mount Hope Catholic Cemetery on Bayview Avenue. His great-granddaughter suspects the plot was likely financed by William's financial legacy. While many O'Connors left Toronto, a large contingent stayed. Thomas's children and their children's children all remained in the city, many of them still living in the same east-end neighbourhood the O'Connors originally called home. Rowing is still part of the family and subsequent generations continued to be members of the Argonaut Rowing Club. The youngest son of William's great-grand-niece, who was not told of

Fig. 6.4i William Joseph O'Connor.

his career until after the fact, has recently taken up rowing. It is in their DNA.

A few years after William's death, his brother Henry installed a stained-glass window in St. Paul's Basilica on Power Street. Its dedication to William is very simple: "In Memory of Wm. J. O'Connor Champion Oarsman of America who died Nov. 23rd, 1892. Erected by His Bro. Henry." The window is a beautiful symbol of William's life in Toronto. It represents his Irish identity, Catholic roots, the pride and glory he felt for his country, his strength, light, and love for and from Torontonians, and his friends and family. As his obituary in the *Globe* stated:

It remains only to be said here that, having attained an eminence where the temptation to wander from the straight path were not few, nor the inducements small, he leaves behind a stainless career. He placed the pursuit of honesty, the glory of his country and the love of victory beyond the prospect of a momentary gain, and set an example that, followed by such as come after him, will bring them the same respect that attended the dead champion. An upright life, in private as in public, was ended when William O'Connor closed his eyes forever. May he rest in peace.[38]

THOMAS T. FERGUSON (1893–1918)

3 (25) Blackburn Street and 218 Munro Street,
28 St. Paul Street, 39 McGee Street, 241 Logan Avenue,
267 Booth Avenue, 38 Strange Street

Thomas T. Ferguson was the eldest of eight siblings. His large Scottish-Irish Protestant family lived in many workers' cottages and Modest Hopes throughout Riverside and Leslieville during the course of his too-short life. The family resided the longest at 3 Blackburn and 218 Munro Streets.

Thomas was the only one of his siblings born in Armagh, Ireland, to an Irish mother (Maggie Ferguson, née Margaret McWilliams) and a Scottish father (Robert Walter Ferguson, a.k.a. Robert Jr.). The rest of his seven siblings were born in Toronto.

Shortly after Thomas's parents married, his father set sail from Ireland aboard the *Oregon* bound for Montreal, leaving behind his wife, Maggie, who was two months' pregnant with Thomas. Robert Jr. sent for Maggie once he found work and laid a foundation for a new life in Canada. Toronto was a long way from home and so different for him, the son of a Scottish country gardener. Robert missed the birth of Thomas on February 1, 1893.

When Thomas was almost six months old, he set sail with Maggie aboard the *Numidian* bound for Montreal, arriving on August 5, 1893. They were processed through immigration and made their way to Toronto, where Robert and Maggie were reunited and Thomas met his father for the first time.

Robert Jr. grew up as a gardener's son in a family of six children in the countryside and small towns of Scotland. His parents, Robert Sr. and Jessie, lived on a variety of large estates, often in small cottages designated for the gardener and family. Robert Sr. was born on July 24, 1833,

Fig. 6.5a Thomas T. Ferguson.

in Lecropt, Perthshire, Scotland, the son of a blacksmith. By 1851, Robert Sr. was working as a farm domestic on the grand 20-acre estate of Wester Ballechin in Perthshire, likely living in one of the outbuildings reserved for servants.[1] Perhaps it was there where he developed an interest in gardening. On February 14, 1861, age 28, Robert Sr. married Jessie Hossack, age 29, in neighbouring Aberfeldy. They had six children in 13 years.

Soon after their marriage, Robert Sr. and Jessie had their first child, Isabella, in 1861. She soon had a sister, Lucy Ann, in 1863 and a brother, John, in 1864. By 1868, the family was living at Cowden Knowes Estate in Earlston, Berwickshire, where Robert Sr. worked as the gardener, with the young family installed in the Gardener's Lodge. It was here where the couple had their fourth child, Robert Jr., Thomas's dad, in 1868. On April 23, 1869, Robert Sr. and Jessie had their fifth child, James, then their sixth, Henry, on November 18, 1870. By 1871, the family was comprised of six children under nine years old at Cowden Knowes's Gardener's Lodge.

In the early 1870s, the Fergusons moved to Kirkfieldbank, Lanark, South Lanarkshire, on the Stonebyres Estate. Once a fortified castle in the 14th century, the estate house was gradually modified over the centuries to become a large mansion with a designed landscape, four entrance lodges, a walled garden, a coach house, laundry, icehouse, barns, and a gardener's cottage, where the Fergusons lived.

Tragedy struck the Ferguson family in 1874. On July 22, 1874, daughter Lucy Ann died, age 10. Just a month later, their son James passed away on August 19, 1874, only five years old. It was no doubt unbearable for Robert and Jessie to cope with the deaths of two children at once and adjust as a family with four kids, not six. Thomas, too, was forced to adapt to the loss of two siblings in a month.

The Fergusons were soon on the move again. By 1881, they were living at 19 West Gate in North Berwick in a modest stone house on the town's High Street, where they likely occupied a flat within a house. Robert Sr. worked as a gardener, while Isabella made dresses, Henry was a student, and Robert Jr. was an apprentice ironmonger.

Between 1867 and into the 1920s, the Canadian government sent agents to Scotland and Ireland to recruit potential immigrants, setting up offices in Ireland and Scotland while "agents went up and down the land pasting up attractive posters, giving lectures, handing out pamphlets," to persuade farmers and labourers of the "virtues of life in Canada." While the agents did not create "emigration fever," they did tap into a sense of restlessness that convinced many to immigrate to Canada during this time. It is highly likely that Robert Jr. and Maggie were inspired like this to seek a new life in North America.[2]

Robert Jr., Maggie, and baby Thomas first show up in Toronto directories in 1894, listed at 28 St. Paul Street in Corktown, a predominately Irish Catholic neighbourhood. Robert had found work as a teamster for Elias Rogers & Company, a large and popular employer in the city.[3]

Toronto Illustrated claimed that [Elias] Rogers owned "the largest yards and the most improved facilities for handling coal in Canada," employed "one of the best arranged telephone systems in the city," and compared his position in the coal trade to that of Macy's in retail in New York City. By the end of 1890, Elias Rogers Coal operated a variety of offices and yards around Toronto, as well as a pair of huge docks on The Esplanade near the St. Lawrence Market, which could process "725 tonnes of coal a day."[4]

The young Ferguson family were not the only residents at 28 St. Paul. They shared the house with other Elias Rogers employees: teamster James Ferguson (no relation), labourer Henry Kirker, and John and

Fig. 6.5b The first home the Fergusons lived in as a family in Toronto: 28 St. Paul Street (left).

Fig. 6.5c The former Ferguson home at 39 McGee Street is marked with an arrow.

Robert Moorcroft. But the Fergusons did not stay at 28 St. Paul for long. By 1895, they had moved out of Corktown and across the Don River to Riverside and 39 McGee Street, a one-storey worker's cottage.

Robert continued to work at Elias Rogers. The move was possibly timed with the arrival of Thomas's sister Mary Jane (Minnie), on February 20, 1895, when 28 St. Paul became too cramped for the expanding family. It was likely that 39 McGee was the Fergusons' first family home, marking the beginning of a long history of their association with Riverside and Leslieville.

The previous occupant of 39 McGee had been the Kelly family, including Hugh Sr. and Hugh Jr., Irish Catholic butchers. Hugh Jr., along with Hugh Wise (a promising athlete who had rowed with Ned Hanlan), Charles Phillips, Samuel Cooper, and James Ferguson (who had boarded with Robert Ferguson at 28 St. Paul and now lived next door at 41 McGee), were accused of beating to death local resident William Long in his mother's back garden. Mysteriously, only Hugh Wise and Charles Phillips were convicted and sent to Kingston Penitentiary. Before dying of brain injuries just days after the vicious attack, Long clearly stated that Hugh Kelly and James Ferguson were among his attackers, so the charges against the other men were dropped. Hugh Jr. and his family continued to live just down the street at 47 McGee.[5]

McGee Street housed many residents employed in local industries. While residential and industrial areas had started to separate in Toronto during the 1850s, at least for the more affluent part of the city, that was not the case east of the Don River in Riverside and Leslieville. William Harris's rendering plants on Pape Avenue coexisted with the neighbourhood's churches and homes, while brickyards were spread throughout Leslieville, employing scores of residents. On Saulter and McGee Streets, residents were uncomfortably close to the stench of Wiliam and George Gooderham's cow barns, the noise and smoke of the train tracks, and the mosquitoes in the nearby marshes.

On October 16, 1897, Thomas's sister Agnes was born. Their one-storey McGee cottage had likely grown too small now that they were a family of five, so the Fergusons moved briefly to 241 Logan Avenue in 1897 (see Fig. 6.5d) and then to 267 Booth Avenue in early 1898 (see Fig. 6.5e). When Robert and Maggie's fourth child, Annie, was born on July 25, 1898, the Fergusons were already living at 38 Strange Street (likely a mansard cottage, now torn down). Sadly, Annie died of meningitis on Strange Street just after her first birthday on September 11, 1899.

The Fergusons left Riverside for a time following the death of Annie, moving to The Esplanade at the foot of Princess Street across from one of Elias Rogers's factories (see Fig. 6.5f). The early 1900s brought the Fergusons back to Riverside. By the end of 1902, they had moved to 3 (25) Blackburn Street, a two-bedroom rowhouse, in time for the birth of Thomas's brother, Robert Walter Edward Ferguson, shortly followed by Grace Fern in 1904. The original row of 12 workers' cottages, numbers 1 to 23, were first built around 1888. Around 1907, a 13th house was added to the end of the row, and shortly after, the house numbers were changed to 21–45 Blackburn Street.

By 1904, this two-bedroom home was alive with the activity of two adults and six children: Thomas (age 11), Minnie (age nine), Agnes (age seven), Violet (age three), Robert (age two), and baby Grace Fern. Three children attended school, while the other three were still at home. These homes were designed with two bedrooms upstairs and two rooms downstairs, earning them the nickname "two-up, two-down" houses.

Thomas and his siblings, Minnie and Agnes, attended Hamilton Street School around the corner at Hamilton and Paul (Kintyre) Streets. In 1904, the school burnt down, so temporary classrooms were set up around the neighbourhood until a new school could be built. By the end of 1905, an all-new Queen Alexandra Public School was built on Broadview Avenue, just south of Wilton (now Dundas) Street.

It is not hard to imagine that 3 Blackburn Street quickly became crowded for a family of eight. So, in 1906, the family moved to 218

Fig. 6.5d The Ferguson family home at 241 Logan Avenue.

Fig. 6.5e The Ferguson family home at 267 Booth Avenue (left).

Fig. 6.5f Toronto Harbour, circa 1894, looking east along The Esplanade. Princess Street is in the foreground. The former Ferguson residence is noted with an arrow, bottom right-hand corner.

Fig. 6.5g (left) Blackburn Street, 1922.

Fig. 6.5h (right) The house in the middle is 25 Blackburn Street, formerly number 3.

Munro Street, a three-bedroom detached cottage, their largest home in Toronto. And it was just in time. On September 12, 1906, their seventh child, Pearl Annie, was born. The move was minimal, since the backyard of their former Blackburn house backed onto the backyard of their new Munro home. The Fergusons lived there for many years. Robert Jr. continued to work at Elias Rogers, while the younger siblings went to school and eventually got jobs of their own. Upon graduation, Thomas found employment at Vokes Hardware at the corner of Queen and Bond Streets, the site of the current St. Michael's Hospital.

In August 1914, Canada entered the First World War, which had an enormous effect on Toronto as a whole and deeply impacted the residents of Riverside and Leslieville.

Thomas's mother, Maggie, died of myocarditis, an inflammation of the heart muscle, in 1915, leaving his father, Robert, to care for six children, age eight to 22. On February 4, 1916, three days after his 23rd birthday, Thomas enlisted in the Canadian Army and went to war. He fought in the Battle of the Somme between July 1 and November 18, 1916.[6] More than three million men took part in the campaign and over a million were wounded or killed. It is considered one of the bloodiest single conflicts in human history.[7]

Fig. 6.5i The Ferguson house at 218 Munro Street today.

While Thomas was overseas, his grandfather, Robert Sr. died on February 15, 1917, in Scotland. The following year, on June 26, 1918, Thomas was granted a 10-day leave to go to England. He returned to the front in France on July 17, 1918. A month later, on August 16, 1918, he was wounded by gunfire in the head and he died on the way to the dressing station.

Robert Ferguson Jr. was notified of the death of his son Thomas at his new home at 79 Allen Avenue (see Chapter Two, Fig. 2.55). He had outlived his daughter Annie, his wife, and now his eldest son, Thomas. On August 27, 1921, Robert Jr. saw his daughter Violet get married, but he died a month later on September 26, 1921, age 53.

Violet appears to be the only one among the remaining Ferguson siblings to stay in Toronto. She married Lisle Thomas Michie and moved into 58 Brookfield Street, her own Modest Hope.

Look closely and there are remnants of Thomas T. Ferguson's legacy and his brief 25 years of life. His name is listed on the honour roll plaque of his former school, Queen Alexandra. In St. John's Presbyterian Church on Broadview Avenue, his name is engraved on a commemorative memorial plaque in the sanctuary. In the First World War *Book of Remembrance*, which memorializes more than 66,000 Canadians who made the ultimate sacrifice for their country, Corporal Thomas Ferguson is inscribed on page 406.

ANNE O'ROURKE (CIRCA1820–1891)

34 Bright Street, 38 St. Paul Street

The story of Anne O'Rourke (née Delaney) of 34 Bright Street and 38 St. Paul Street in Corktown is drawn from correspondence with her great-great-granddaughter Vickie Wybo-Yuhase as well as from additional research.

Anne[1] Delaney was born in Ireland around 1820. In her late teens, she married Martin O'Rourke (born 1806) of Ballyfin, Mountrath, Laois, Ireland, who was almost 15 years older than she was. Correspondence with the O'Rourke family suggests that Anne and Martin came to Canada, circa 1847, in connection with the Irish Potato Famine. They would have seven children in Toronto.

By 1848, the O'Rourkes were in Toronto, though their first address has proven difficult to track down. It is not until 1856 that they appear

Fig. 6.6a 32 Bright Street, present day.

in the Toronto directories, living in Toronto's east end. On July 29, 1848, Martin and Anne gave birth to Mary in Toronto, the first of Anne's children to be born in Canada. Two years later, on August 1, 1850, the couple had Bridget. Sadly, this baby died on March 26, 1851, less than a year old.

The O'Rourke family continued to grow. In 1852, Anne gave birth to their third child in Toronto, also named Anne, soon followed by James on March 30, 1854. In less than a decade after their arrival in Toronto, the O'Rourkes were now a family of five.

In 1856, the O'Rourkes finally show up in Toronto directories.[2] Martin "Rourke" is listed on North Park (Shuter) Street between Pine (Sackville) and Sumach Streets. Like many of his neighbours, Martin worked as a labourer. That same year, their daughter Catherine was born. Godparents listed on their children's baptismal records are fellow Irish immigrants as well as neighbours on North Park Street (such as Joseph Costigan[3] and Patrick Coulehan), suggesting the strength of their new community and its deep roots in their homeland. Costigan and Coulehan are recorded on North Park Street in 1850, hinting that the O'Rourkes could also have lived there as early as 1850. As well as being godfather to their second-youngest son, Joseph Costigan became an important neighbour to Anne in the years to come.

While living on North Park Street, the O'Rourke family expanded again. In 1858, Martin Jr. was born (neighbour Joseph Costigan is named as godfather) and their youngest and final child, John, followed in 1861. Sadly, on February 20, 1861, Martin Sr. died and Anne was left a widow with six children.

Tiny, crooked Bright Street first appears on a Toronto map in 1862. That year, two small one-storey side-by-side cottages were the first on the street. Joseph Costigan, Anne's former neighbour on North Park Street, occupied the first cottage, while newly widowed Anne lived in the two-bedroom cottage directly beside him, lwith her six children. This Bright Street cottage represented a new chapter for Anne at age 42: her first house alone, her own Modest Hope.

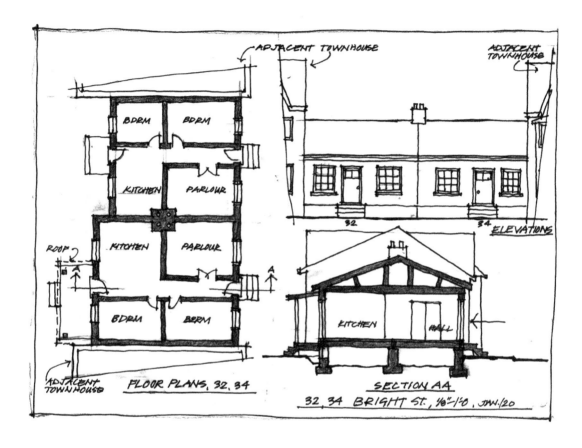

BDRM   BDRM

KITCHEN   PARLOUR

KITCHEN   PARLOUR

ROOF

BDRM   BERM

ADJACENT TOWNHOUSE   FLOOR PLANS, 32, 34

ADJACENT TOWNHOUSE

ADJACENT TOWNHOUSE

ELEVATIONS

32   34

KITCHEN   HALL

SECTION AA
32, 34 BRIGHT St., ⅛"=1'-0, JAN./20

Anne found work as a dairywoman or milkwoman. It is likely that she did so at the Gooderham & Worts dairy located just blocks from her Bright Street cottage. William Gooderham's business had begun as a flour mill; he then added a distillery to his operation in 1837 after a year of surplus grain harvests, initiating the basis for the production of his first whiskey. As manufacturing expanded, so did the company's wastes, which Gooderham initially sold to farmers for feed. He then recognized the revenue that could be made by keeping his own cows and pigs, so just as the distillery had grown out of the mill, a livestock operation sprouted from the spirits business.[4]

Fig. 6.6b Plan, section, and elevation of 32 and 34 Bright Street.

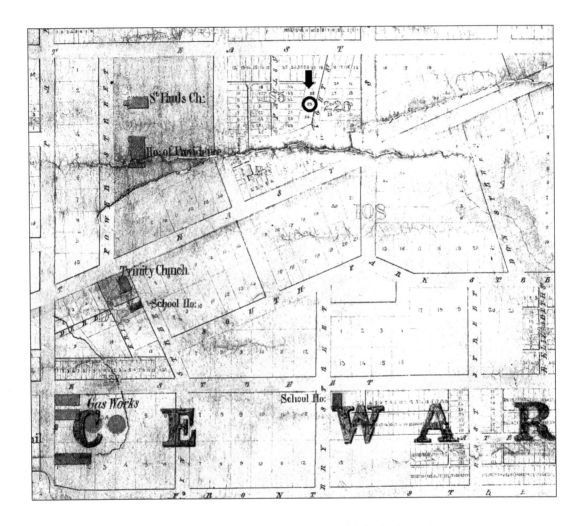

Fig. 6.6c H.J. Browne's 1862 plan of Toronto. Joseph Costigan's and Anne O'Rourke's cottages occupied Lot 23.

By 1841, Gooderham had established a large dairy on a nine-acre site between Trinity and Cherry Streets across from his mill.[5] Both the dairy and the distillery employed many residents in Corktown. "A business tycoon with a social conscience," Gooderham "also financed the building of small, affordable cottages" on Corktown streets such as Trinity and Sackville "for many of his workers and the city's growing working class."[6] Gooderham also saw the benefit of having his employees live close to work.

In late 1867, Anne and Joseph, Bright Street's sole occupants, were joined by another neighbour, Edwin Apted, who moved into a cottage across the street. By 1871, Anne was still sharing the compact one-storey, two-bedroom cottage with her six children, which likely included her recently widowed eldest daughter, Mary, and Mary's two children.[7] Space and money was tight. Anne continued to work as a dairywoman, her daughters, Anne and Mary, found jobs as servants, and her son James became a tinsmith.[8]

Around 1872, philanthropist and music dealer Richard Brooking Butland purchased numerous lots in Corktown as well as several pieces of land to the north and south of Joseph's and Anne's cottages, with the vision of creating a newer and better Bright Street. He demolished many of the existing cottages that had been built on the street and began construction of Victorian two-storied, brick-fronted terraced homes. But Anne and Joseph refused to sell their cottages. Butland's dream of a newly terraced Bright Street was derailed by their holding out, which remained stuck in the middle of the streetscape on the west side. Instead, he developed terraced rowhouses to the north and south of Anne's and Joseph's cottages. In 1872, he first constructed five rough-cast cottages to the south of Joseph and Anne, selling them for $500 each.

By 1875, Butland had erected terraced rowhouses to the north of Joseph's and Anne's cottages, as well. Housing on Bright Street mushroomed in the 1870s, and by the early 20th century, similar rowhouses also lined the east side of the street. Joseph's cottage became 32 Bright while Anne's became 34 Bright.

Compact and densely populated, Bright Street was at the centre of impoverished Corktown, a predominately Irish working-class enclave. Many residents lived in houses originally built for single families, but poverty often forced multiple families into one home. Bright Street appears not to have had the best reputation, either. Mentions of it in the *Globe* and *Toronto Star* newspaper archives feature reports of petty

Fig. 6.6d Toronto insurance plan for 1884, showing R.B. Butland's new development on Bright Street, built to the north and south of the original cottages of Anne O'Rourke and Joseph Costigan.

crime, unfortunate accidents, and personal tragedies. Mary Metcalf was arrested for stripping a Bright Street clothesline in 1879; John Evoy, at number 28, was arrested in 1883 "on a charge of drunkenness and larceny of various articles to procure liquor"; Peter Currant, at number 23, was arrested in 1896 for assaulting two "Chinamen." The most troubling mention of the street came in 1908 when Matthew and Alma Mathieson were found huddled for warmth in an empty house on Bright Street. The Mathiesons had been homeless since Matthew had lost his job at Conboy Carriage Company. They had not eaten in three days.[9]

There were also mentions of dog-related crimes. In 1875, a fight over a stolen dog led to murder next door to Joseph Costigan's house.[10] And in 1881, eight-year-old John Burns was badly bitten by a bulldog, its owner charged for not having a licence. That owner was Anne O'Rourke, now living a block away on St. Paul Street.

Anne had moved off Bright Street in 1874 to 38, formerly 10, St. Paul Street, one block away. The two Bright Street cottages remained side by side, surrounded by the curved terraced rowhouses that followed the arc of the street. Joseph Costigan remained at 32 Bright until his death in 1879, and his wife, Julia, and their son continued to live there for many years after he died. Just up the street from Julia at number 42 Bright lived the noted Henry Box Brown, a Virginia slave who escaped to freedom at the age of 33 by having himself mailed in a wooden crate to freedom in Philadelphia in 1849. Upon his delivery to liberty, he first moved from the United States to England where he toured as a magician, entertainer, and abolitionist speaker before immigrating to Toronto. He lived at 42 Bright from 1890 to 1893 and died in Toronto in 1897.

The cottage at 34 Bright Street, once the home of Anne O'Rourke, remained side by side with Julia Costigan's for a few more years. However, by 1910, it was finally sold to a developer and demolished. In its place, 34–36 Bright went up, blending in with its terraced neighbours to the north. The cottage at 32 Bright became the only remaining one of its kind on the west side and eventually the sole one on the whole street.

Anne's time on St. Paul Street began in 1874 when she moved to a new Modest Hope, number 38, formerly 10. While the St. Paul cottage was still two bedrooms, it was slightly larger than her Bright Street home. She continued to work as a dairywoman, while the children who still lived with her helped pay the bills. Catherine, now 23, was a seamstress, while sons Martin, 21, and John, 19, followed in their father's footsteps and worked as labourers, John at the dairy with his mother, Martin eventually becoming a teamster for P. Burns & Company.

Fig. 6.6e Anne O'Rourke's home at 38 St. Paul Street.

Fig. 6.6f The home of Anne O'Rourke's youngest son, John, at 31 St. Paul Street.

Fig. 6.6g Bright Street today, with the last cottage holdout remaining (32 Bright Street).

In 1885, Anne's youngest son, John, married Catherine Prior, and they moved across the street to 31 St. Paul, formerly number 13, where they started a family in their own Modest Hope. Anne continued to live at 38 St. Paul with her son Martin until 1890. The next year, Martin was listed at 93 Parliament Street, while Anne disappeared from the city's directories. It has been difficult to determine if this was the year she died.

Anne's son Martin moved back to St. Paul Street in 1892 and into number 26, now demolished, but he lived there for only a year, dying of Bright's disease on October 11, 1893, age 34. Her son John continued to own properties on St. Paul Street, eventually purchasing 31 and 31½, which he turned into rental units. He also appeared to still own his mother's former home at 38 St. Paul, since he is listed at that address for a few years before moving to 73 Frizzell Street near Pape and Danforth Avenues. Upon his death in 1917, John had amassed a modest estate, a far cry from his family's humble roots as Irish Famine immigrants to Toronto.

THE MOORE FAMILY

551, 543, 539, 745, 759 Craven Road,
Formerly Erie Terrace

If you walk up Craven Road once, it is unforgettable. In its long history, the street has had two names: Erie Terrace and then Craven Road. But early in its inception, it had been known as "The Street with the Fence." On Craven Road, houses are on one side, a fence on the other. The long wooden fence creeps and weaves its way along the west side of the street from Queen Street north to Danforth Avenue, breaking only for the railway tracks and very few cross streets. It is the longest municipally maintained wooden fence in Toronto.[1]

The roots of the fence run almost as deep as the history of the dense, mostly detached houses that line the east side. Craven Road holds Toronto's highest concentration of detached homes under 500 square feet. Many of the structures are the houses first built by the original "shackers" who once lived on Craven Road, and while none of them are exactly alike, there is a unity and evolution in their design that connects them. These houses tell the story of Toronto's development, of the wave of largely Protestant British families that settled in Toronto's east end at the beginning of the 20th century. The Moore family was one of those families.

Before it was Craven Road, it was Erie Terrace. The Moore family started to come to Toronto in 1907 at the beginning of Erie Terrace's development. The head of the family, George Edward Moore, born in 1860 on the Isle of Man, was the first and only of his siblings to cross the Atlantic and settle in Toronto.[2]

George's father, Samuel Moore, was an Irish farmer, while his mother, Jane Gawne, hailed from the Isle of Man. George lived with his family on a 12-acre farm near Ballakaighen, Isle of Man, but by his late teens was ready for change. By 1881, he had moved to West Ham, London,

Fig. 6.7a Craven Road, formerly Erie Terrace, "The Street with the Fence."

where he lived among other boarders with the Powell family, honing his skills as a carpenter. It was likely here that George met Ellen Jane Hudson, born in 1861. They were married in July 1882 in West Ham, London, and soon had five children, all of them boys.

In the early years of their marriage, Ellen and George moved frequently, likely timed with the arrival of each new son. They had a succession of January babies. In January 1884, their first, George Jr., was born in Leyton, East London. Exactly three years later, in January 1887, Edward Arthur was born at 72 Danbrook Road in Streatham, East London, a two-storey, two-bedroom, brick-terraced rowhouse. They appeared to have shared it with another family.[3] And in January 1890, their third son, William Gawne, was born there.

By 1891, George and Ellen and their three boys were living at 62 Danbrook Road, a similar two-storey brick rowhouse with two bedrooms, yet no longer shared with another family.[4] In December 1891, Philip John was born, followed by their fifth and final son, Herbert

AN APPEAL.

I bring you what you want—the English speech,
  The good old British fashion of a Home ;
A sturdy family, healthy all and each—
  Now tell me, shall I workless, homeless roam ?

Is there no farmer who shall welcome me,
  And say, "My brother, take this little place—
This cottage for your blooming family,
  And as my helper start your prosperous race ! "

Or is there not some owner of a mill
  Who'll serve himself by giving me a start ?
Or some good quarry-man who has the will
  To put the joy of hope within my heart ?

Here am I and the souls to me most dear,
  Eager to grow into Canadians true ;
Say, shall we sit and mope in want and fear,
  Or will you give me honest work to do ?

You say you prize the English mother-tongue,
  And the domestic virtues of our breed ;
Yet foreign jargons shall prevail ere long
  Here in your land unless you take good heed !

We're grateful for the kindly sympathy
  We've known in Shacktown ; now we make appeal
For leave to work—for opportunity
  The Briton's joy of self-support to feel.
                                        J.W.B.

Fig. 6.7b *"An Appeal"* printed in the *Globe* on March 19, 1908, to entice British emigrants to come to Canada.

Walker, on March 22, 1894. With five boys, 62 Danbrook Road was a full and energetic household.

Death struck the Moore family in 1894. George's father, Samuel, died on the Isle of Man on July 6, 1894. Still mourning the death of his father, George had to then face the passing of his brother, John, soon afterward. John's death came just months after the birth of John's son, Ernest. Sadly, this nephew of George's grew up never knowing his father and was raised by his maternal grandparents.

By 1901, the Moore family of seven had moved to 76 Besley Street, a two-storey, two-bedroom, brick rowhouse in Streatham, London. George Jr., 17, and Edward, 14, now contributed to the household income as a carpenter and a porter, respectively, while William, 11, Philip, nine, and Herbert, seven, went to the local Eardley Road School.[5]

In 1902, tragedy struck the Moore family once again. In April 1902, son William died, only 12 years old,[6] and George's mother, Jane, died a few months later. Perhaps with the recent deaths of his son, parents, and brother, or maybe attracted by the promise of greater opportunities, George Moore prepared for a move to Canada, a land where British immigrants were welcome, labourers were needed, and land was cheap.

In the early 1900s, Canada launched a campaign to entice British immigrants with "British ideals" to come to the country to help out short-handed farms and reverse a rural depopulation to Toronto. The campaign reached out to the poor suburbs of East London, among other targeted areas, and advertised that money problems would disappear in Canada and that jobs, land, and housing were abundant. The Canadian government's Immigration Branch paid organizations such as the Salvation Army as well as steamship lines to encourage immigration to Canada, paying a commission or "British Bonus" to steamship booking agents for each "suitable immigrant" who purchased a ticket to sail to Canada. While the Moores were not involved in this scheme, since they likely intended to stay in Toronto, they were still part of the huge British wave of immigrants to Canada in the early 20th century.

So, in 1907 at age 44, George Moore set sail for Canada, travelling solo and leaving his wife, Ellen, and their four sons behind in London. He boarded the SS *Sardinian*, a British passenger ship bound for Halifax, then made his way to Toronto by rail. His son George Jr., age 23, followed a few months later aboard the SS *Lake Erie* bound for Quebec, then went by train to Toronto. Although lured by the promised land of opportunity, they had no idea what to expect when they got to their new city.

The Canadian immigration campaign was a success, and scores of British migrants came to Canada, but problems with the program soon surfaced. Steamships agents were supposed to recruit farm labourers and rural-bound settlers, not urban factory workers, mechanics, and skilled tradesmen, since there was little demand for them.[7] As a result, a steady stream of British immigrants poured into Toronto and stayed. What was worse, the city had no effective system to deal with the massive influx and soon found itself in a "house famine." As the *Toronto Daily Star* reported: "For the first eight months of 1907, the total immigration to Canada was 216,865, an increase of 50,058 as compared with the first eight months of 1906. The total for the eight months is more than the total immigration during the whole six years, 1896 to 1902."[8]

In the early 20th century, eight "shacktowns," which included Erie Terrace, developed just outside Toronto's city limits in a sort of "horseshoe of poverty,"[9] where city regulations did not reach. Erie Terrace, the first road east of Ashdale Avenue, which was the eastern city limit, became a linear slum around 1906, just outside the city. It provided cheap building lots for new homes in a housing shortage and quickly became populated with young couples and new immigrants from Britain, some experiencing unexpected lives of poverty in their new country.

George Sr. and George Jr. arrived in Toronto in 1907[10] amid the wave of British immigrants streaming out of Union Station, landing in the middle of the city's housing crisis. But then father and son mysteriously disappear from public records. It is not until 1910 that they resurface, listed at 128 Erie Terrace. Where were the father-and-son carpenters living from 1907 to 1910? While not confirmed, there is a possibility that George and his son were residing on Erie Terrace before 1910, undocumented, since the history of Erie Terrace stretches back earlier than the official record began. Perhaps they were there all along in a shacktown. Meanwhile, Ellen, wife of George Sr., and their three remaining children joined him and George Jr. in 1910.

In the 1908 *Toronto Directory*, which reflects 1907, Erie Terrace is claimed as "not built on," though houses and occupants were not listed in the directories until 1909. However, lots on Reid (Rhodes) Avenue and "a new street to the west" (Erie Terrace) were already being sold in 1906, and tents, shacks, and owner-built houses were everywhere. It is possible that the city officials who created the directories did not venture up the shacktown street to take note of its inhabitants. Nevertheless, by 1907, Erie Terrace was abuzz with activity. New British immigrants turned a dirt laneway into a street, houses into homes, and as carpenters, it is probable that the two George Moores were highly sought-after neighbours.

Leslieville and Toronto's east end were transformed in 1906 as farm lots were quickly sold and exploited to meet the needs of thousands of new immigrants. One large farm lot instrumental in the development of eastern Leslieville was the 600-acre Ashbridge Estate owned by brothers Jesse and Wellington Ashbridge. The estate, which had been in the family since the 1790s, extended from Greenwood to Coxwell Avenues, Queen

Street to Danforth Avenue. Influential real estate tycoon Frederick B. Robins, who played a hand in creating subdivisions throughout Toronto before the First World War, acted as the agent for much of the Ashbridge Estate and helped sell lots carved out of the brothers' land.[11]

The Ashbridge brothers kept a close eye on the evolution of their property and ensured its modest redevelopment, even making their mark with namesake Ashdale Avenue on its eastern edge. The restructuring of Erie Terrace took hold in 1906 thanks to Robins and his Erie Realty Company. In the early 1900s, Reid (Rhodes) Avenue and Erie Terrace went on the market, and Robins set his sights on its development. Erie Terrace, one block to the east and thus just outside city limits, was almost half the size of the average Toronto street, but it became Ashdale Avenue's uncomfortable neighbour nevertheless. In fact, unlike Ashdale, Erie Terrace was most likely intentionally planned and conceived to be a shacktown.[12]

Lots on Erie Terrace were affordable and available. Maximizing their profits, developers divided the street into as many parcels of lands as possible, some only 10 feet wide. Too narrow and close to the backyards of neighbouring Ashdale Avenue, Erie Terrace was developed only on the east side of the street. Soon tents, shacks, and small houses haphazardly stared into the backyards of their neighbours on Ashdale, who watched the shacktown rising behind them.

As Erie Terrace expanded, it evolved into a unique and varied streetscape. Some houses were owner-built with a "homemade" quality culled from available materials, others were constructed simply by local carpenters and tradespeople, still more were erected by small developers from basic kits. While landowners turned their lots into homes, many lived in tents on their properties, or in the basement foundations of their houses while they built their homes.

Although shacktowns were often criticized in the city's newspapers, the Standard and Loan Company, which purchased and took over the assets of Erie Realty, sang their praises and congratulated themselves on the Erie Terrace development. Erie Terrace's position outside city limits meant that it was largely "off the grid," but the benefits of that situation soon became part of the problem because the amenities to support the ballooning community were lacking. There were no water mains, sewers, drains, police and fire services, paved roads, or even a sidewalk.[13] And with so many kids in the growing neighbourhood, the need for a school soon became apparent. Norway Public School was too far to walk to and too crowded, thus a single room in Rhodes Avenue Church was created in November 1906. It was soon enlarged to a four-room school building in May 1907, formally opening in 1908 and christened Roden Public School.[14]

The Erie Terrace shacktown continued to build up and put down roots. The first Canadian winter in 1906 was mild and manageable for the unacclimatized immigrants in their tents, shacks, and uninsulated homes, perhaps giving a false sense of security. The densely packed street of predominately British immigrants evolved into a close-knit community. As they settled into their new city, they enjoyed the fresh air and nature still within reach, watched their children play on the street, established churches, enjoyed sports, and built more houses in community-led bees. It was a street full of skilled tradespeople eager to work and grow their investments. It is not hard to imagine George Sr. and George Jr., carpenter father and son, living in this community.

The end of 1907 brought a perfect storm for the "shackers" on Erie Terrace. A financial crisis caused a stock market crash, the economy plummeted, factories closed, and jobs were lost. With the financial loss came the taste of the immigrants' first real Canadian winter, one of the coldest on record. The shacker tents, tarpaper shacks, and uninsulated houses offered little protection against the Canadian cold. Without jobs, food, fuel, and proper winter clothing, they began to starve and freeze. Those residents who could got off the street as quickly as possible, selling their lots at a loss, even offering free lumber. Yet many more had no choice but to stay, since all their money was tied up in their plots of land. Aided by community support and the creation of the Shacktown Relief Fund, many families were able to pull through on Erie Terrace. The economic crisis was short-lived. By the spring of 1908, the economy bounced back, jobs returned, and emptied lots on Erie Terrace filled up again.

In 1909, Erie Terrace residents voted to join the City of Toronto, which brought proper services such as water mains, sewers, fire and police services, a paved road, and a suitable sidewalk. While Erie Terrace had been growing since 1906, it was finally acknowledged in the 1909 *Toronto Directory*.

Carpenters George Sr. and George Jr. first appear in the 1911 *Toronto Directory*, reflecting 1910, living at 128 Erie Terrace (551 Craven Road). Perhaps they were already boarding on Erie Terrace undetected while they built their own house. Or maybe they were attracted to Erie Terrace by a newspaper advertisement and could finally send word to Ellen, Philip, Herbert, and Edward that they were settled in Toronto. This house at 128 Erie Terrace was their first Modest Hope.

From 1910 to 1912, the rest of the Moore family arrived in Toronto. In 1910, Ellen Moore, now age 49, with son Herbert, age 15, joined her husband and eldest son in Toronto. Their son Philip, age 19, joined them soon after. Reunited, George and Ellen, with their three boys, began their Toronto life together at 128 Erie Terrace. The house contained three main rooms: a living room in the front with two bedrooms in the middle and back, with a washroom and small kitchen at the back. The rooms were connected by a long hall that ran along one side of the house from front to back. Everyone contributed to the household: George Sr. and George Jr. as carpenters, Ellen running the house, Philip as a blacksmith, and Herbert as a labourer for the railway.

In 1912, the Moore family's migration was complete. Edward, his pregnant wife, Jessie, and their three-year-old son, George Arthur Charles, arrived in Toronto and joined the others on Erie Terrace. Split up for many years, they now lived together in close quarters on a tightly knit street. Likely, they all resided at 128 Erie Terrace for the first year, nine of them in a two-bedroom house, including boarder Henry Farrow, until Edward moved his family two doors north to 159 Erie Terrace (563 Craven Road).

Fig. 6.7c Craven Road today looking north, showing (from right to left) the various Moore family homes at 539 Craven Road, 543 Craven Road, and 551 Craven Road (formerly Erie Terrace).

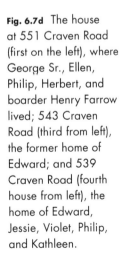

Fig. 6.7d The house at 551 Craven Road (first on the left), where George Sr., Ellen, Philip, Herbert, and boarder Henry Farrow lived; 543 Craven Road (third from left), the former home of Edward; and 539 Craven Road (fourth house from left), the home of Edward, Jessie, Violet, Philip, and Kathleen.

The narrow dirt laneway that once lay outside city limits was now a busy residential street within Toronto, but its narrow width and impassable muddy roadway with a makeshift three-plank wooden sidewalk caused endless problems for its residents and became a headache for the city.

In December 1911, the City of Toronto authorized the widening of Erie Terrace to improve the conditions of the street by taking land from Ashdale residents' backyards. Works Commissioner R.C. Harris had deemed that "the conditions of life on Erie Terrace were anything but satisfactory" and that its widening was a "necessity."[15] At a cost of $6,000, it was proposed that the city would pay $2,400 and Erie Terrace's residents would pay the remaining $3,600, but for the latter, this was a steep price.[16] The widening also meant Ashdale residents would lose chunks of their backyards and yet there still would not be enough room to build on both sides of Erie Terrace.

This "undesirable,"[17] almost one-and-a-half-mile strange little laneway with backyards and houses bewildered city politicians and bureaucrats.[18] But it was a desirable street for the Moores and their Erie Terrace neighbours. It was their community, their home.

The Moores had been reunited in Canada for only a couple of years when tragedy struck once more. On January 1, 1914, Edward's son, George Arthur Charles, died in the isolation hospital of heart failure. He was only four. The death of his grandson at such a young age must have sparked painful flashbacks for George Sr. of the loss of his own son, William, just 12 years earlier.

Edward, Jessie, and one-year-old Violet left 159 Erie Terrace (563 Craven Road) and the ghosts and moved to the newly numbered 483 Erie Terrace (543 Craven Road), two doors south of his father, mother, and brothers, George Jr., Philip, and Herbert, as well as boarder Henry Farrow.

On August 4, 1914, Britain entered the First World War, with Canada soon following suit. The pull to enlist was disproportionately high on Erie Terrace.[19] Patriotism was one motivation, economic necessity another. Having endured years of low pay or no pay, army pay was often more money than many had earned before the war. As a result, Erie Terrace emptied of men who enlisted. Many never returned, dying in action, from wounds, or from disease in the trenches. Others who did come back were often injured or psychologically broken.

One by one, Ellen saw all four of her sons enlist. First, Philip on September 22, 1914, age 22, followed by George Jr. the next day, age 29. They made $10 per month. Eight months later, on May 3, 1915, Herbert joined them, age 21, though he lied and said he was 24. He was soon followed by Edward on July 6, 1915, age 28, who left behind his young daughter, Violet, and his pregnant wife, Jessie. Edward, the only son who was married, earned upward of $20 per month, which included a "separation payment" because he was leaving a wife and children behind. Their boarder, Henry Farrow, enlisted, as well.

Finally, George Sr. departed, too, travelling to Russia in 1915 to assist in the construction of a railway through Finland.[20] Ellen, who had for so long been surrounded by her husband, four sons, and a boarder, was now alone, living next door to her daughter-in-law, Jessie, and granddaughter, Violet. Their absence must have been felt acutely, worry and anxiety ever-present while they waited for news of their sons and husbands.

While the war raged overseas, the Erie Terrace debate continued at City Hall. Toronto wanted to "clean up" Erie Terrace by improving and widening the road and bringing in a water main, but the latter could not be done without grading the thoroughfare first. That would cost Erie Terrace residents money, which they did not have to spare. Furthermore, widening the road meant taking 10 to 14 feet off the backyards of Erie Terrace's Ashdale neighbours, not something that would please them. In the end, Erie Terrace residents had to pay a sizable portion of the bill to the city to make these changes. In 1916, the street was widened and graded, leaving a reserve strip along the west side so that Ashdale residents could not build structures in their now-smaller backyards, nor have access to their backyards from Erie Terrace. The residents of Erie Terrace had paid quite a lot for their new road and did not want Ashdale using their street as a rear access. In the end, "a complicated problem was made simple by a fence."²¹ Along the reserve strip, the city erected a long, continuous fence, a soft yet hard dividing line between the residents of Erie Terrace and the backyards of Ashdale Avenue.

Ellen's husband, George Sr., returned from Russia earlier than planned, an injury forcing him to do so.²² He was greeted with a widened and paved street and a fence that now ran the length of it. And his house number had changed once more. It was now 551 Erie Terrace.

On June 30, 1916, Ellen and George's son Corporal George Moore Jr. died of wounds to the head, left eye, and chest at No. 13 Stationary Hospital in Boulogne, France. They received notification of his death at 551 Erie Terrace.

Their youngest son, Gunner Herbert Walter Moore, got into lots of trouble in the war. He was penalized for misconduct several times during service and had a colourful record.

In 1916, Herbert suffered illnesses and was wounded "but not seriously and went almost

Fig. 6.7e (top) Unsightly sheds and outbuildings in the backyards of Ashdale Avenue, which Erie Terrace residents' front yards looked onto.

Fig. 6.7f (bottom) The various separate fences of Ashdale backyards before the municipal fence was built.

immediately back on duty."[23] He was not so lucky the next time. On August 5, 1917, he died following shrapnel wounds that led to the amputation of his left leg and left arm. He passed away at No. 1 Canadian Field Ambulance and was buried in Noeux-les-Mines Communal Cemetery in France. His parents received notification of his death at 551 Erie Terrace.

Ellen and George Moore once had five sons. One died age 12 and two were killed in the First World War.

On February 18, 1919, Sergeant Philip John Moore was discharged and returned home, deemed "medically unfit to be treated as an out-patient." He came back to Toronto with "gassed lungs and bronchitis."[24] Age 28, single, and disabled, Philip moved back into 551 Erie Terrace with his parents.

On April 7, 1919, Private Edward Arthur Moore was discharged and returned home, deemed to have defective hearing and badly crippled. The only Moore son who ever married, Edward came back to 543 Erie Terrace to his wife, Jessie, daughter, Violet, and infant son, Philip, who had been born while he was overseas. They soon had another baby, Kathleen, and moved to 539 Erie Terrace, newly vacated by recent widow Phoebe Hunter and her eight children.

The vacant houses of Erie Terrace filled up again with returning veterans, and what lots remained soon had new houses and families. In 1923, the street was renamed Craven Road.

In 1923, Ellen and George moved to 91 Stacy Street near Coxwell and Danforth Avenues and then to Goodwood, Ontario. When Ellen and George left Erie Terrace, so, too, did their son, Philip, who had been living with his parents since his return from the war. He accepted a job in Detroit as a structural draftsman.

Edward, his wife, Jessie, and their three children, Violet, Philip, and Kathleen were the only ones remaining on Craven Road at number 539. On June 13, 1929, Edward died of pulmonary tuberculosis, likely a residual effect of his time in the war, and was buried at St.

John's Norway Cemetery on Kingston Road in Toronto. Jessie continued to live on Craven Road with her children, eventually moving to 759 Craven in 1936.

Ellen Moore had outlived four of her five children. She also outlasted her husband, George, who died in 1936 in Goodwood. He, too, is buried at St. John's Norway Cemetery, near his son Edward.

Ellen returned in 1940 to the Toronto street that had been her first home in Canada, moving back to Craven Road beside her daughter-in-law, Jessie, and her grandkids at 745 Craven Road. Side by side, the two women were perched on Craven Road, surrounded by neighbours and shared experiences and memories. Ellen died there in 1953 and is buried with Edward and her husband at St. John's Norway Cemetery. Jessie continued to live on Craven Road until her death in 1973. Philip John Moore died on February 1, 1978, the only son to survive his mother. Although he passed away in the United States, he is buried in Toronto.

Craven Road has a long and complicated history. In recent years, many of the original working-class residents have yielded to newcomers, resulting in gentrification, expansion, and the destruction of some of the original dwellings.[25] The street was developed as a shacktown whose residents, new immigrants, claimed a wedge of Toronto real estate with their "starter homes." But as their structures became houses, the houses became homes, and the homes became Modest Hopes, their fence unified and identified them. Their street became their community, their life stories, their homes.

Ellen Moore lost three boys on this street, two during the war. "However," she once said, "I know they have all done what they consider their duty. And that, at least, is some satisfaction."[26]

ALBERT JACKSON (1857–1918)

213 Brunswick Avenue

> Albert Jackson and his family came to Canada for a
> better life. They stayed to make it a better place.
> — Karolyn Smardz Frost[1]

This is the story of Albert Calvin Whitley Jackson, his large family,
and many generations of descendants. In 1914, Albert and his wife,
Henrietta, purchased 213 Brunswick Avenue (see Fig. 6.8a); this Modest
Hope would go on to house Albert Jackson's descendants, including his
nephew and niece, grandchildren, and great-grandchildren. It was the
first of many homes that the Jackson family bought in the Bathurst and

Fig. 6.8a 213 Brunswick
Avenue (left) as it would
have looked when
it was purchased. A
second storey has since
been added.

Bloor neighbourhood. Jackson's legacy highlights the history of Black immigration to Toronto in the 19th century.

In the Town of York, the first Black people were Loyalists, free men and women, and the enslaved servants of wealthy white families. They were joined by freedom seekers, who sought Toronto as a place to build a new life, new home, and future.[2]

As recounted in Chapter Three, in 1793, the Act to Limit Slavery (also known as the Act Against Slavery) in Upper Canada was given royal assent by Lieutenant Governor John Graves Simcoe to abolish slavery in the colony. However, he could do little against the "property rights" of slave owners within the confines of the law. Nevertheless, the Act to Limit Slavery, and the British Empire's Slavery Abolition Act in 1833, set the stage for the extension of the Underground Railroad farther north into Canada. As runaways became free upon arrival in Upper Canada, many enslaved African Americans made the difficult passage north. Although exact figures are uncertain, it is believed that as many as 30,000 refugees from U.S. enslavement found liberty in Canada either by the Underground Railroad or on their own. The railroad's traffic reached its peak between 1840 and 1860 and particularly after the United States passed the Fugitive Slave Act on September 10, 1850.[3]

Fig. 6.8b Albert Calvin Whitley Jackson.

In 1799, only 15 Black people were counted in York. Early colonialists in the town continued to own slaves into the early 19th century, but judicial rulings gradually constrained the practice.[4] By the 1820s, slavery in Canada had all but ended, almost a decade before the British Empire's abolition of it was formally declared on August 1, 1834.

By 1837, there were around 50 Black families living in Toronto.[5] These early settlers were centred around the St. Lawrence Market area at the foot of Church Street, near Queen and Richmond Streets, and close to the African Baptist Church founded in 1826.[6] By the 1830s, the city had two Black churches, the second located on what became Chestnut Street.[7] These churches served as spiritual and political hubs for the city's growing Black community, which was asserting its voice in the abolitionist movement and welcoming an influx of families seeking freedom via the Underground Railroad.[8]

In 1840, John Strachan, Toronto's Anglican archbishop, commissioned former student Peter Gallego to conduct a census of Toronto's Black residents. He counted 525.[9] By 1855, that number had almost doubled to 973. A year later, Toronto had a population of 47,000,[10] of which approximately 1,000 were Black.[11]

The expanding Black community began to shift west and then north to streets such as York, Sayer (Chestnut), Elizabeth, and Centre in Macaulaytown (The Ward). Over half the Black population chose The Ward, the most crowded neighbourhood in the city, as their home.[12] At that time, it was dominated by Protestants who ran Toronto's public life and was known for its rowdy saloons and the Orange Lodges that catered to its Protestant clientele.[13] Centrally located, it became an initial starting point for many immigrants throughout the 19th century, providing newcomers with fresh starts and opportunities.[14]

As their new city became home, the members of the Black community in Toronto opened barbershops, restaurants, lumber yards, and construction companies, and took in laundry, offered dressmaking and housekeeping services, and formed the city's first taxi company. In short, they invested in social democracy, business, politics, and real estate.

Thornton Blackburn and his wife, Lucie, were among Toronto's earliest Black residents and were instrumental in paving the way for future Black freedom-seekers in the city. They were at the heart of the first fugitive slave extradition case between Canada and the United States.[15]

As a fugitive slave from Louisville, Kentucky, Thornton saw his case establish the precedent that Canada would not return slaves to their former masters in the United States, thus making the Americans' northern neighbour a safe terminus. In 1831, Thornton and his wife fled from Kentucky to Pennsylvania to Detroit, where they were arrested. Aided by 400 of Detroit's Black residents who stormed the prison, the Blackburns escaped and arrived in Toronto in 1834 to begin their free lives.

Soon, Thornton found work as a waiter in the Osgoode Hall dining room, and while waiting tables there, discovered an empty niche in Toronto — a taxi service. With a one-horse cab painted yellow and red that could accommodate four passengers, he started the first taxi service in Toronto in 1837, calling it The City, which became remarkably successful.

The Blackburns settled on a lot on South Park Street, where they built a small one-storey frame cottage. It became 54 Eastern Avenue and was at the corner of that road and Sackville Street (now the southeast corner of Inglenook Community School's playground), where they lived for over 50 years. The Blackburns became active members in the anti-slavery movement as well as leaders in the Black community, along with fellow citizens such as Francis Simpson and John Meriwether Tinsley. In addition, the handful of Black churches played a crucial social and political role, providing space and resources for education and support for Black refugees coming to Toronto from the United States.[16] When Thornton died in 1890, he left a small fortune of $18,000 to Lucie, along with several houses he owned all over Toronto.

The Blackburns' first humble home welcomed freedom seekers arriving via the Underground Railroad, helping them get on their feet and acclimatize to their new land. In 1858, they assisted Ann Maria Jackson (née Emery), a widow who arrived in Toronto with seven of her nine children via the Underground Railroad, taking the family into their home until Ann Maria had enough money to start a new life.

Albert Calvin Whitley Jackson was born in 1857 in Milford, Delaware, the youngest of nine children of Ann Maria and John Jackson.

John, a blacksmith, was a free man, but his wife was a slave who was permitted to live with her husband and children. Constantly concerned for her children's safety, Ann Maria repeatedly pleaded with her husband to escape the slave state in which they lived, but John feared the risk. Ann Maria's fear soon became reality when two of her nine children, her eldest sons, James and Richard, were sold by their master, causing John to suffer a nervous breakdown.

Ann Maria later said, as recounted by historian Karolyn Smardz Frost in *I've Got a Home in Glory Land*:

> It almost broke my heart when he came and took my children away as soon as they were big enough to hand me a drink of water. My husband was always very kind to me, and I had often wanted him to run away with me and the children, but I could not get him in the notion; he did not feel that he could, and so he stayed, and died broken-hearted, crazy.[17]

When her owner made plans to sell four more of her children, Ann Maria immediately mobilized and "took destiny into her own hands and escaped from her Maryland slave owner." With children ages 1 to 16 — Mary Ann, Frances, William, John, Wilhelmina, Thomas, and Albert, the youngest   the family made their way through the slave state of Delaware, terrified of discovery. Finally, just outside Wilmington, Delaware, they were picked up by Underground Railroad agents in a horse-drawn carriage.[18]

Ann Maria and her children were then transported to a second carriage and driven across the state line into Chester County in free Pennsylvania. From there, they were moved to Philadelphia, where they met William Still, secretary of Pennsylvania's Anti-Slavery Society. Still was a businessman, writer, historian, civil-rights activist, and "conductor" on the Underground Railroad who had helped as many as 800 slaves escape to freedom. He sent them on through Pennsylvania and

Fig. 6.8c An image of Ann Maria Jackson with seven of her nine children featured in abolitionist William Still's *The Underground Rail Road* (1872).

New York State and eventually to St. Catharines, Canada West, where they met Reverend Hiram Wilson, who transferred them to Toronto in 1858.[19] The Jacksons were one of the largest families ever to travel together on the Underground Railroad and were welcomed by the Blackburns at 54 Eastern Avenue, where they stayed until they got on their feet.[20] By 1859, Ann Maria had rented rooms for her family in The Ward. Their first address was 8 Terauley Street, now Bay Street, near the corner of Queen Street West. Ann Maria took in laundry as a washer-woman to support her family, and likely, the younger children went to school while the older ones worked to contribute to the household.[21]

According to Goad's Insurance Plan for 1880, 8–10 Terauley Street was a pair of two-storey cottages. Ann Maria and her children were not the only tenants in the small cottage. Listed also at this address, which was demolished by 1890, were William Brown (cab driver), Thaddeus Cable (stage driver), Harman Knox (shoemaker), John Ryan (labourer), James Wright (whitewasher), and Mrs. McNicolls (widowed nurse).

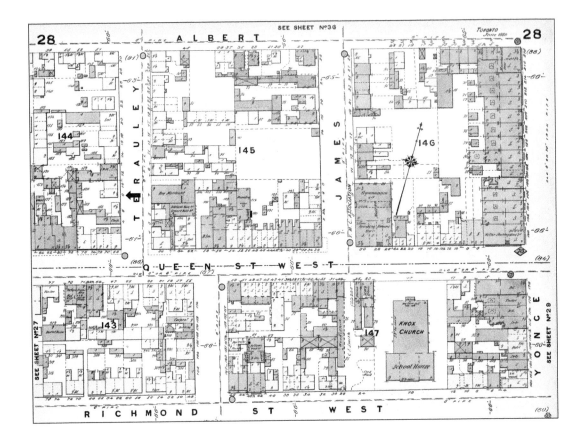

Fig. 6.8d Insurance plan for 1880, showing 8 Terauley (Bay) Street, probably a two-storey cottage, near what is now Bay and Queen Streets on the grounds of present-day Nathan Phillips Square.

By 1861, Ann Maria and her children had moved a couple of blocks north in The Ward to a one-storey cottage at 232 Sayer (now Chestnut) Street,[22] where they appear to have occupied the entire home as the sole family. It was likely here that Ann Maria was joyfully reunited with her son James, who had been sold into slavery. He, too, had found freedom on the Underground Railroad, and likely reconnected with his mother with the help of William Still, who had met and documented Ann Maria a few years earlier as part of work done for Pennsylvania's Anti-Slavery Society.

The reunited family relocated to 104 Edward Street by the mid-1860s. Shortly after this move, another of Ann Maria's missing sons,

Fig. 6.8e Chestnut Street, north from Christopher Street, 1907. About two-thirds up Chestnut (then called Sayer Street) was number 232 (see black arrow), where Ann Maria lived with her children.

Richard, joined her in Toronto. He had been sold into slavery almost a decade earlier. She now had all of her nine children together again.

By the 1870s, as Ann Maria's children grew up, the family continued to disperse throughout The Ward, developing their own livelihoods, careers, and families to become prominent residents of the neighbourhood. The youngest, Albert, attended the local school, getting the education that would have been denied him in slavery. His sister Wilhelmina followed in their mother's footsteps and became a laundress, marrying Henry Bacon in 1872, and had two children. Albert's brothers, William, Richard, and James, established themselves as barbers, a field that offered one of the most popular jobs in the Black community, serving both white and Black customers. Although there were white and Black barbers in the city, Black barbers operated more consistent, successful operations.[23] Toronto barbers had a significant culture in the 19th century. They did more than just cut hair. Their full-service operations featured shaves, too, and frequently catered to a wealthy clientele; their shops were meeting grounds for the community to explore politics, race relations, and identity.

Fig. 6.8f This address, 47–49 Laplante Avenue (formerly Emma Street and Mission Avenue), 1914, was possibly once home to Ann Maria's son Thomas. Similar-style houses were also occupied by Wilhemina Bacon (née Jackson) at 39 Laplante (Emma Street), while James Jackson lived at 51 Laplante (Emma Street).

Albert's brother Richard became a popular and well-liked barber, his establishments frequented by prominent Torontonians, making him a sort of "barber to the stars." While Richard "deftly scraped their faces, he entertained them with the latest gossip of the day — political, personal, and social."[24]

He started a barbershop with Reuben Custaloe, called "Jackson and Custaloe," on King Street West, or "Dick and Rube's," as the advertisements read in the city's newspapers in the 1870s. Custaloe was the grandson of John Meriwether Tinsley, a prosperous Black building contractor on Agnes Street, often described as the "celebrated patriarch of the coloured community." Tinsley was a free-born African-American carpenter from Richmond, Virginia, who was the first Black Canadian to start a construction company in Toronto. His firm provided scores of fugitive slaves with their first jobs in the city.[25] Tinsley died at age 109.[26]

As their Toronto lives developed, members of the Jackson family occupied a patchwork of addresses throughout The Ward, often living at numerous addresses on the same street. In addition to Terauley (Bay), Sayer (Chestnut), and Edward Streets, they resided at 39, 47, and 51 Emma Street (Laplante Avenue, Mission Avenue); 20, 21, 40, 91, and 147 Elizabeth Street; Centre Avenue; and 97 and 95 Chestnut Street. And brothers William, Richard, and James had barbershops on King Street West, as well as Church, Queen, and Yonge Streets. Each and every one of these properties are now gone.

Ann Maria died on April 28, 1880, and was buried in the Necropolis in a plot that was the property of Thornton Blackburn. She left behind nine children whom she had delivered from slavery to Toronto and had helped cultivate into free and productive citizens in their new city. Sadly,

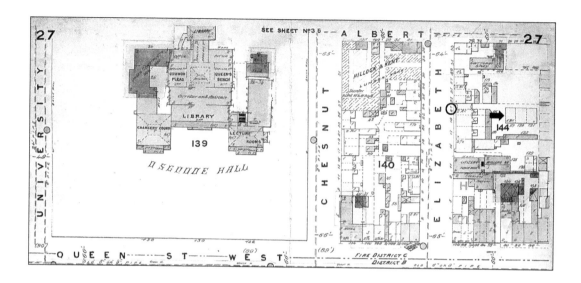

she missed the legacy that her youngest son, Albert, soon created.

By the early 1880s, Albert and his successful barber brother, Richard, were living together at the rear of 21 Elizabeth Street, a few years before Old City Hall was built a block away, almost literally in their backyard. It was here that Albert applied for the job that changed his life forever.

In 1882, Albert Jackson applied by mail to the government for employment as a letter carrier and got the job. But when he showed up for work to start his new career, his first day almost never happened.

In "Blacks in 1880s Toronto: The Search for Equality," Colin McFarquhar

Fig. 6.8g (top) Map of Toronto, 1883, showing 21 Elizabeth Street. Richard and Albert Jackson were listed as living at the "rear of 21 Elizabeth Street," where a row of three one-storey workers' cottages existed.

Fig. 6.8h (bottom) The rear of 21 Elizabeth Street, circa 1913, where Albert and Richard Jackson once lived, with Old City Hall in the background.

Fig. 6.8i Albert Jackson, postman, along with his letter-carrier peers, 1882. Jackson stands in the fifth row from the bottom, eighth person from the left.

writes that "The City of Toronto had a total of 2,363 commercial clerks in 1881, but only one clerk was African Canadian. There were no Black agents, accountants, book-keepers, physicians, or surgeons."[27]

Albert's appointment caused friction among white postal workers in lesser positions, and fellow white postmen refused to train him. He was quickly relegated to inside, lesser positions. News of this racially motivated demotion quickly spread and became widely covered in the Toronto press for the next couple of weeks. There were accounts of postal employees calling Albert an "objectionable African" and an "obnoxious coloured man," while a flurry of letters to the editor escalated the debate over so-called "scientific racism" in relation to Albert's suitability for the job.[28] The Black community insisted Jackson be given his proper appointment, while letters from the white community argued that white letter carriers should not be forced to work with him. The Jackson issue became highly charged in Toronto, then quickly intensified politically. The people of St. John's Ward launched a public inquiry, and a committee was formed.

The Jackson controversy was so contentious that the *Globe* expressed concern that a race war might occur.[29] This public debate coincided with an upcoming federal election campaign, and Prime Minister John A. Macdonald, who was courting Black voters,[30] was made aware of the brewing controversy and intervened, as did the white press and leaders in the community to alleviate personal or civic embarrassment.[31] Eventually, Albert won the job back that he had been hired for and went on to work as a postman for 36 years. He earned a minimum of $1.25 daily in 1902 and $3 per day in 1913. Churchgoing Jackson became a pillar of Toronto's Black community as the first Black postal worker in Toronto.

In 1883, Albert married Henrietta Elizabeth Jones, and the next year, their son Alfred Burasides Jackson was born. By the mid-1880s, the young couple had moved, along with brother Richard, up the street to 91 Elizabeth Street.

At age 38, in 1885, Albert's brother Richard died.[32] According to the *Toronto World* newspaper, "a thousand people were at the funeral, including aldermen and military officers, former mayors of the city, and a host of the town's notables," such as

William Maclean and John Ross Robertson, the publishers of the *Toronto World* and *Toronto Telegram*, respectively. It was a "remarkable tribute to a man whose virtue to the community clearly transcended any divisions of race or class that existed in the highly stratified late-nineteenth-century city."[33] The service took place at the British Methodist Episcopal Church on Chestnut Street on June 2, 1885, and he was buried at the Necropolis.

Albert and Henrietta purchased their first family home at 95 Chestnut Street around 1890. Here, they raised Alfred, who was a talented painter and fine artist, and three more boys: Ernest Bruce (born 1891), Richard (born 1893), and Harold (born 1894). Albert continued working as a postman, while Henrietta was a talented seamstress who also loved music and played the harp.[34] Sadly, in 1901, tragedy struck Albert's family again when Alfred died at age 17. He, too, was buried at the Necropolis.

In 1914, Albert and Henrietta bought a second house at 213 Brunswick Avenue in the Annex (see Figs. 6.8a and 6.8l), their first property outside The Ward. But they continued to live at 95 Chestnut Street, choosing to rent out the Brunswick Avenue home.

On January 14, 1918, Albert Jackson collapsed after dinner and died. He was 61.

Fig. 6.8j (top) The house at 91 Elizabeth Street where Albert Jackson lived with his wife, Henrietta, circa 1885, corner of Elizabeth Street and Foster Place.

Fig. 6.8k (bottom) Albert Jackson and his wife, Henrietta, with their four children: Alfred, Ernest Bruce, Richard, and Harold.

Albert's widow, Henrietta, continued to reside at 95 Chestnut Street for a few more years with her three sons, Ernest Bruce, a printer at W.R. Phillips & Company; Richard, a jeweller at Frederick A. Parkinson; and Harold, a driver for Fred W. Halls Paper Company. In 1921, Harold married Julia Anderson. As a wedding present, Henrietta gave them the house she owned at 238 Brunswick Avenue, across the street from 213 Brunswick, selling it to them for a dollar.[35]

In the early 1920s, Henrietta purchased 277 Palmerston Avenue and moved in there with sons Bruce and Richard. In 1924, Bruce married Ethel Graham. As a wedding gift, Henrietta gave them her property at 234 Brunswick Avenue, the house next door to Bruce's brother Harold, selling it to the couple once again for a dollar.[36]

Henrietta and her son Richard continued to live around the corner at 277 Palmerston Avenue. Richard never married and looked after his widowed mother. Eventually, he became the owner of 213 Brunswick Avenue, which he rented out while continuing to live with Henrietta.[37]

Three Jackson homes now lined this stretch of Brunswick Avenue, while Henrietta resided nearby on Palmerston Avenue. Eventually, eight or nine houses were owned by various members of the Jackson family on Borden Street, Brunswick Avenue, and Palmerston Avenue.

Albert and Henrietta's son Ernest Bruce had a son also named Ernest Bruce, who like his father was simply called Bruce. Bruce Jr. married Faith, and in 1950 they were renting a small flat on Harbord Street but needed more space when they wanted to start a family.

Richard, "Uncle Dick" to Bruce Jr. and Faith, decided to rent 213 Brunswick Avenue to the young couple, who moved into the one-storey, two-bedroom cottage, which had no basement. Uncle Dick tried unsuccessfully to dig out a basement in 1951 to make the house warmer, but the walls caved in and it became only a crawlspace. The house was heated with coal but still felt cold. One bedroom was at the front of the house, beside the front living room; the other was at the back of the house, beside the kitchen. The dining room was in the middle of the house.[38]

Bruce Jr. and Faith lived at 213 Brunswick Avenue from 1950 to

1972, raising five children there: Marva, Donna, Wayne, Glenn, and Michele, Albert's great-grandchildren. Two boys were in the back bedroom, two girls in the front bedroom. Bruce Jr. and Faith, and for a time the youngest child, were in the living room, adapted into a third bedroom. Their family home was a full house. Faith Jackson has outlived two of her children as well as husband Bruce Jr.[39]

Many descendants of Ann Maria Jackson are still in Canada today. Albert's wife, Henrietta, died in 1958, age 99. Grandchildren, great-grandchildren, even great-great-grandchildren of Albert and Henrietta still live in Toronto and surrounding areas, many raised in the houses Albert, Henrietta, and their sons purchased around Bloor and Bathurst Streets.

Albert's great-grandchildren, Jay and Shawne Jackson, descendants of Albert's son Harold, were members of the popular band The Majestics, a 13-piece rhythm-and-blues band that recorded several albums for ARC Records in the late 1960s.[40] Jay Jackson began singing at the First Baptist Church on Huron Street when he was 12 years old.[41] When family matters brought Jay back to Toronto in the 1980s, cutting his music and television career short, he took a job at the Ontario Ministry of Citizenship and Culture, and in 1985, approved an archeological dig at the former Blackburn property on the grounds of Inglenook Community School, led by historian Karolyn Smardz Frost and supported by the Toronto Board of Education. The initiative was called the Lucie and Thornton Blackburn Public Archaeology Project.

To Jay's amazement, the dig turned up several artifacts, including birth and marriage certificates linked to his own family. While there had always been stories of his great-grandmother's connection to the Blackburn family and the Underground Railroad, this dig made their association to this history tangible. Documents supporting evidence of their family's history were quite literally unearthed. "We just couldn't get over the coincidences that kept happening," Jackson has said. "A lot of it we knew orally. When you support it with documentation, it's more valid."[42] On September 15, 2020, Jay Jackson, singer, television host, and effervescent bandleader, died of congestive heart failure, age 78.[43]

Fig. 6.81 The house at 213 Brunswick Avenue after the renovation in the 1980s, now owned by book publisher Patrick Crean and author Susan Swan.

The Lucie and Thornton Blackburn Public Archaeology Project began a path for further historic research and recognition that spurred more ideas to honour Albert Jackson. In 2007, Karolyn Smardz Frost published the compelling *I've Got a Home in Glory Land: A Lost Tale of the Underground Railroad*, which painstakingly details the gripping story and context of Lucie and Thornton Blackburn's escape from the United States to Toronto via the Underground Railroad. Smardz Frost's book also reveals the previously untold account of Albert Jackson and the journey his mother took to come to Toronto with seven of her children.

In "an unusual twist of fate,"[44] the publisher of *I've Got a Home in Glory Land*, Patrick Crean, learned from Smardz Frost that Albert Jackson had once owned a house on Brunswick Avenue, and in fact, Patrick and his partner, author Susan Swan, were living in it. In the 1990s, Crean and Swan had moved into the house, which had been extensively renovated, with a second storey and rear addition added.

At the book launch for *I've Got a Home in Glory Land*, Crean was introduced to Faith Jackson, who asked Crean what number his house was. When he told her, she burst into tears and said she had raised five children there "with a lot of love." Crean responded that "Love was still there." According to Crean, it remains so — 213 Brunswick is a happy place.[45]

In 2012, Crean proposed to Toronto's City Council that a neighbourhood laneway that runs behind Brunswick Avenue be named after Albert Jackson, which was approved by the council in October of that year.[46]

The next year, in March, the Canadian Union of Postal Workers (CUPW) presented a commemorative poster to the Jackson family. Mark Brown, CUPW's Toronto regional education and organizing officer, said, "When you look at [Jackson's] story, it's not just about a struggle about the obvious: racism. It's also a struggle for dignity, respect, and

fairness in the workplace — something that not just CUPW but the labour movement fights for to this very day."[47]

After two years in the making, Heritage Toronto honoured Albert's memory in 2017 with a commemorative plaque at the former site of the Toronto Post Office on Toronto Street. At the national level, Canada Post released a commemorative stamp recognizing Albert Jackson as the first Black letter carrier in the country — a fitting tribute.[48]

As Patrick Crean has said,

> We often fail to remember heroic stories in this great country of ours. I think Albert Jackson embodied what this country is all about which is courage and persistence in the face of injustice, honourable behaviour and the rights of all citizens. He was an early pioneer in the struggle for a nation that holds pluralism and acceptance of all people as its highest virtue.[49]

Fig. 6.8m (left) Albert Jackson Lane.

Fig. 6.8n (right) Canada Post's Albert Jackson stamp.

Fig. 7.1 Heritage Roadkill:
Broadview Avenue, at
Eastern Avenue.

CONCLUSION

Why Are Modest Hopes
Important Today?

Magnificent old buildings may define our past and
new monuments may house our future, but only people
can give structure to structure. If we are to seek out a
bold and beautiful future, we must look to each other.
That's the lesson of Toronto's past.
   — Adam Vaughan, *Utopia: Towards a New Toronto*

The central theme of *Modest Hopes* is the idea that the rental
or even ownership of narrow one- and two-storey brick-and-
frame workers' cottages built from the early 19th century to the 1920s
represents an outstanding achievement at that time for all of the families
who managed to make them their homes. Examples of these houses exist
today throughout the former industrial and working-class neighbourhoods of Toronto and are a template for similar homes across Canada
in cities such as Montreal, Hamilton, Winnipeg, and Vancouver, as

well as in smaller communities across the country such as Stratford, St. Catharines, Westport, and Dundas in Ontario; St. Stephen in New Brunswick; Fort Macleod in Alberta; and Tofino in British Columbia.

When these Modest Hopes, nestled singly between their larger neighbours or in rows along inner-city streets, are encountered, they reflect a number of values and associations that make them important contributors to the quality of life and history of Toronto. Embedded in them are the stories of the thousands of immigrants who came to the city: those who fled famine and disease in Ireland; the Scottish families evicted from their homes during the Highland Clearances; the jobless victims of the Industrial Revolution's redistribution of labour; those who escaped the urban slums of the British Isles and Europe; Jewish refugees from Eastern Europe; economic migrants from Southeast and East Asia; and Black people escaping slavery in the United States. All sought better lives in Canada.

What has emerged from the study and research for this book and from the resulting close familiarity and admiration for so many of these workers' houses that have been toured, studied, and measured, and whose owners were interviewed, are some important conclusions. The following assumptions and attributes that are shared by all these houses sum up many of the reasons why Modest Hopes are valuable, why they should be preserved, and why they continue as homes for people building today's Toronto.

They represent a thematic arc connecting housing and hope: Many immigrants came from very little and were displaced peasants or serfs who farmed the estates of lords in exchange for small pieces of land to live on and grow their own food. Or they were transient labourers following jobs in towns and villages. Often they were people who raised their families in small stone, thatched-roof, rural cottages, or they were workers and tradesmen residing in one-storey rowhouses on crowded streets in towns and cities in the Old World. What connected all these various people was the shared knowledge and hope that a better life was possible for them and their families in the New World. Toronto's Modest Hopes are a reminder of the connection between housing and hope.

Their architectural and symbolic meanings have heritage value: The form, architectural style, and detailing of Modest Hopes reflect and honour their British roots, and the application of these elements was often an expression of patriotism and loyalty to the British Crown. Built by colonial carpenters and masons, these houses convey the influence and power of the British Empire and echo its imperialism in their details and styles. Their architecture is also a manifestation of the knowledge and experience of the craftsmen and builders who constructed them.

Design and construction materials reflect their social value: Logs versus planks, wooden shacks versus brick homes, small versus large, single detached versus attached doubles and rowhouses, architectural details and brick for all four sides of a complete house, or only on the front elevation — all these differences reflect cost, value, status, and an owner's income. What is important about identifying these differences is that they help us understand the socio-cultural values they represent and illustrate the story of the life/class differences of that period. The tangible, physical form of these Modest Hopes speaks to the intangible values they represented when they were constructed, which is an important part of comprehending the heritage of Toronto. What are the equivalent expressions today?

Their location reflects aspects of their intangible socio-cultural heritage: Although the built expression of these Modest Hopes is a manifestation of the socio-cultural values of Toronto, another important but elusive part of the city's narrative is about where they were actually built. The geographic location of the workers' housing within the city clearly indicates the homes' value and/or status at the time. Generally, they were sited close to the industries where their residents were employed and were often built on the least-desirable sites — low-lying, boggy land and areas generally downwind from the noxious smoke of Toronto's industries. These building sites were often underserviced by civic amenities such as paved roads, sewers, water, schools, and parks, and sometimes they were just outside the city's limits.

These small workers' cottages are not just "cute": The cuteness of these cottages helped elevate their status in the 1970s, 1980s, and 1990s so that intact enclaves in Cabbagetown, on Draper Street, and in parts of Leslieville were recognized and preserved. Besides their cuteness, a more significant and inclusive reason for their value and preservation today is to understand and recognize how important the lives were that were sheltered and contained within them. It is also essential to realize that the vast majority of Toronto's residents in the middle and late 19th and early 20th centuries, either resided in these houses or were saving in the hope that one day they and their families could live in one of them. In terms of sacrifice and achievement, the act of working and saving to finally rent or own one of these Modest Hopes reflects people's immense commitment and hope for the future.

The people who built Toronto lived in these Modest Hopes: What about all those people who weren't famous or rich? Much has been made of movie actress Mary Pickford who grew up in The Ward at University Avenue and Elm Street, or former Ontario lieutenant governor Lincoln Alexander who was raised on Draper Street. But what about those thousands who grew up in shacks and cottages in other working-class neighbourhoods and who managed to succeed as tradespeople, shopkeepers, teachers, lawyers, restaurateurs, doctors, nurses, factory workers, and even architects? These are the people who built Toronto, and the houses they lived in are the Modest Hopes celebrated in this book.

Their small size and compact form is important today: When they were built, these homes' sizes and forms were reflections of the economic and social statuses of their working-class residents or owners. But what is interesting today is that excessive private space is considered environmentally and socially unsustainable and irresponsible. As such, these Modest Hopes from the late 19th century are being validated for reasons that extend beyond their economical size and considerable but underappreciated heritage and social attributes. They are also important because they are usually well located near established schools, parks, commercial areas, and transit. Also, their "small" footprints address many people's commitment to environmental sustainability and the need for affordability.

The evolution of Modest Hopes and what it means today: As the 18th century ended, the increasing size and more elaborate architectural details of these houses reflected both the growing prosperity of the labourers who lived in them and the gentrification of working-class districts. Did the decorative bracketing, turret dormers, buff-brick quoins, and arched door and window openings raise the purchase prices and affordability of these houses? If that were so, did workers have to move out of Toronto's core to find housing more within their means? Unfortunately, this pattern continues today as the cost of urban housing, modest or otherwise, is out of the reach of so many. The preservation of Toronto's Modest Hopes can serve as a reminder that healthy communities can be inclusive and successfully combine living, working, shopping, education, and recreation for everyone.

Modest Hopes today: This book set out to describe what Toronto's Modest Hopes were like in the 1820s to the 1920s and to highlight the important role they played in fostering and supporting the families who lived in them. "Home" continues to be the dream for successive generations, but as the cost of "starter" houses in the downtowns of cities escalates and the supply of those homes decreases, where are the Modest Hopes of today? What do they look like? How big are they? What social values do they represent? What sacrifices are necessary to live in them and how do they contribute to livable, sustainable communities today?

The small cottages discussed in this book express the durable and consistent hope and belief in the ideal of family and "home and hearth." The amazing trajectory of the lives and progress of immigrants to Toronto should be contemplated and appreciated. After long and arduous journeys, they arrived in Canada with only what they could carry and then, in many cases, made their way to Toronto. After sharing a variety of crowded housing in the city's neighbourhoods of shacks and tenements, the fact that some were able to work and save enough money to move into their own house, maybe a Modest Hope, was the result of an unshakable commitment to the dream of "home" and the importance of family.

For such early Toronto workers, these rowhouses, couplets, and cottages were far from modest. They improved their lives, they were symbols of their family values, they showed the community the level of their success and social and economic advancement, and most importantly, they embodied their hopes for the future. Today, in Toronto, the traditionally long-held disdain for these "small and cramped shacks" is changing as our comprehension of the history of the people who came to Canada and built this city deepens.

The intent of *Modest Hopes* is to provide a better grasp of, and appreciation for, these houses by introducing through their stories some of the original generations who lived in them. The hope is that the narratives of their lives will help us understand more thoroughly the immense impact these people had on the Toronto we know today and shed more light on the contributions they made to the city. The ink-sketch "portraits" and photographs of some of these beautiful houses, combined with a greater validation of the houses themselves, as well as the lives lived in them, may contribute to the preservation and reuse of Modest Hopes in Toronto and across Canada in the future.

ACKNOWLEDGEMENTS

W e would like to thank our families for their support, all the people whose stories are in *Modest Hopes*, and everyone who helped us create this book. They include: Monika Ahmad, Colin Baird, Chris Bell, Murray Buchman, Dennis Chow, Patrick Crean, Dundurn Press, Joanne Doucette, Patrick Farrell, Tony Harwood-Jones, Faith Jackson, Marva Jackson, Shawne Jackson-Troiano, Zelinde Kaiser, Robert Kearns, Yew-Thong Leong, Dr. Mark McGowan, Doug McTaggart, Barb Myrvold, Marylee O'Neill (O'Connor story), Daniel Parkinson, Jacqueline Perry, Queen Alexandra Public School, Jim Retallack, Karolyn Smardz Frost, Terry Smith (Treacy story), Connor Ishiguro Turnbull, Amanda Valpy, Michael Valpy, Diane Walton, Vickie Wybo-Yuhase (O'Rourke story), and all the owners of Modest Hopes which we featured in this book.

NOTES

Introduction: Home Is Where the Heart Is

1. John Doyle, "Return to Park Ex: A Beautiful, Bittersweet Story of Urban Canada," *Globe and Mail*, October 5, 2017.
2. George H. Rust-D'Eye, *Cabbagetown Remembered* (Erin, ON: Boston Mills Press, 1984).
3. The Osterhout Log Cabin plaque reads: "The oldest building in Scarborough built in 1795 by Augustus Jones who was commissioned by John Graves Simcoe — first Lieutenant-Governor of Upper Canada — to survey Scarborough. William Osterhout later received the first crown grant of the land from King George III in 1805." Conflicting accounts claim the building was built in 1845.
4. Lombard is a short west-east street between Victoria and Jarvis Streets a block north of Adelaide Street East in downtown Toronto.
5. The boundaries of The Junction on the west side of Toronto are generally considered to be north of Annette Avenue, south of St. Clair Avenue, east of Runnymede Road, and west of Keele Street and the junction of the Canadian National and Canadian Pacific railway lines, hence its name.
6. St. John's Ward, simply The Ward, once Macaulaytown, was a downtown Toronto neighbourhood centred on the intersection of Bay (formerly Terauley) and Albert (now mostly gone) Streets, bounded by College Street to the north, Queen Street West to the south, Yonge Street to the east, and University Avenue to the west. It was once the most densely populated area of the city and home to many of Toronto's early immigrants. Almost all of The Ward's original buildings, even some of its streets, are now gone, replaced by Toronto General Hospital, Hospital for Sick Children, Nathan Phillips Square, New City Hall, and the Eaton Centre. Today, very few buildings on Dundas West and Elizabeth Streets still exist.
7. The boundaries of Cabbagetown, a central-east neighbourhood, have shifted over time. Today, it is generally considered to be bounded by Wellesley Street and Rosedale Valley Road on the

north, Shuter and Gerrard Streets on the south, Sherbourne Street on the west, and the Don River on the east. Originally, the boundaries were considered a little south: Gerrard Street to the north, Queen Street to the south, Sherbourne Street to the west, and the Don River to the east. Parliament Street remains the "main-street" hub.

8. Corktown is south of Cabbagetown and Regent Park. Its boundaries are Berkeley Street to the west, the Don River to the east, Shuter Street to the north, and Front Street East to the south.

9. Leslieville, east of the Don River, is bounded by the Canadian National Railway line and Gerrard Street to the north, Eastern Avenue to the south, Empire Avenue to the west, and Coxwell Avenue to the east.

10. Riverside, on the east side, is bounded by the Don River to the west, Gerrard Street to the north, Empire Avenue to the east, and Eastern Avenue to the south.

Chapter 1: Origins: The History and Antecedents of Workers' Housing Movements

1. Nathaniel Kent, *Hints to Gentlemen of Landed Property* (London: J. Dodsley, 1775), 230.
2. Kent, *Hints to Gentlemen of Landed Property*, 228.
3. Kent, *Hints to Gentlemen of Landed Property*, 229.
4. Kent, *Hints to Gentlemen of Landed Property*, 231.
5. Barbara Leckie, "Prince Albert's Exhibition Model Dwellings," BRANCH, April 17, 2020, branch-collective.org/?ps_articles=barbara-leckie-prince-alberts-exhibition-model-dwellings; Dino Franco Felluga, ed., "Britain, Representation, and Nineteenth-Century History," BRANCH, branchcollective.org.
6. The mansard roof allows a full floor of living space above the cornice line of a building without increasing the technical number of stories in the structure.
7. Fretwork: Ornamental interlaced work in relief.
8. See thelondonphile.com/2012/05/02/prince-alberts-model-cottages.
9. Mark Kishlansky, Patrick Geary, and Patricia O'Brien, *Civilization in the West*, 7th ed., vol. C (New York: Pearson Education, 2008).
10. Kishlansky, Geary, and O'Brien, *Civilization in the West*.
11. See "View from the Knightsbridge Road of the Crystal Palace in Hyde Park for Grand International Exhibition of 1851" (London: Read & Co. Engravers & Printers, 1851), en.wikipedia.org/wiki/The_Crystal_Palace#/media/File:The_Crystal_Palace_in_Hyde_Park_for_Grand_International_Exhibition_of_1851.jpg.
12. See mcgill.ca/mchg/pastproject/cristal.
13. "Prince Albert's Cottages," *Spectator Archives*, archive.spectator.co.uk/article/14th-june-1851/12/prince-alberts-cottages.
14. See branchcollective.org/?ps_articles=barbara-leckie-prince-alberts-exhibition-model-dwellings.

15. *Plans and Suggestions for Dwellings Adapted to the Working Classes, Including the Model Houses for Families* (London: Society for Improving the Condition of the Labouring Classes, 1884).

16. Leckie, "Prince Albert's Exhibition Model Dwellings"; Felluga, "Britain, Representation, and Nineteenth-Century History."

17. Karen Elizabeth Armstrong, "The Late Nineteenth-Century Stone Farmhouses of John Thompson Crellin," *Journal of the Society for the Study of Architecture in Canada* 43, no. 2 (2018): 27–41, erudit.org/en/journals/jssac/2018-v43-n2-jssac04441/1058037ar.pdf.

18. Jessica Mace, "Beautifying the Countryside: Rural and Vernacular Gothic in Late Nineteenth-Century Ontario," *Journal of the Society for the Study of Architecture in Canada* 38, no. 1 (2013): 29–36, dalspace.library.dal.ca/bitstream/handle/10222/65242/vol38_no1_29_36.pdf?sequenc1&isAllowed=y.

19. Mace, "Beautifying the Countryside: Rural and Vernacular Gothic in Late Nineteenth-Century Ontario," 29–36.

20. Mace, "Beautifying the Countryside: Rural and Vernacular Gothic in Late Nineteenth-Century Ontario," 29–36.

21. Armstrong, "The Late Nineteenth-Century Stone Farmhouses of John Thompson Crellin."

22. Mace, "Beautifying the Countryside, Rural and Vernacular Gothic in Late Nineteenth-Century Ontario," 29–36.

23. See archiseek.com/2017/1875-labourers-dwellings-co-mayo.

24. G.A. Dean, "Essay on Cottages," in *Essays on the Construction of Farm Buildings and Labourers' Cottages* (London: Waterlow and Sons, 1849), 2–3, 14.

25. See jamieoneill.com/atswim/resources/slums.html.

26. See census.nationalarchives.ie/exhibition/dublin/poverty_health.html.

27. See folkloreproject.ie/tenement-life.

28. See webs.bcp.org/sites/vcleary/ModernWorldHistoryTextbook/IndustrialRevolution/IREffects.html.

29. Joanne Harrison, "The Origin, Development and Decline of Back-to-Back Houses in Leeds, 1787–1937," *Industrial Archaeology Review* 39, no. 2 (2017): 101–16, doi: 10.1080/03090728.2017.1398902.

30. Geoff Timmins, "Housing Industrial Workers During the 19th Century: Back-to-Back Housing in Textile Lancashire," *Industrial Archaeology Review* 35, no. 2 (2014): 111–27.

31. Frank Murphy, "Dublin Slums in the 1930s," *Dublin Historical Record* 37, nos. 3–4 (June–September 1984), 105.

32. Kevin C. Kearns, *Dublin Tenement Life: An Oral History* (Dublin: Gill & Macmillan, 1994), 1.

33. Judith Flanders, "Slums," British Library, britishlibrary.cn/en/articles/slums.

34. *First Report of Her Majesty's Commissioners for Inquiring into the Housing of the Working Classes* (London: Eyre and Spottiswoode, 1885), 7.

35. E.P. Thompson, *The Making of the English Working Class* (London: Victor Gollancz, 1963), 267.

36. Thompson, *The Making of the English Working Class*, 267.

37. See londonist.com/2014/04/punished-for-being-poor-londons-forgotten-workhouses.

38. Thompson, *The Making of the English Working Class*, 268.

39. See webs.bcp.org/sites/vcleary/ModernWorldHistoryTextbook/IndustrialRevolution/IREffects.html.

40. Dennis J. Pogue and Douglas Sanford, "Slave Housing in Virginia," *Encyclopedia Virginia*, encyclopediavirginia.org/slave_housing_in_virginia.

41. "The Edisto Island Slave Cabin, Communities, and Collecting," National Museum of African American History & Culture, South Carolina, nmaahc.si.edu/edisto-island-slave-cabin -communities-and-collecting.

42. See flickr.com/photos/joeross/4178675841.

Chapter 2: The Architecture: Five Modest Hope House Types

1. Derek Flack, "This Is Why Some Toronto Homes Look Like Tiny Cottages," *blogTO*, blogto.com/ city/2015/12/torontos_lost_cottage_architecture_hides_in_plain_sight.

2. Flack, "This Is Why Some Toronto Homes Look Like Tiny Cottages."

3. Christine Stanshell, *City of Women: Sex and Class in New York, 1789–1860* (Urbana: University of Illinois Press, 1987), 41.

4. Christopher Alexander, *The Timeless Way of Building* (New York: Oxford University Press, 1979), 106.

5. An architectural style of the Western European Middle Ages.

6. Joanne Doucette, *Pigs, Flowers and Bricks: A History of Leslieville to 1920* (Toronto: Joanne Doucette, 2016).

7. Soldier course: where brick is set vertically in rows.

8. Blind arch: an arch in which the opening is permanently closed by wall construction.

9. *Globe*, March 16, 1883; *Globe*, July 14, 1871; *Toronto Daily Mail*, July 20, 1882; *Globe*, August 21, 1880; *Toronto Daily Mail*, July 24, 1882; *Globe*, July 22, 1882.

10. "Arrest of Supposed Fenians: The President and Secretary of the Hibernian ..." *Globe*, May 6, 1868.

11. Mark McGowan, "Boyle, Patrick," *Dictionary of Canadian Biography*, biographi.ca/en/bio /boyle_patrick_13E.html.

Chapter 3: The Newcomers: Early Immigrants to Toronto Who Built and Lived in Modest Hopes

1. Robert F. Harney and Harold Troper, *Immigrants: A Portrait of the Urban Experience, 1890-1930* (Toronto: Van Nostrand Reinhold, 1975).

2. Patrick A. Dunae and George Woodcock, "English Canadians," *The Canadian Encyclopedia*, thecanadianencyclopedia.ca/en/article/english.

3. Dunae and Woodcock, "English Canadians."

4. Dunae and Woodcock, "English Canadians."

5. See leslievillehistory.com/the-great-shacktown-crisis.

6. Dunae and Woodcock, "English Canadians."

7. Censuses of Canada, 1901 and 1911, mdl.library.utoronto.ca/collections/numeric-data/census -canada/1901, mdl.library.utoronto.ca/collections/numeric-data/census-canada/1911.

8. Allan Levine, *Toronto: Biography of a City* (Toronto: Douglas & McIntyre, 2013), 122–23.

9. As quoted in Levine, *Toronto: Biography of a City*, 123.

10. Levine, *Toronto: Biography of a City*, 123.

11. Dunae and Woodcock, "English Canadians."

12. J.M. Bumsted, *The Scots in Canada* (Ottawa: Canadian Historical Association, 1982), 5–6.

13. J.M. Bumsted, "Scottish Canadians," *The Canadian Encyclopedia*, thecanadianencyclopedia.ca/en/article/scots.

14. Bumsted, "Scottish Canadians."

15. Bumsted, *The Scots in Canada*, 7.

16. "Highland Clearances," *Encyclopaedia Britannica*, britannica.com/event/Highland-Clearances.

17. "Highland Clearances," *Encyclopaedia Britannica*.

18. "Highland Clearances," *Encyclopaedia Britannica*.

19. Bumsted, *The Scots in Canada*, 11.

20. Bumsted, *The Scots in Canada*, 11.

21. "Scottish Genealogy and Family History," Library and Archives Canada, bac-lac.gc.ca/eng/discover /immigration/history-ethnic-cultural/Pages/scottish.aspx.

22. Bumsted, *The Scots in Canada*, 13.

23. Bumsted, *The Scots in Canada*, 10–11.

24. Censuses of Canada, 1901 and 1921, bac-lac.gc.ca, mdl.library.utoronto.ca/collections/numeric -data/census-canada/1921.

25. Dunae and Woodcock, "English Canadians."

26. See irelandparkfoundation.com/great-famine-history.

27. See irelandparkfoundation.com/great-famine-history/?doing_wp_cron=1600998299.551825046539 3066406250.

28. Kerby A. Miller, *Emigrants and Exiles: Ireland and the Irish Exodus to North America* (New York: Oxford University Press, 1985), 103.

29. Miller, *Emigrants and Exiles*, 103.

30. Mark G. McGowan, *Death or Canada: The Irish Migration to Toronto, 1847* (Toronto: Novalis, 2009), Introduction.

31. Mark G. McGowan, "Famine, Facts and Fabrication: An Examination of Diaries from the Irish Famine Migration to Canada," *The Canadian Journal of Irish Studies* 33, no 2 (Fall 2007): 48.

32. McGowan, *Death or Canada*.

33. John Crowley, William J. Smyth, and Mike Murphy, *Atlas of the Great Irish Famine* (Cork: University College Cork, 2012).

34. Crowley, Smyth, and Murphy, *Atlas of the Great Irish Famine.*

35. William Jenkins, "Poverty and Place: Documenting and Representing Toronto's Catholic Irish, 1845–1890," in *At the Anvil: Essays in Honour of William J. Smyth*, eds., Patrick J. Duffy and William Nolan (Dublin: Geography Publications, 2012), 477.

36. McGowan, "Famine, Facts and Fabrication," 49.

37. Reverend John O'Hanlon, *The Irish Emigrant's Guide for the United States* (Boston: Patrick Donahoe, 1851), 33.

38. O'Hanlon, *The Irish Emigrant's Guide for the United States.*

39. McGowan, "Famine, Facts and Fabrication," 49.

40. Brian Murphy with Toula Vlahou, *Adrift: A True Story of Tragedy on the Icy Atlantic and the One Who Lived to Tell About It* (New York: Da Capo Press, 2018), 68.

41. Mark G. McGowan and Michael Chard, "Great Famine History," Canada Ireland Foundation, irelandparkfoundation.com/great-famine-history.

42. Jenkins, "Poverty and Place," 493.

43. Eric Andrew-Gee, "19th-Century Toronto Irish Immigrants a Lesson in Upward Mobility," *Toronto Star*, March 14, 2015, thestar.com/news/gta/2015/03/14/19th-century-toronto-irish-immigrants-a-lesson-in-upward-mobility.html.

44. See canada.ca/en/immigration-refugees-citizenship/services/refugees/canada-role/timeline.html.

45. See canada.ca/en/immigration-refugees-citizenship/services/refugees/canada-role/timeline.html.

46. Levine, *Toronto: Biography of a City*, 121.

47. See canada.ca/en/immigration-refugees-citizenship/services/refugees/canada-role/timeline.html.

48. See canada.ca/en/immigration-refugees-citizenship/services/refugees/canada-role/timeline.html.

49. Levine, *Toronto: Biography of a City*, 120.

50. Levine, *Toronto: Biography of a City*, 122.

51. See thecanadianencyclopedia.ca/en/timeline/black-history.

52. See thecanadianencyclopedia.ca/en/timeline/black-history.

53. *An Autobiography of the Rev. Josiah Henson: (Mrs. Harriet Beecher Stowe's "Uncle Tom") from 1789 to 1876* (London: Christian Age, 1876), 23.

54. Debra Thompson, "My Black Ancestors Fled America for Freedom …" *Globe and Mail*, June 5, 2020, theglobeandmail.com/opinion/article-my-black-ancestors-fled-america-for-freedom-i-left-canada-to-find-a.

55. Anne Milan and Kelly Tran, "Blacks in History: A Long History," www150.statcan.gc.ca/n1/en/pub/11-008-x/2003004/article/6802-eng.pdf?st=lDAACQdo

56. Arlene Chan, *The Chinese in Toronto from 1878: From Outside to Inside the Circle* (Toronto: Dundurn Press, 2011), 17.

57. See bac-lac.gc.ca/eng/discover/immigration/history-ethnic-cultural/early-chinese-canadians/Pages /history.aspx#whyb2.

58. Chan, *The Chinese in Toronto from 1878*, 17.

59. See gov.bc.ca/gov/content/governments/multiculturalism-anti-racism/chinese-legacy-bc/history /building-the-railway.

60. See sfu.ca/chinese-canadian-history/chart_en.html#.

61. See sfu.ca/chinese-canadian-history/chart_en.html#.

62. See sfu.ca/chinese-canadian-history/chart_en.html#.

Chapter 4: Toronto: 1820–1920

1. See blogto.com/city/2015/12/torontos_lost_cottage_architecture_hides_in_plain_sight.

2. March Street was renamed Stanley Street in 1850, then became Lombard Street in the 1880s.

3. Dummer Street was renamed William Street, then became St. Patrick Street.

4. See cabbagetownpa.ca/heritage/architectural-styles.

5. Christine Stansell, *City of Women: Sex and Class in New York, 1789–1860* (Urbana: University of Illinois Press, 1987), 41.

6. Stansell, *City of Women*, 41.

7. Derek Hayes, *Historical Atlas of Toronto* (Vancouver: Douglas & McIntyre, 2009), 6.

8. Carl Benn, "First Peoples, 9000 BCE to 1600 CE," *The History of Toronto: An 11,000-Year Journey*, toronto.ca/explore-enjoy/history-art-culture/museums/virtual-exhibits/history-of-toronto /first-peoples-9000-bce-to-1600-ce.

9. C.E. Heidenreich, "Huron-Wendat," *The Canadian Encyclopedia*, thecanadianencyclopedia.ca/en/article/huron.

10. Carl Benn, "Natives and Newcomers, 1600–1793," *The History of Toronto: An 11,000-Year Journey*, toronto.ca/explore-enjoy/history-art-culture/museums/virtual-exhibits/history-of-toronto/ natives-and-newcomers-1600-1793.

11. J.M.S. Careless, "Toronto," *The Canadian Encyclopedia*, thecanadianencyclopedia.ca/en/article/toronto.

12. Levine, *Toronto: Biography of a City*, 13–15.

13. See torontopubliclibrary.typepad.com/local-history-genealogy/2018/06/remembering-the-toronto -purchase-and-its-settlement-june-8-snapshots-in-history.html.

14. Douglas Laforme, "What Could Canada Have Been If the Treaty Process Was Fair? *Torontoist*, June 7, 2017, torontoist.com/2017/06/canada-treaty-process-fair.

15. "The Toronto Purchase — Contg. 250,880 Acres," Toronto Public Library, torontopubliclibrary.ca /detail.jsp?Entt=RDMDC-MAPS-R-140&R=DC-MAPS-R-140.

16. Levine, *Toronto: Biography of a City*, 25.

17. Levine, *Toronto: Biography of a City*, 25.

18. Eric Arthur, *Toronto, No Mean City*, 3rd ed., rev. Stephen A. Otto (Toronto: University of Toronto Press, 2003), 16–17.

19. Levine, *Toronto: Biography of a City*, 27.

20. Robert M. MacIntosh, *Earliest Toronto* (Renfrew, ON: General Store, 2006).

21. MacIntosh, *Earliest Toronto*.

22. Levine, *Toronto: Biography of a City*, 32.

23. Levine, *Toronto: Biography of a City*, 28.

24. Edith G. Firth, ed., *The Town of York 1793–1815: A Collection of Documents of Early Toronto* (Toronto: Champlain Society/University of Toronto Press, 1962), xlix.

25. Careless, "Toronto."

26. James H. Marsh and Pierre Berton, "War of 1812," *The Canadian Encyclopedia*, thecanadianencyclopedia.ca/en/article/war-of-1812.

27. Antonio S. Thompson and Christos G. Frentzos, eds., *The Routledge Handbook of American Military and Diplomatic History: The Colonial Period to 1877* (New York: Routledge, 2015), 196.

28. Levine, *Toronto: Biography of a City*, 40.

29. See opentextbc.ca/preconfederation/chapter/10-3-immigration.

30. Levine, *Toronto: Biography of a City*, 45.

31. Levine, *Toronto: Biography of a City*, 44–45.

32. Marian A. Patterson, "The Cholera Epidemic of 1832 in York, Upper Canada," *Bulletin of the Medical Library Association* 46, no. 2 (April 1958): 165–84. ncbi.nlm.nih.gov/pmc/articles/PMC233409/pdf/mlab00208-1001.pdf.

33. Levine, *Toronto: Biography of a City*, 45.

34. Levine, *Toronto: Biography of a City*, 45.

35. Levine, *Toronto: Biography of a City*, 51.

36. McGowan, "Famine, Facts and Fabrication," 48.

37. McGowan, *Death or Canada*, Chapter 2.

38. McGowan, "Famine, Facts and Fabrication," 49.

39. McGowan, *Death or Canada*, Introduction.

40. Mark McGowan, *Creating Canadian Historical Memory: The Case for the Famine Migration of 1847* (Ottawa: Canadian Historical Association, 2006), 4, cha-shc.ca/_uploads/5c374f5883075.pdf.

41. McGowan, *Death or Canada*, Chapter 3.

42. See irelandparkfoundation.com/great-famine-history.

43. McGowan, *Death or Canada*, Introduction.

44. Jenkins, "Poverty and Place."

45. As quoted in Levine, *Toronto: Biography of a City*, 75.

46. See irishtocanada.com/canada-s-irish-immigrants.

47. Canada Census, 1851, bac-lac.gc.ca/eng/census/1851/Pages/about-census.aspx.

48. Canada Census, 1871, bac-lac.gc.ca/eng/census/1871/Pages/about-census.aspx.

49. Levine, *Toronto: Biography of a City*, 73.

50. Levine, *Toronto: Biography of a City*, 69.

51. Levine, *Toronto: Biography of a City*, 80.

52. Levine, *Toronto: Biography of a City*, 83.

53. As quoted in Levine, *Toronto: Biography of a City*, 83.

54. See toronto.ca/explore-enjoy/history-art-culture/black-history-month/the-black-community-in-st -johns-ward.

55. Julia Roberts, *In Mixed Company: Taverns and Public Life in Upper Canada* (Vancouver: University of British Columbia Press, 2009), 108–9.

56. Kristin McLaren, "'We Had No Desire to Be Set Apart': Forced Segregation of Black Students in Canada West Public Schools and Myths of British Egalitarianism," *Social History* 37, no. 73 (2004): 28, hssh.journals.yorku.ca/index.php/hssh/article/view/4373/3571.

57. See toronto.ca/explore-enjoy/history-art-culture/black-history-month/the-black-community-in-st -johns-ward.

58. See thestar.com/life/2018/02/01/first-census-of-torontos-black-population-in-1840-counted-525 -people.html.

59. "The Census of Toronto," *Globe*, October 15, 1856.

60. Benjamin Drew, *The Refugee, or, the Narratives of Fugitive Slaves in Canada* (Boston: J.P. Jewett and Company, 1856), 112.

61. Arthur, *Toronto, No Mean City*, 226.

62. Levine, *Toronto: Biography of a City*, 69.

63. Levine, *Toronto: Biography of a City*, 72.

64. United Empire Loyalists' Association of Canada, *Loyal She Remains: A Pictorial History of Ontario* (Toronto: United Empire Loyalists' Association of Canada, 1984), 336.

65. United Empire Loyalists' Association of Canada, *Loyal She Remains*, 348.

66. United Empire Loyalists' Association of Canada, *Loyal She Remains*, 348.

67. Careless, "Toronto."

68. As quoted in Levine, *Toronto: Biography of a City*, 85.

69. William Kilbourn, *Toronto Remembered: A Celebration of the City* (Toronto: Stoddart, 1984), 110.

70. Bill Rawling, "Technology and Innovation in the Toronto Police Force, 1875–1925," *Ontario History* 80, no. 1 (March 1988): 53–71.

71. Careless, "Toronto."

72. Bryan D. Palmer and Gaétan Héroux, *Toronto's Poor: A Rebellious History* (Between the Lines, 2016), 41.

73. Mark G. McGowan, *The Waning of the Green: Catholics, the Irish, and Identity in Toronto, 1887–1922* (Montreal: McGill-Queen's University Press, 1999).

74. Chan, *The Chinese in Toronto from 1878*, 17.

75. Chan, *The Chinese in Toronto from 1878*, 40.

76. See bac-lac.gc.ca/eng/discover/immigration/history-ethnic-cultural/early-chinese-canadians/Pages /history.aspx#ac1.

77. Franc Sturino, *Forging the Chain: A Case Study of Italian Migration to North America, 1880–1930* (Toronto: Multicultural History Society of Ontario, 1990), 168.

78. Careless, "Toronto."

Chapter 5: The Neighbourhoods: A Selection of Historic Toronto Areas Where Modest Hopes Were Concentrated

1. "Once Upon a City: Poor House Helped Toronto's Destitute," *Toronto Star*, spon.ca/once -upon-a-city-poor-house-helped-torontos-destitute/2017/08/27.

2. *Globe*, October 27, 1849.

3. Jenkins, *Poverty and Place*, 488.

4. See onegalstoronto.wordpress.com/2017/02/11/by-any-other-name.

5. City of Toronto Council Minutes, April 22, 1850, Item 248, City of Toronto Archives.

6. See onegalstoronto.wordpress.com/2017/02/11/by-any-other-name.

7. Levine, *Toronto: Biography of a City*, 77.

8. See onegalstoronto.wordpress.com/2017/02/11/by-any-other-name.

9. See onegalstoronto.wordpress.com/2017/02/11/by-any-other-name.

10. See torontoist.com/2017/09/walking-the-ward.

11. See torontoist.com/2017/09/walking-the-ward.

12. Holly Martelle, Michael McClelland, Tatum Taylor, and John Lorinc, eds., *The Ward Uncovered: The Archaeology of Everyday Life* (Toronto: Coach House Press, 2018), 19.

13. Levine, *Toronto: Biography of a City*, 79.

14. See thestar.com/life/2018/02/01/first-census-of-torontos-black-population-in-1840-counted-525 -people.html.

15. John Lorinc, Michael McClelland, Ellen Scheinberg, and Tatum Taylor, eds., *The Ward: The Life and Loss of Toronto's First Immigrant Neighbourhood* (Toronto: Coach House Press, 2015), 35.

16. Lorinc, McClelland, Scheinberg, and Taylor, *The Ward*, 240.

17. Lorinc, McClelland, Scheinberg, and Taylor, *The Ward*, 34–35.

18. Lorinc, McClelland, Scheinberg, and Taylor, *The Ward*, 34–35.

19. Martelle, McClelland, Taylor, and Lorinc, *The Ward Uncovered*, 20.

20. Reverend H.S. Magee, *The Christian Guardian*, 1911, as quoted in Levine, *Toronto: Biography of a City*, 123.

21. Lorinc, McClelland, Scheinberg, and Taylor, *The Ward*, 35.

22. Lorinc, McClelland, Scheinberg, and Taylor, *The Ward*, 91.

23. *Toronto Daily Star*, July 11, 1911.

24. Levine, *Toronto: Biography of a City*, 126.

25. See thestar.com/yourtoronto/once-upon-a-city-archives/2017/08/27/once-upon-a-city-poor -house-created-to-help-torontos-destitute.html.

26. Lucille H. Campey, *Ontario and Quebec's Irish Pioneers: Farmers, Labourers, and Lumberjacks* (Toronto: Dundurn Press, 2018), 149.

27. Coralina R. Lemos, *Corktown: The History of a Toronto Neighbourhood and the People Who Made It* (Toronto: Coralina R. Lemos, 2018), 27.

28. See cbc.ca/news/canada/toronto/graves-discovered-beneath-downtown-elementary-school-mean -no-expansion-1.3962758.

29. See theglobeandmail.com/news/toronto/regent-park-a-look-back-through-the-years-at-canadas -oldest-social-housing-project/ article27612426.

30. Colleen Kelly, *Cabbagetown in Pictures* (Toronto: Toronto Public Library Board, 1984), 3.

31. Kelly, *Cabbagetown in Pictures*, 3.

32. Kelly, *Cabbagetown in Pictures*, 3.

33. See lostrivers.ca/points/donvalehs.htm.

34. J.M.S. Careless, *Careless at Work: Selected Canadian Historical Studies* (Toronto: Dundurn Press, 1990), 309.

35. See ipfdev.develops.technology/architectural-heritage-exhibition/5-preserved-histories.

36. See ipfdev.develops.technology/architectural-heritage-exhibition/5-preserved-histories.

37. See ipfdev.develops.technology/architectural-heritage-exhibition/5-preserved-histories.

38. See ipfdev.develops.technology/architectural-heritage-exhibition/5-preserved-histories.

39. See cabbagetownpa.ca/ufaqs/workers-cottage.

40. See cabbagetownpa.ca/ufaqs/from-prosperity-to-decline.

41. See theglobeandmail.com/news/toronto/regent-park-a-look-back-through-the-years-at-canadas -oldest-social-housing-project/article27612426.

42. See torontopubliclibrary.ca/detail.jsp?Entt=RDMDC-PICTURES-R-1201&R=DC -PICTURES-R-1201.

43. See leslievillehistory.com/2017/12.

44. Doucette, *Pigs, Flowers and Bricks*, 30.

45. Doucette, *Pigs, Flowers and Bricks*, 32.

46. Doucette, *Pigs, Flowers and Bricks*, 32.

47. See the 1861 Canada Census, bac-lac.gc.ca/eng/census/1861/Pages/about-census.aspx.

48. *Mitchell & Co.'s General Directory for the City of Toronto and Gazetteer of the Counties of York and Peel* (Toronto: Mitchell & Co., 1866).

49. Doucette, *Pigs, Flowers and Bricks*, 18.

50. Doucette, *Pigs, Flowers and Bricks*, 18.

51. Doucette, *Pigs, Flowers and Bricks*, 47.

52. Doucette, *Pigs, Flowers and Bricks*, 75.

53. Doucette, *Pigs, Flowers and Bricks*, 141, 144.

54. Doucette, *Pigs, Flowers and Bricks*, 144.

55. See 1901 Canada Census, bac-lac.gc.ca/eng/census/1901/Pages/about-census.aspx.

Chapter 6: The Stories: Portraits of the People and Their Modest Hopes Homes

BRIDGET ANN TREACY McTAGUE (1840–1924)

1. There are differing spellings of her name in records: Tracey, Tracy, or Treacy.

2. See irelandparkfoundation.com/great-famine-history.

3. McGowan, *Creating Canadian Historical Memory*, 2.

4. McGowan, "Famine, Facts and Fabrication," 48.

5. McGowan, "Famine, Facts and Fabrication," 48.

6. McGowan, *Creating Canadian Historical Memory*, 4.

7. See irelandparkfoundation.com/great-famine-history.

8. Leslie Scrivener, "Remnants of Toronto's History," *Toronto Star*, March 11, 2007.

9. See irelandparkfoundation.com/great-famine-history.

MURRAY BUCHMAN (1923–)

1. There are various spellings of the surname Haimovitch. The name is derived from Yiddish in which it was spelled Chaimovich — *Chaim* is a given name, *ovich* means "the son of." Murray Buchman's recollection is that the name was spelled interchangeably Haimovich and Haimovitch. In the *Toronto Directories*, the name is spelled Helmowich, Heimowich, Himowitch, Haimovitch, et cetera. For this story, we have spelled it Haimovitch, since that is the one on the gravestones of Harry and Hannah.

SAM CHING AND DENNIS CHOW

1. Jan Wong, "'No Tickee' No More," *Globe and Mail*, June 30, 2001, theglobeandmail
.com/incoming/no-tickee-no-more/article4149856.

2. See sfu.ca/chinese-canadian-history/chart_en.html.

3. See gov.bc.ca/gov/content/governments/multiculturalism-anti-racism/chinese-legacy-bc/history
/building-the-railway.

4. See sfu.ca/chinese-canadian-history/chart_en.html#.

5. See sfu.ca/chinese-canadian-history/chart_en.html#.

6. Chan, *The Chinese in Toronto from 1878*, 21–22.

7. See sfu.ca/chinese-canadian-history/chart_en.html.

8. Wong, "'No Tickee' No More."

9. See countercultures.net/design/portfolio-item/the-hand-laundry-a-chinese-legacy-2.

10. Chan, *The Chinese in Toronto from 1878*, 24.

11. According to the 1881 Canada Census, bac-lac.gc.ca/eng/census/1881/Pages/about-census.aspx.

12. The listing first appears in the 1878 *Toronto Directory*, static.torontopubliclibrary.ca/da/pdfs /758720002.pdf.

13. Chan, *The Chinese in Toronto from 1878*, 40.

14. See bac-lac.gc.ca/eng/discover/immigration/history-ethnic-cultural/early-chinese-canadians/Pages /history.aspx#ac1.

15. "Chinamen in Toronto: Extraordinary Funeral at the Necropolis," *Globe*, October 25, 1877.

16. Death certificate, "Deaths in York," 1877.

17. See mhso.ca/ggp/Polyphony/ChineseLaundries.html.

18. Chan, *The Chinese in Toronto from 1878*, 23.

19. See mhso.ca/ggp/Polyphony/ChineseLaundries.html.

20. Based on a phone interview with Dennis Chow, September 19, 2020.

21. See mhso.ca/ggp/Polyphony/ChineseLaundries.html.

22. Dora Nipp, "The Chinese in Toronto," in *Gathering Place: Peoples and Neighbourhoods of Toronto, 1834–1945*, ed. Robert F. Harney (Toronto: Multicultural Society of Ontario, 1985), 149.

23. See mhso.ca/ggp/Polyphony/ChineseLaundries.html.

24. Chan, *The Chinese in Toronto from 1878*, 41.

25. See mhso.ca/ggp/Polyphony/ChineseLaundries.html.

26. See leslievillehistory.com/2017/09/25/chinese-immigrants-the-old-east-end.

27. The 1911 Canada Census, bac-lac.gc.ca/eng/census/1911/Pages/about-census.aspx.

28. See torontoist.com/2016/02/shaping-toronto-chinatowns.

29. Chan, *The Chinese in Toronto from 1878*, 32.

30. Wong, "'No Tickee' No More."

31. Telephone conversation with Dennis Chow, September 18, 2020.

32. Wong, "'No Tickee' No More."

33. Wong, "'No Tickee' No More."

34. Wong, "'No Tickee' No More."

35. Wong, "'No Tickee' No More."

WILLIAM JOSEPH O'CONNOR (1862–1892)

1. Goca Lebl, *Don Rowing Club: The First 140 Years* (Toronto: Don Rowing Club, 2020), 21.

2. From email correspondence with Marylee O'Neill, William J. O'Connor's great-grand-niece.

3. From email correspondence with Marylee O'Neill, William J. O'Connor's great-grand-niece.

4. See jpeg2000.eloquent-systems.com/toronto.html?image=s0726\s0726_it0005 .jp2#xd_co_f=MTc1MGViMTktMTQ0ZS00YjY3LWI1YzgtMmMxNDZlNGU5NDBh-.

5. See the 1862 *Toronto Directory*, static.torontopubliclibrary.ca/da/pdfs/1363386.pdf.

6. Toronto Historical Association, *A Glimpse of Toronto's History: Opportunities for the Commemoration of Lost Historical Sites* (Toronto: City Planning Division/Urban Development Services, 2001); troymedia.com/business/a-brief-history-of-canadian-meat-processing. Built in 1879, at one time,

the William Davies Company was the largest pork packer in Canada. It is now known around the world as Maple Leaf Foods.

7. See maps.library.utoronto.ca/dvhmp/davies.html.

8. See gencat4.eloquent-systems.com/webcat/systems/toronto.arch/resource/fo1244/f1244_it0371.jpg.

9. Mike Filey, "Within the Hallowed Walls of Old St. Michael's Cemetery," *The Catholic Register*, 1992.

10. See cbc.ca/sportslongform/entry/the-scandalous-sculler-150-years-ago-ned-hanlan-canada-first -superstar.

11. Lebl, *Don Rowing Club*, 16.

12. See leslievillehistory.com/timeline-ashbridges-bay/#_ftn71.

13. Captain Thomas Blackwell, "The Rowing Clubs of Canada," *Outing: An Illustrated Monthly Magazine of Sport, Travel, and Recreation* 18 (April–September 1891), 245.

14. Lebl, *Don Rowing Club*, 16.

15. See archive.org/stream/stpaulsparish00kelluoft/stpaulsparish00kelluoft_djvu.txt.

16. See biographi.ca/en/bio/o_connor_william_joseph_12E.html.

17. Lebl, *Don Rowing Club*, 21.

18. "The Late Champion Oarsman of America," *The Illustrated American*, vol. 12 (New York: Illustrated American Publishing Company, 1892), books.google.ca/books?id=rHRNAAAAYAAJ.

19. Lemos, *Corktown*, 117.

20. See biographi.ca/en/bio/o_connor_william_joseph_12E.html.

21. Lemos, *Corktown*, 117.

22. "With Heart and Hand," *Globe*, December 4, 1888, 3.

23. *New York Times*, November 13, 1889.

24. "Knows No Champion: King Death Conquers Our Famous Oarsman," *Globe*, November 24, 1892.

25. Lebl, *Don Rowing Club*, 24.

26. See biographi.ca/en/bio/o_connor_william_joseph_12E.html.

27. *Globe*, June 23, 1890.

28. See biographi.ca/en/bio/o_connor_william_joseph_12E.html.

29. "William as a Walker," *Globe*, December 10, 1891.

30. Lemos, *Corktown*, 119.

31. Lebl, *Don Rowing Club*, 23.

32. *Globe*, November 24, 1892.

33. See biographi.ca/en/bio/o_connor_william_joseph_12E.html.

34. "The Oarsman at Rest," *Globe*, November 28, 1892.

35. Lebl, *Don Rowing Club*, 21.

36. See evanescenttoronto.wordpress.com/tag/sackville-street-public-school.

37. From email correspondence with Marylee O'Neill, William O'Connor's great-grand-niece.

38. *Globe*, November 24, 1892.

THOMAS T. FERGUSON (1893–1918)

1.   The 1851 Scotland Census, nrscotland.gov.uk/research/guides/census-records/1851-census.
2.   Marjory Harper, "Enticing the Emigrant: Canadian Agents in Ireland and Scotland, c. 1870–c. 1920," *Scottish Historical Review* 83, no. 1 (2004): 41–58.
3.   The 1894 *Toronto Directory*, static.torontopubliclibrary.ca/da/pdfs/tcd1894.pdf.
4.   See torontoist.com/2010/01/historicist_a_business_quartet.
5.   *Globe*, March 16, 1883; *Globe*, July 14, 1871; *Toronto Daily Mail*, July 20, 1882; *Globe*, August 21, 1880; *Toronto Daily Mail*, July 24, 1882; *Globe*, July 22, 1882.
6.   See ancestry.ca/family-tree/person/tree/491063/person/6112318852/gallery.
7.   David Frum, "The Lessons of the Somme," *The Atlantic*, July 1, 2016, theatlantic.com /international/archive/2016/07/somme-centennial/489656.

ANNE O'ROURKE (CIRCA 1820–1891)

1.   Some references call her Anna or Ann.
2.   Tracking down the O'Rourke name in Toronto's directories is difficult. Various spellings of the O'Rourke name include Rourke, Rorke, Roark, Rourk, and finally O'Rourke.
3.   Costigan is sometimes spelled "Castigan" in Toronto's directories and Canada Censuses.
4.   See biographi.ca/en/bio/gooderham_william_1790_1881_11E.html.
5.   See maps.library.utoronto.ca/dvhmp/gooderham-dis.html.
6.   Levine, *Toronto: Biography of a City*, 72.
7.   This is an educated guess based on the 1871 Canada Census, bac-lac.gc.ca/eng/census/1871/Pages /about-census.aspx.
8.   The 1871 Canada Census, bac-lac.gc.ca/eng/census/1871/Pages/about-census.asp.
9.   See blogto.com/city/2014/04/why_did_bright_street_get_so_bent.
10 . *Globe*, May 28, 1875.

THE MOORE FAMILY

1.   See blogto.com/city/2014/02/is_craven_road_the_weirdest_street_in_toronto.
2.   The 1911 and 1921 Canada Censuses, bac-lac.gc.ca/eng/census/1911/Pages/about-census.aspx and bac-lac.gc.ca/eng/census/1921/Pages/introduction.aspx. Also ship passenger lists sourced through ancestry.ca.
3.   The address is listed on Edward Arthur Moore's baptism record.
4.   The address is listed on baptismal records of Philip John Moore and Herbert Walter Moore.
5.   The address is listed in Eardley Road School records.
6.   See ancestry.ca/family-tree/person/tree/72954510/person/400068942357/facts.
7.   See leslievillehistory.com/the-great-shacktown-crisis.
8.   *Toronto Daily Star*, October 4, 1907.
9.   See leslievillehistory.com/the-great-shacktown-crisis.

10. The 1911 and 1921 Canada Censuses, bac-lac.gc.ca/eng/census/1911/Pages/about-census.aspx and bac-lac.gc.ca/eng/census/1921/Pages/introduction.aspx. Also ship passenger lists sourced through ancestry.ca.

11. See leslievillehistory.com/2016/05/08/the-fence.

12. See leslievillehistory.com/2016/05/08/the-fence.

13. See leslievillehistory.com/2016/05/08/the-fence.

14. See torontoplaques.com/Pages/Roden_Public_School.htm.

15. leslievillehistory.com/craven-rd-fence.

16. *Toronto Star*, December 16, 1911.

17. *Toronto Star*, October 2, 1912.

18. See leslievillehistory.com/craven-rd-fence.

19. See leslievillehistory.com/craven-rd-fence.

20. George Moore's obituary, *Globe*, July 6, 1916.

21. See leslievillehistory.com/craven-rd-fence.

22. George Moore's obituary, *Globe*, July 6, 1916.

23. Herbert Walter Moore's Attestation Papers.

24. First World War Attestation Papers for Philip John Moore.

25. See blogto.com/city/2014/02/is_craven_road_the_weirdest_street_in_toronto.

26. Herbert Walter Moore obituary, *Toronto Daily Star*, August 28, 1917.

ALBERT JACKSON (1857–1918)

1. See ronfanfair.com/home/2016/12/25/laneway-honours-torontos-first-black-postman.

2. See omeka.tplcs.ca/virtual-exhibits/exhibits/show/freedom-city/stories-of-freedom.

3. Natasha L. Henry, "Chloe Cooley and the Act to Limit Slavery in Upper Canada," *The Canadian Encyclopedia*, thecanadianencyclopedia.ca/en/article/chloe-cooley-and-the-act-to-limit-slavery-in-upper-canada.

4. Robin Winks, *The Blacks in Canada: A History*, 2nd ed. (Montreal: McGill-Queen's University Press, 1997), 110–11.

5. See thecanadianencyclopedia.ca/en/collection/black-history-in-canada?id=194&themeid=9.

6. Lorinc, McClelland, Scheinberg, and Taylor, *The Ward*, 66–70.

7. The African Methodist Church on the north side of Richmond Street, just east of York Street, was located at what is now the south driveway entrance of the Sheraton Hotel.

8. See thespec.com/news/ontario/2016/02/15/landmark-church-with-ties-to-underground-railroad-unearthed-in-toronto.html.

9. See the Toronto Public Library's "Freedom City" exhibit, omeka.tplcs.ca/virtual-exhibits/exhibits/show/freedom-city/stories-of-freedom.

10. *Globe*, October 10, 1856.

11. The 1861 Canada Census, bac-lac.gc.ca/eng/census/1861/Pages/about-census.aspx.

12. *Globe*, October 15, 1856.

13. John Lorinc, "The Black Community in St. John's Ward: An Essay Marking Black History Month in the City of Toronto," February 2017, toronto.ca/explore-enjoy/history-art-culture /black-history-month/the-black-community-in-st-johns-ward.

14. See omeka.tplcs.ca/virtual-exhibits/exhibits/show/freedom-city/stories-of-freedom.

15. See omeka.tplcs.ca/virtual-exhibits/exhibits/show/freedom-city/stories-of-freedom.

16. See lostrivers.ca/points/blackburn.htm.

17. Karolyn Smardz Frost, *I've Got a Home in Glory Land: A Lost Tale of the Underground Railroad* (Toronto: Thomas Allen, 2007), 301.

18. See tubman.info.yorku.ca/educational-resources/breaking-the-chains/toronto/ann-maria-jackson.

19. See tubman.info.yorku.ca/educational-resources/breaking-the-chains/toronto/ann-maria-jackson.

20. Smardz Frost, *I've Got a Home in Glory Land*, 301.

21. See canadianstampnews.com/family-cheers-stamp-honouring-likely -first-black-canadian-letter-carrier.

22. The 1861 Canada Census and Goad's Insurance Plan for 1880, bac-lac.gc.ca/eng/census/1861 /Pages/about-census.aspx and static.torontopubliclibrary.ca/da/pdfs/37131055452510d.pdf.

23. Douglas Bristol Jr., "From Outposts to Enclaves: A Social History of Black Barbers from 1750 to 1915," *Enterprise & Society* 5, no. 4 (December 2004): 594–606.

24. *Toronto World*, June 3, 1885.

25. See toronto.ca/explore-enjoy/history-art-culture/black-history-month/the-black-community -in-st-johns-ward.

26. *Globe*, October 6, 1892.

27. Colin McFarquhar, "Blacks in 1880s Toronto: The Search for Equality," *Ontario History* 99, no. 1 (Spring 2007): 66, erudit.org/en/journals/onhistory/2007-v99-n1-onhistory04967/1065797ar.pdf.

28. McFarquhar, "Blacks in 1880s Toronto," 64–76.

29. McFarquhar, "Blacks in 1880s Toronto," 64–76.

30. See memorialogy.com/pages/entries/entries.php?post=n137.

31. McFarquhar, "Blacks in 1880s Toronto," 64–76.

32. Smardz Frost, *I've Got a Home in Glory Land*, 334.

33. *Toronto World*, June 3, 1885.

34. See ronfanfair.com/home/2016/12/25/laneway-honours-torontos-first-black-postman.

35. Details noted from a conversation with Faith Jackson, January 2021.

36. Based on email correspondence with Marva Jackson, Albert and Henrietta's great-granddaughter.

37. Based on email correspondence with Marva Jackson, Albert and Henrietta's great-granddaughter.

38. Based on email correspondence with Marva Jackson, Albert and Henrietta's great-granddaughter.

39. Details noted from a conversation with Faith Jackson, January 2021.

40. Details noted from a conversation with Faith Jackson, January 2021.

41. See ronfanfair.com/home/2016/12/25/laneway-honours-torontos-first-black-postman.

42. Brad Wheeler, "Debonair Singer Jay Jackson Co-Fronted R&B Group the Majestics," *Globe and Mail*, September 30, 2020, theglobeandmail.com/arts/music/article-debonair-singer-jay-jackson-co-fronted-rb-group-the-majestics.

43. See cbc.ca/news/canada/toronto/first-black-mailman-honoured-1.4217353.

44. Wheeler, "Debonair Singer Jay Jackson."

45. See thestar.com/life/2013/03/22/union_honouring_family_of_albert_jackson_torontos_first_black_postman.html.

46. From email correspondence with Patrick Crean.

47. See thestar.com/life/2013/03/22/union_honouring_family_of_albert_jackson_torontos_first_black_postman.html.

48. See thestar.com/life/2013/03/22/union_honouring_family_of_albert_jackson_torontos_first_black_postman.html.

49. See canadianstampnews.com/wp-content/uploads/sites/3/2019/01/OFDC.jpeg.

BIBLIOGRAPHY

Articles

Armstrong, Karen Elizabeth. "The Late Nineteenth-Century Stone Farmhouses of John Thompson Crellin." *Journal of the Society for the Study of Architecture in Canada* 43, no. 2 (2018): 27–41. erudit.org/en/journals/jssac/2018-v43-n2-jssac04441/1058037ar.pdf.

Bateman, Chris. "Is Craven Road the Weirdest Street in Toronto?" *blogTO* February 19, 2014. blogto.com/city/2014/02/is_craven_road_the_weirdest_street_in_toronto.

——. "Why Did Bright Street Get So Bent? April 23, 2014. blogto.com/city/2014/04/why_did_bright_street_get_so_bent.

Belshaw, John Douglas. "10.3 Immigration." BC Campus Open Publishing. opentextbc.ca/preconfederation/chapter/10-3-immigration.

Benn, Carl. "First Peoples, 9000 BCE to 1600 CE." *The History of Toronto: An 11,000 Year Journey.* toronto.ca/explore-enjoy/history-art-culture/museums/virtual-exhibits/history-of-toronto/first-peoples-9000-bce-to-1600-ce.

——, "Natives and Newcomers, 1600–1793." *The History of Toronto: An 11,000 Year Journey.* toronto.ca/explore-enjoy/history-art-culture/museums/virtual-exhibits/history-of-toronto/natives-and-newcomers-1600-1793.

Blackwell, Captain Thomas. "The Rowing Clubs of Canada." *Outing: An Illustrated Monthly Magazine of Sport, Travel and Recreation* 18 (April–September 1891).

Bonnell, Jennifer, and Marcel Fortin. "Gooderham & Worts Distillery." Don Valley Historical Mapping Project. maps.library.utoronto.ca/dvhmp/gooderham-dis.html.

Bradburn, Jamie. "Historicist: An Illustrated Business Quartet." *Torontoist*, January 23, 2010. torontoist.com/2010/01/historicist_a_business_quartet.

——. "Shaping Toronto: Chinatowns." *Torontoist*, February 4, 2016. torontoist.com/2016/02/shaping-toronto-chinatowns.

Bristol, Douglas, Jr. "From Outposts to Enclaves: A Social History of Black Barbers from 1750 to 1915." *Enterprise & Society* 5, no. 4 (December 2004): 594–606.

Bumsted, J.M. "Scottish Canadians." *The Canadian Encyclopedia*. thecanadianencyclopedia.ca/en/article
/scots.

Cabbagetown Preservation Association. "Architectural Styles." cabbagetownpa.ca/heritage
/architectural-styles.

_____."From Prosperity to Decline." cabbagetownpa.ca/ufaqs/workers-cottage.

_____. "Worker's Cottage." cabbagetownpa.ca/ufaqs/workers-cottage.

Campey, George, and Lucille Campey. "Canada's Irish Immigrants." irishtocanada.com
/canada-s-irish-immigrants.

Canadian Encyclopedia, The. "Black History in Canada." thecanadianencyclopedia.ca/en/collection
/black-history-in-canada?id=194&themeid=9.

_____. "Timeline: Black History." thecanadianencyclopedia.ca/en/timeline/black-history.

Canadian Stamp News. "Albert Jackson Stamp Issued Today." January 25, 2019. canadianstampnews
.com/albert-jackson-stamp-issued-today.

Careless, J.M.S. "Toronto." *The Canadian Encyclopedia*. thecanadianencyclopedia.ca/en/article/toronto.

Doucette, Joanne. "Chinese Immigrants and the Old East End." September 25, 2017. leslievillehistory
.com/2017/09/25/chinese-immigrants-the-old-east-end.

_____. "The Fence." May 8, 2016. leslievillehistory.com/2016/05/08/the-fence.

_____. "From Farm to Shacktown to Bungalowland: Gerrard-Coxwell." February 9, 2021.
leslievillehistory.com/timeline-ashbridges-bay/#_ftn71.

_____. "The Great Shacktown Crisis." 2017. leslievillehistory.com/the-great-shacktown-crisis.

_____. "Lumber Yards from Mud Roads and Plank Sidewalks, Part 13." December 2017.
leslievillehistory.com/2017/12.

_____. "The Story of the Craven Road Fence." leslievillehistory.com/craven-rd-fence.

Dunae, Patrick A., and George Woodcock. "English Canadians." *The Canadian Encyclopedia*.
thecanadianencyclopedia.ca/en/article/english.

Fanfair, Ron. "Laneway Honours Toronto's First Black Postman." ronfanfair.com/home/2016/12/25
/laneway-honours-torontos-first-black-postman.

Felluga, Dino Franco, ed. "Britain, Representation, and Nineteenth-Century History." BRANCH.
branchcollective.org.

Filey, Mike. "Within the Hallowed Walls of Old St. Michael's Cemetery. *The Catholic Register* (1992).

Flack, Derek. "This Is Why Some Toronto Homes Look Like Tiny Cottages." *blogTO* November 1,
2020. blogto.com/city/2015/12/torontos_lost_cottage_architecture_hides_in_plain_sight.

_____. "Toronto's Lost Cottage Architecture Hides in Plain Sight." *blogTO* August 11, 2017. blogto
.com/city/2015/12/torontos_lost_cottage_architecture_hides_in_plain_sight.

Flanders, Judith. "Slums." British Library. bl.uk/romantics-and-victorians/articles/slums#.

Frum, David. "The Lessons of the Somme." *Atlantic* July 1, 2016. theatlantic.com/international
/archive/2016/07/somme-centennial/489656.

Giddens, David. "The Scandalous Sculler: Almost 150 Years Ago, Ned Hanlan Became Canada's First Superstar." *CBC* cbc.ca/sportslongform/entry/the-scandalous-sculler-150-years-ago-ned-hanlan-canada-first-superstar.

Government of British Columbia. "Building the Railway." gov.bc.ca/gov/content/governments /multiculturalism-anti-racism/chinese-legacy-bc/history/building-the-railway.

Government of Canada. "Canada: A History of Refugees." canada.ca/en/immigration-refugees-citizenship /services/refugees/canada-role/timeline.html.

Hare, Peter. "Don Vale House." lostrivers.ca/points/donvalehs.htm.

———. "Thornton and Lucie Blackburn House." lostrivers.ca/points/blackburn.htm.

Harper, Marjory. "Enticing the Emigrant: Canadian Agents in Ireland and Scotland, c. 1870–c. 1920." *Scottish Historical Review* 83, no. 1 (2004): 41–58.

Harriet Tubman Institute for Research on Africa and its Diasporas. "Ann Maria Jackson." March 14, 2013. tubman.info.yorku.ca/educational-resources/breaking-the-chains/toronto/ann-maria-jackson.

Harrison, Joanne. "The Origin, Development and Decline of Back-to-Back Houses in Leeds, 1787–1937." *Industrial Archaeology Review* 39, no. 2 (2017): 101–16.

Henry, Natasha L. "Chloe Cooley and the Act to Limit Slavery in Upper Canada." *The Canadian Encyclopedia*. thecanadianencyclopedia.ca/en/article/chloe-cooley-and-the-act-to-limit-slavery-in -upper-canada.

"Highland Clearances." *Encyclopaedia Britannica*. britannica.com/event/Highland-Clearances.

Ireland Park Foundation. "Preserved Histories." ipfdev.develops.technology/architectural-heritage -exhibition/5-preserved-histories.

Kidd, Bruce. "O'Connor, William Joseph." *Dictionary of Canadian Biography*. biographi.ca/en/bio/o _connor_william_joseph_12E.html.

Laforme, Douglas. "What Could Canada Have Been If the Treaty Process Was Fair?" *Torontoist*, June 7, 2017. torontoist.com/2017/06/canada-treaty-process-fair.

Leckie, Barbara. "Prince Albert's Exhibition Model Dwellings." BRANCH. April 17, 2020. branchcollective.org/?ps_articles=barbara-leckie-prince-alberts-exhibition-model-dwellings.

Lee, Wai-Ma. "Dance No More: Chinese Hand Laundries in Toronto." *Polyphony* (Summer 1984): 32–34. mhso.ca/ggp/Polyphony/ChineseLaundries.html.

Levesque, André M. "Did You Ever Wonder Who Was the First Black Letter Carrier in Canada?" memorialogy.com/pages/entries/entries.php?post=n137.

Library and Archives Canada. "History of Canada's Early Chinese Immigrants." bac-lac.gc.ca/eng/discover /immigration/history-ethnic-cultural/early-chinese-canadians/Pages/history.aspx#whyb2.

———. "Scottish Genealogy and Family History." bac-lac .gc.ca/eng/discover/immigration/history-ethnic-cultural/Pages/scottish.aspx.

Londonist. "Punished for Being Poor: London's Forgotten Workhouses." londonist.com/2014/04 /punished-for-being-poor-londons-forgotten-workhouses.

Lorinc, John. "The Black Community in St. John's Ward: An Essay Marking Black History Month in the City of Toronto." toronto.ca/explore-enjoy/history-art-culture/black-history-month/the-black-community-in-st-johns-ward.

Mace, Jessica. "Beautifying the Countryside: Rural and Vernacular Gothic in Late Nineteenth-Century Ontario." *Journal of the Society for the Study of Architecture in Canada* 38, no. 1 (2013): 29–36. dalspace.library.dal.ca/bitstream/handle/10222/65242/vol38_no1_29_36.pdf?sequenc1&isAllowed=y.

Marsh, James H., and Pierre Berton. "War of 1812." *The Canadian Encyclopedia.* thecanadianencyclopedia.ca/en/article/war-of-1812.

McFarquhar, Colin. "Blacks in 1880s Toronto: The Search for Equality." *Ontario History* 99, no. 1 (Spring 2007): 64–76. erudit.org/en/journals/onhistory/2007-v99-n1-onhistory04967/1065797ar.pdf.

McGill School of Architecture, Minimum Cost Housing Group. "Crystal Palace." mcgill.ca/mchg/pastproject/cristal.

McGillivray, Kate. "Revealing Downtown Toronto's Irish Roots, One Hidden House at a Time." *CBC.* cbc.ca/news/canada/toronto/toronto-irish-history-1.4028360.

McGowan, Mark. "Boyle, Patrick." *Dictionary of Canadian Biography.* biographi.ca/en/bio/boyle_patrick_13E.html.

McGowan, Mark G. "Famine, Facts and Fabrication: An Examination of Diaries from the Irish Famine Migration to Canada." *The Canadian Journal of Irish Studies* 33, no. 2 (Fall 2007).

McGowan, Mark G., and Michael Chard. "Great Famine History." Canada Ireland Foundation. irelandparkfoundation.com/great-famine-history.

McLaren, Kristin. "'We Had No Desire to Be Set Apart': Forced Segregation of Black Students in Canada West Public Schools and Myths of British Egalitarianism." *Social History* 37, no. 73 (2004): 27–50. hssh.journals.yorku.ca/index.php/hssh/article/view/4373/3571.

Minton, Maurice. "The Late Champion Oarsman of America." In *The Illustrated American*, vol. 12. New York: Illustrated American Publishing Company, 1892.

Murphy, Frank. "Dublin Slums in the 1930s." *Dublin Historical Record* 37, nos. 3–4 (June-September 1984): 104–11.

Nankivel, Anne-Marie. "Prince Albert's Model Cottages." thelondonphile.com/2012/05/02/prince-alberts-model-cottages.

National Archives of Ireland. "Poverty and Health. census.nationalarchives.ie/exhibition/dublin/poverty_health.html.

Newell, Dianne. "Gooderham, William." *Dictionary of Canadian Biography.* biographi.ca/en/bio/gooderham_william_1790_1881_11E.html.

Patterson, Marian A. "The Cholera Epidemic of 1832 in York, Upper Canada." *Bulletin of the Medical Library Association* 46, no. 2 (April 1958): 165–84. ncbi.nlm.nih.gov/pmc/articles/PMC233409/pdf/mlab00208-1001.pdf.

Pogue, Dennis J., and Douglas Sanford. "Slave Housing in Virginia." *Encyclopedia Virginia.* encyclopediavirginia.org/slave_housing_in_virginia.

"Prince Albert's Cottages." *Spectator Archives.* http://archive.spectator.co.uk/article/14th-june-1851/12
/prince-alberts-cottages.

Rawling, Bill. "Technology and Innovation in the Toronto Police Force, 1875–1925." *Ontario History*
80, no. 1 (March 1988): 53–71.

"Remembering the Toronto Purchase and Its Settlement: June 8: Snapshots in History." John P. Blog,
June 10, 2918. torontopubliclibrary.ca. torontopubliclibrary.typepad.com/local-history-genealogy
/2018/06/remembering-the-toronto-purchase-and-its-settlement-june-8-snapshots-in-history.html.

Robertson, Ian. "Family Cheers Stamp Honouring Likely First Black Canadian Letter Carrier."
canadianstampnews.com/family-cheers-stamp-honouring-likely-first-black-canadian-letter-carrier.

"Roden Public School." torontoplaques.com/Pages/Roden_Public_School.html.

Simon Fraser University. "A Brief Chronology of Chinese Canadian History: From Segregation to
Integration. sfu.ca/chinese-canadian-history/chart_en.html#.

Smee, Michael. "Graves Discovered Beneath Downtown Elementary School Mean No Expansion."
CBC February 1, 2017. cbc.ca/news/canada/toronto/graves-discovered-beneath-downtown-
elementary-school-mean-no-expansion-1.3962758.

Stewart, Terry. "The Highland Clearances." historic-uk.com/HistoryUK/HistoryofScotland/The
-Highland-Clearances.

Sylvester, Erin. "Walking the Ward." *Torontoist*, September 6, 2017. torontoist.com/2017/09/walking
-the-ward.

Taylor, Katherine. "By Any Other Name." February 11, 2017. onegalstoronto.wordpress.com
/2017/02/11/by-any-other-name.

"Toronto's Huron-Wendat Heritage." Torontoplaques.com. torontoplaques.com/Pages/Torontos_Huron_
Wendat_Heritage.html.

Toronto Public Library. "Uncovering the Stories of Freedom." omeka.tplcs.ca/virtual-exhibits/exhibits
/show/freedom-city/stories-of-freedom.

Walker, Sheryl. "John Meriwether Tinsley." findagrave.com/memorial/166870385/john-merriwether
-tinsley.

Yee, Paul. "History of Canada's Early Chinese Immigrants." bac-lac.gc.ca/eng/discover/immigration
/history-ethnic-cultural/early-chinese-canadians/Pages/history.aspx#ac1.

Books

Alexander, Christopher. *The Timeless Way of Building.* New York: Oxford University Press, 1979.

Arthur, Eric. *Toronto, No Mean City.* Revised by Stephen A. Otto. 3rd ed. Toronto: University of
Toronto Press, 2003.

Autobiography of the Rev. Josiah Henson: (Mrs. Harriet Beecher Stowe's "Uncle Tom") from 1789 to 1876.
London: Christian Age, 1876.

Bumsted, J.M. *The Scots in Canada*. Ottawa: Canadian Historical Association, 1982.

Campey, Lucille H. *Ontario and Quebec's Irish Pioneers: Farmers, Labourers, and Lumberjacks*. Toronto: Dundurn Press, 2018.

Careless, J.M.S. *Careless at Work: Selected Canadian Historical Studies*. Toronto: Dundurn Press, 1996.

Chan, Arlene. *The Chinese in Toronto from 1878: From Outside to Inside the Circle*. Toronto: Dundurn Press, 2011.

Crowley, John, and William J. Smyth and Mike Murphy. *Atlas of the Great Irish Famine*. Cork: University College Cork, 2012.

De Botton, Alain. *The Architecture of Happiness*. Toronto: McClelland & Stewart, 2008.

Doucette, Joanne. *Pigs, Flowers and Bricks: A History of Leslieville to 1920*. Toronto: Joanne Doucette, 2016.

Firth, Edith, ed. *The Town of York 1793–1815: A Collection of Documents of Early Toronto*. Toronto: University of Toronto Press, 1962.

Fryer, M.B., and Charles J. Humber, eds. *Loyal She Remains: A Pictorial History of Ontario*. Toronto: The United Empire Loyalists' Association of Canada, 1984.

Harney, Robert F., and Harold Troper. *Immigrants: A Portrait of the Urban Experience, 1890–1930*. Toronto: Van Nostrand Reinhold, 1975.

Hastings, Dr. Charles. *Report of the Medical Health Officer Dealing with the Recent Investigation of Slum Conditions in Toronto …* Toronto: Department of Public Health, 1911.

Hayes, Derek. *Historical Atlas of Toronto*. Vancouver: Douglas & McIntyre, 2009.

Jenkins, William. "Poverty and Place: Documenting and Representing Toronto's Catholic Irish, 1845–1890." In *At the Anvil: Essays in Honour of William J. Smyth*, edited by Patrick J. Duffy and William Nolan. Dublin: Geography Publications. 2012.

Kearns, Kevin C. *Dublin Tenement Life: An Oral History*. Dublin: Gill & Macmillan Ltd., 1994.

Kelly, Colleen. *Cabbagetown in Pictures*. Toronto: Toronto Public Library Board, 1984.

Kelly, Reverend E. *The Story of St. Paul's Parish, Toronto: Commemorating the Centenary of the First Parish Church in the Archdiocese of Toronto, 1622–1922*. Toronto, 1922.

Kenny, Nicolas. *The Feel of the City: Experiences of Urban Transformation*. Toronto: University of Toronto Press, 2014.

Kent, Nathaniel. *Hints to Gentlemen of Landed Property*. London: J. Dodsley, 1775.

Kilbourn, William. *Toronto Remembered: A Celebration of the City*. Toronto: Stoddart, 1984.

Kishlansky, Mark, and Patrick Geary and Patricia O'Brien. *Civilization in the West*. 7th Edition. Vol. C. New York: Pearson Education, 2008.

Lebl, Goca. *Don Rowing Club: The First 140 Years*. Toronto: Goca Lebl, 2020.

Lemos, Coralina R. *Corktown: The History of a Toronto Neighbourhood and the People Who Made It*. Toronto: Coralina R. Lemos, 2018.

Levine, Allan. *Toronto: Biography of a City*. Toronto: Douglas & McIntyre, 2013.

Lorinc, John, and Michael McClelland, Ellen Scheinberg, and Tatum Taylor, eds. *The Ward: The Life and Loss of Toronto's First Immigrant Neighbourhood*. Toronto: Coach House Press, 2015.

MacIntosh, Robert. *Earliest Toronto*. Toronto: General Publishing Co., 2006.

Magee, Reverend H.S. *The Christian Guardian*. 1911.

Martelle, Holly, and Michael McClelland, Tatum Taylor, and John Lorinc, eds., *The Ward Uncovered: The Archaeology of Everyday Life*. Toronto: Coach House Press, 2018.

Mays, John Bentley. *Emerald City: Toronto Visited*. Toronto: Viking, 1994.

McCourt, Malachy. *Malachy McCourt's History of Ireland*. Philadelphia: Running Press, 2008.

McGowan, Mark. *Creating Canadian Historical Memory: The Case for the Famine Migration of 1847*. Ottawa: Canadian Historical Association, 2006. cha-shc.ca/_uploads/5c374f5883075.pdf.

McGowan, Mark G. *Death or Canada: The Irish Migration to Toronto, 1847*. Toronto: Novalis, 2009.

_____. *The Waning of the Green: Catholics, the Irish, and Identity in Toronto, 1887–1922* (Montreal: McGill-Queen's University Press, 1999).

Miller, Kerby A. *Emigrants and Exiles: Ireland and the Irish Exodus to North America*. New York: Oxford University Press, 1985.

Murphy, Brian, with Toula Vlahou. *Adrift: A True Story of Tragedy on the Icy Atlantic and the One Who Lived to Tell About It*. New York: Da Capo Press, 2018.

Myrvold, Barbara. *The Danforth in Pictures: A Brief History of the Danforth*. Toronto: Toronto Public Library, 1979.

Nipp, Dora. "The Chinese in Toronto." In *Gathering Place: Peoples and Neighbourhoods of Toronto, 1834–1945*, edited by Robert F. Harney. Toronto: Multicultural Society of Ontario, 1985.

O'Connell, Michael. "The Dublin Slums." In *Shadows: An Album of the Irish People 1841–1914*. Dublin: The O'Brien Press, 1985.

O'Hanlon, Reverend John. *The Irish Emigrant's Guide for the United States*. Boston: Patrick Donahoe, 1851.

Palmer, Bryan D., and Gaétan Héroux. *Toronto's Poor: A Rebellious History*. Toronto: Between the Lines, 2016.

Roberts, Julia. *In Mixed Company: Taverns and Public Life in Upper Canada*. Vancouver: University of British Columbia Press, 2009.

Sewell, John. *The Shape of the City: Toronto Struggles with Modern Planning*. Toronto: University of Toronto Press, 1993.

Smardz Frost, Karolyn. *I've Got a Home in Glory Land: A Lost Tale of the Underground Railroad*. Toronto: Thomas Allen, 2007.

Society for Improving the Condition of the Labouring Classes. *Plans and Suggestions for Dwellings Adapted to the Working Classes, Including the Model Houses for Families*. London: Society for Improving the Condition of the Labouring Classes, 1884.

Stanshell, Christine. *City of Women: Sex and Class in New York, 1789–1860*. Urbana: University of Illinois Press, 1987.

Sturino, Franc. *Forging the Chain: A Case Study of Italian Migration to North America, 1880–1930.* Toronto: Multicultural History Society of Ontario, 1990.

Thompson, Antonio S., and Christos G. Frentzos, eds. *The Routledge Handbook of American Military and Diplomatic History: The Colonial Period to 1877.* New York: Routledge, 2015.

Thompson, E.P. *The Making of the English Working Class.* London: Victor Gollancz, 1963.

Toronto Historical Association. *A Glimpse of Toronto's History: Opportunities for the Commemoration of Lost Historic Sites.* Toronto: City Planning Division/Urban Development Services, 2001.

Wilcox, Alana, and Jason McBride, eds. *UTOpia: Towards a New Toronto.* Toronto: Coach House, 2005.

Winks, Robin. *The Blacks in Canada: A History.* Montreal: McGill-Queen's University Press, 2000.

Databases

Canada Censuses, 1825–1926. Library and Archives Canada. bac-lac.gc.ca/eng/census/Pages/census.aspx.

City of Toronto Council Minutes. April 22, 1850. Item 248. City of Toronto Archives.

Herbert Walter Moore First World War Attestation Papers. bac-lac.gc.ca/eng/discover/military-heritage /first-world-war/personnel-records/Pages/search.aspx.

Phillip John Moore. First World War Attestation Papers. bac-lac.gc.ca/eng/discover/military-heritage/first -world-war/personnel-records/Pages/search.aspx.

Scotland Census (1851). nrscotland.gov.uk/research/guides/census-records/1851-census.

Directories

Brown's Toronto City and Home District Directory, 1846–47, 1856, 1861. Toronto: George Brown, 1846.

Caverhill's Toronto City Directory for 1859–60. Toronto: W.C.F. Caverhill. 1859.

Cherrier, Kirwin and McGown's Toronto Directory for 1873. Toronto: Cherrier, Kirwin & McGown, 1873.

City of Toronto and the Home District Commercial Directory and Register. Toronto: T. Dalton and W.J. Coates, 1837.

City of Toronto Directory for 1867–68. Toronto: W.C. Chewett & Co., 1867–69.

City of Toronto Illustrated Business Directory for 1865. Toronto: A.S. Irving, 1865.

Fisher and Taylor's Toronto Directory for 1874–76. Toronto: Fisher & Taylor.

Hutchinson's Toronto Directory, 1862–63. Toronto: Lovell & Gibson. 1862.

Mitchell & Co's General Directory for the City of Toronto and Gazetteer of the Counties of York and Peel, 1864–66. Toronto: Mitchell & Company, 1866.

Robertson & Cook's Toronto City Directory for 1870–72. Toronto: Daily Telegraph Printing House.

Rowsell's City of Toronto and County of York Directory for 1850–51. Toronto: Henry Rowsell, 1851.

Toronto City Directory for 1872–73. Toronto: Telegraph Printing House.

Toronto City Directory for 1883–90. Toronto: R.L. Polk & Co.

Toronto City Directory for 1891–1969. Toronto: Might's Directory Company.

Toronto Directory and Street Guide for 1843–44. Toronto: H&W Rowsell, 1843.

Toronto Directory for 1877–82. Toronto: Might & Taylor Publishers.

York Commercial Directory, Street Guide and Register, 1833–34. York, Upper Canada: Thomas Dalton 1834.

Newspapers

"Arrest of Supposed Fenians: The President and Secretary of the Hibernian Benevolent Society in Gaol."
Globe, May 6, 1868.

Bradbeer, Janice. "Once Upon a City: Poor House Helped Toronto's Destitute." *Toronto Star*, August 27,
2017. thestar.com/yourtoronto/once-upon-a-city-archives/2017/08/27/once-upon-a-city-poor
-house-created-to-help-torontos-destitute.html.

"The Census of Toronto." *Globe*, October 10, 1856.

"Chinamen in Toronto: Extraordinary Funeral at the Necropolis." *Globe*, October 25, 1877.

"City News." *Globe*, June 25, 1881.

Globe, October 27, 1849.

Globe, July 14, 1871.

Globe, August 21, 1880.

Globe, July 22, 1882.

Globe, March 16, 1883.

Globe, June 23, 1890.

Jacques, Steve. "Regent Park — A Look Back Through the Years at Canada's Oldest Social Housing
Project." *Globe and Mail*, January 13, 2016. theglobeandmail.com/news/toronto/regent
-park-a-look-back-through-the-years-at-canadas-oldest-social-housing-project/article27612426.

"Knows No Champion: King Death Conquers Our Famous Oarsman." *Globe*, November 24, 1892.

"LD John M. Tinsley Dead: The Patriarch of Toronto Quietly Passes Away." *Globe*, October 6, 1892.

Lorinc, John. "First Census of Toronto's Black Population in 1840 Counted 525 People." *Toronto Star*,
February 1, 2018. thestar.com/life/2018/02/01/first-census-of-torontos-black-population-in-1840
-counted-525-people.html.

———. "Landmark Church with Ties to Underground Railroad Unearthed in Toronto." *Hamilton
Spectator*, February 15, 2016. thespec.com/news/ontario/2016/02/15/landmark-church-with-ties
-to-underground-railroad-unearthed-in-toronto.html.

New York Times, November 13, 1889.

"The Oarsman at Rest." *Globe*, November 28, 1892.

"Obituary of Corporal George Moore." *Globe*, July 6, 1916.

"Obituary of Herbert Walter Moore." *Toronto Daily Star*, August 28, 1917.

"One Block to Turn a Whole City Sick." *Toronto Daily Star*, July 11. 1911.

"The Outrage on Bright Street: The Inquest." *Globe*, May 28, 1875.

Scrivener, Leslie. "Remnants of Toronto's History." *Toronto Star*, March 11, 2007. thestar.com /news/2007/03/11/remnants_of_torontos_history.html.

Teotonio, Isabel. "Union Honouring Family of Albert Jackson, Toronto's First Black Postman." *Toronto Star*, March 22, 2013. thestar.com/life/2013/03/22/union_honouring_family_of_albert_jackson_ torontos_first_black_postman.html.

Toronto Daily Mail, July 20, 1882.

Toronto Daily Mail, July 24, 1882.

Toronto Daily Star, May 29, 1906.

Toronto Daily Star, October 4, 1907.

Toronto Star, December 16, 1911.

Toronto Star, October 2, 1912.

Toronto World, June 3, 1885.

Wheeler, Brad. "Debonair Singer Jay Jackson Co-Fronted R&B Group the Majestics." *Globe and Mail*, September 30, 2020.

"William as a Walker." *Globe*, December 10, 1891.

"William O'Connor's Death." *Globe*, November 24, 1892.

"With Heart and Hand." *Globe*, December 4, 1888.

Wong, Jan. "'No Tickee' No More." *Globe and Mail*, June 30, 2001. theglobeandmail.com/ incoming/no-tickee-no-more/article4149856.

IMAGE CREDITS

Alamy: Figs. 1.8 (KGPA Ltd/Alamy Stock Photo PGRJ0B), 1.11 (Photo by Tom Corban, ID D87A43), 1.13 (Photo by Cliff Green, ID R365Y8), 1.15 (Photo by John Barron, ID PPK7AP), 6.3d (Photo by Charles Phelps Cushing, ID FPW2F7), 6.4f (Lithograph by Lindner, Eddy & Claus).

Archiseek: Fig. 1.6.

Canada Farmer: Figs. 1.3, 1.5 (vol. 1, no. 22, Nov. 15, 1864. Toronto: G. Brown).

Canada Post: Fig. 6.8n.

City of Toronto Archives: Figs. 3.2 (Photo by William James, Fonds 1244, Item 102), 3.3 (Fonds 1244, Item 107), 4.2 (Fonds 1498, Item 16), 4.3 (Series 372, Subseries 32, Item 45), 4.7 (Series 88, Item 13), 5.5 (Fonds 1244, Item 596), 5.6 (Photo by Arthur Goss, Fonds 200, Series 372, Subseries 32, Item 246), 5.7 (Photo by Arthur Goss, Fonds 200, Series 372, Subseries 32, Item 25), 5.8 (Photo by Arthur Goss, Fonds 200, Series 372, Subseries 32, Item 40), 5.9 (Fonds 200, Series 372, Subseries 33, Item 97), 5.10 (Fonds 200, Series 372, Subseries 33, Item 62), 5.11 (Housing Dept. 9), 5.12 (Fonds 200, Series 372, Subseries 33b, Item 127), 5.14 (Fonds 200, Series 372, Subseries 84, Item 82), 5.15 (Fonds 1244, Item 24), 6.2c (Series 372, Item 732), 6.2d (Fonds 200, Series 372, Item 167), 6.3e (Fonds 200, Series 372, Subseries 55, Item 43), 6.3f (Fonds 200, Series 372, Subseries 33, Item 175), 6.3g (Fonds 200, Series 372, Subseries 33, Item 173), 6.5g (Fonds 200, Series 372, Subseries 27, Item 20), 6.6c, 6.7e (Fonds 200, Series 372, Subseries 3, Item 207), 6.7f (Fonds 200, Series 372, Subseries 3, Item 205), 6.8d (Goad's Insurance Map 1880), 6.8f (Fonds 200, Series 372, Subseries 32, Item 195), 6.8h (Fonds 200, Series 372, Subseries 32, Item 187), 6.8j (Fonds 1244, Item 341).

Don Loucks: Figs. i, ii, 1.1, 1.7, 2.1, 2.3–2.5, 2.12, 2.19–2.21, 2.28–2.30, 2.39–2.42, 2.48–2.50, 3.1, 4.1, 5.1, 6, 6.1e, 6.2f, 6.3h, 6.4c, 6.5i, 6.6b, 6.6e, 6.6g, 6.7c, 6.8a, 7.1.

Don Rowing Club, The First 140 Years: Figs. 6.4a, 6.4d.

Edward Lumb: Fig. 6.3a.

Ellen Buchman: Fig. 6.2p.

Elmer Chickering: Fig. 6.4i

Globe: Fig. 6.7b.

Illustrated London News: Figs. 3.5, 6.4g.

J. Taylor, Architectural Library: Fig. 1.2.

Jackson family: Fig. 6.8k.

Leslie Valpy: Fig. 1.9.

Library and Archives Canada: Figs. 3.4 (Box 00600B, copy negative, PA-010226), 4.65 (NMC 16819), 6.2b (Goad's Insurance Map, 1903), 6.8i (Kennedy & Bell, e010963829).

Murray Buchman: Figs. 6.2a, 6.2g, 6.2i, 6.2j, 6.2k, 6.2l, 6.2m, 6.2n, 6.2o.

National Museum of African American History and Culture: Fig. 1.14.

Patrick Crean: Fig. 6.8l.

Royal British Columbia Museum and Archives: Fig. 3.6 (BCA D-07548).

Royal Society of Antiquaries of Ireland (RSAI), Georgina McMahon: Fig. 1.10.

Simon Pulsifer: Fig. 5.2.

Terry Smith: Fig. 6.1a.

Toronto Evening Star: Fig. 2.2.

Toronto Public Library: Figs. 4.4 (T 17931/5 Large), 4.5 (JRR 905 FRA), 5.4 (Goad's Insurance Plan, 1890, Plate 7), 5.13 (B 13-38), 5.16 (Y 23), 6.1b (Goad's Insurance Plan, 1884, Plate 10), 6.1c, 6.1d (Series 65, File 693, Item 5), 6.3c (Goad's Insurance Plan, 1884), 6.4b (Toronto Goad's Insurance Map, 1884), 6.4e (B11-28A), 6.5f, 6.6d (Toronto Goad's Insurance Map, 1884), 6.8b, 6.8c, 6.8e, 6.8g (Toronto Goad's Map, 1883).

Toronto Star: Fig. 6.2h.

Valpy family: Fig. 1.4.

Veterans Affairs Canada: Fig. 6.5a.

Victoria and Albert Museum: Fig. 1.12 (H.J. Malby for National Photographic Record and Survey, E.3596-2000).

Vik Pahwa: Figs. 2.6–2.11, 2.13–2.18, 2.22–2.27, 2.31–2.38, 2.43–2.47, 2.51–2.59, 5.3, 5.17, 6.2e, 6.3b, 6.4h, 6.5b, 6.5c, 6.5d, 6.5e, 6.5h, 6.6a, 6.6f, 6.7a, 6.7d.

INDEX

Page numbers in italics refer to illustrations.